Rethinking Strategic Management

EDITORIAL ADVISORS

Rethinking Strategic Management

Ways to Improve Competitive Performance

Edited by

D. E. Hussey

JOHN WILEY & SONS

CHICHESTER · NEW YORK · BRISBANE · TORONTO · SINGAPORE

Other Wiley Editorial Offices

John Wiley & Sons, Inc., 605 Third Avenue,
New York, NY 10158-0012, USA

Jacaranda Wiley Ltd, 33 Park Road, Milton,
Queensland 4064, Australia

John Wiley & Sons (Canada) Ltd, 22 Worcester Road,
Rexdale, Ontario M9W 1L1, Canada

John Wiley & Sons (SEA) Pte Ltd, 37 Jalan Pemimpin #05-04,
Block B, Union Industrial Building, Singapore 2057

British Library Cataloguing in Publication Data

A catalogue record for this book is available from the British Library

ISBN 0-471-95908-1

Typeset in 11/12pt Palatino by Mackreth Media Services, Hemel Hempstead
Printed and bound in Great Britain by Biddles Ltd, Guildford and King's Lynn
This book is printed on acid-free paper responsibly manufactured from sustainable forestation,
for which at least two trees are planted for each one used for paper production.

CONTENTS

ABOUT THE CONTRIBUTORS

GRAHAM BEAVER is a principal lecturer in strategic management and the MBA programme director at Nottingham Business School. He is responsible for much of the academic and consultancy work on business development and small business management.

CHARLES JEAN-NOEL DESPRES is currently a Research Fellow at the International Institute for Management Development (IMD), specialising in organisational theory, organisational behaviour and organisational development. His research emphasis includes information systems, knowledge-age organisational forms and the socio-cultural changes occasioned by the move into a *post-industrial* era. He is a consultant to US and European organisations in these areas, and in matters related to human resource development.

JEAN M. HILTROP is Professor of Human Resource Management at the International Institute for Management Development (IMD) in Switzerland. He has been involved in executive education for many years at the management centre of the University of Bradford and at the Department of Applied Economic Sciences of the Katholieke Universiteit Leuven in Belgium. He has extensive experience as a human resource manager and consultant for several large companies in Europe, Asia and the United States. He is currently leading an international research project, which examines the impact of human resource practices on the global strategy and competitiveness of European organisations.

HANS H. HINTERHUBER is Professor of Business Administration and the Director of the Department of Management at the University of Innsbruck, Austria. He also teaches Strategic Management at the University of Milan, Italy. He holds an MS degree in petroleum engineering from the Mining University of Loeben, Austria, and a PhD in business administration from the University of Venice, Italy.

Dr Hinterhuber has worked in management in Italian and German companies. He now serves as a director of a number of companies in Austria, Germany and Italy. His research and consulting work focus on strategy, strategic management and the management of organisational evolution in different cultures.

DAVID HUSSEY has had many years of experience in corporate planning, as a practitioner in industry from 1964 to 1975, and as a consultant since 1976. Prior to moving into corporate planning, he was engaged in industrial development work in a developing country. He was managing director of the European operations of a well-known US consultancy from 1980 to 1994, and now runs his own consulting business. He is the author of several books on the subject of strategic management, including *Corporate Planning: Theory and Practice* (Pergamon, 1974), which won the John Player management author of the year award. He was one of the founders of the Society for Strategic Planning, and has been associated with the official journal of the society, *Long Range Planning*, since its foundation. He is a member of the editorial board of *Strategic Directions*, and is a director of the Japanese Society of Strategic Management. He is editor of the *Journal of Strategic Change*, which was launched in 1992.

PETER JENNINGS is a senior lecturer in management strategy at Sheffield Business School. His specialist subjects include strategic management with particular reference to the small business sector.

BENGT KARLÖF is the senior partner and chairman of Karlöf and Partners, a Swedish-based consultancy with world-wide interests. He is well known for his work in the area of strategic development, and has undertaken numerous consultancy assignments, as well as lecturing widely in academic and professional seminars. He has written many books which tackle strategy and related management subjects from a practical viewpoint. He is a member of the editorial board of the *International Review of Strategic Management*.

BORIS LEVIN has degrees from Dartmouth College and Wharton (USA), and is completing a PhD at Innsbruck (Austria). After working with Boston Consulting Group, Munich, from 1989–1991, he became partner and co-founder of a German industrial holding company, Beteiligungsgesellschaft mbH.

DIANNE LEWIS originally trained as a secondary school teacher and has taught in tertiary institutions for the past fifteen years. She completed her PhD in Organisational Theory and Behaviour in 1992 and currently lectures in Management at the Queensland University of Technology. She has had wide experience in public administration and has been engaged as a consultant by a number of state government departments to assist senior and middle management in the organisation and development of their communications. Her research interests are organisational culture, organisational change and transformational leadership, all areas in which she has published.

MARIE McHUGH is a lecturer in organisation studies at the University of Ulster. Upon joining the university's Centre for Research in Management in 1987 she worked on a number of research projects on competitive strategy. Since her appointment as lecturer in 1989, she has combined her research interests in strategic management with organisational behaviour, particularly employee stress and its impact on performance. She has published widely, and in addition to teaching on a range of courses she has been a consultant to organisations in the UK and Scandinavia.

ROBERT MOCKLER is a Professor of Business at St John's University Graduate School of Business. He is director of the Strategic Management Research Group and its Centres of Knowledge-Based Systems for Business and of Case Study Development. He is author or co-author of 36 books and monographs, some 100 case studies and over 120 articles and presentations covering a wide range of management and educational topics. His first articles on strategic management and situational decision theory were published in *Harvard Business Review* in 1970 and 1971. His first book was published by Prentice Hall in 1969, and his latest in 1994. He has lectured and consulted world-wide, has received national awards for innovative teaching (Decision Sciences Institute) and has been a Fulbright scholar. He also started, managed and eventually sold, multi-million-dollar business ventures.

DOLORES O'REILLY is a lecturer in the School of Public Policy, Economics and Law at the University of Ulster. She specialises in Public Policy and European Studies. Her current research work focuses on the competitive strategies adopted by industries pre- and post-deregulation. She is Chairman of the Public Affairs Committee of the United Kingdom's Air Transport Users' Council (AUC) and represents the AUC in Brussels at the regular consultative meetings between the European Commission and the European Air Transport user groups. She also sits on the Irish Air Transport Users' Committee (ATUC) in Dublin.

JOHN PRESCOTT is Professor of Business Administration at the Joseph Katz Graduate School of Business Administration at the University of Pittsburgh. Dr Prescott's research interests focus on the network of relationships among a firm's industry strategy, organisational processes and performance. A specific focus is the design and implementation of competitive intelligence systems. He has published numerous articles in leading journals, and is editor of two books on competitive intelligence. He is also editor of *The Competitive Intelligence Review*. In 1994 he was selected for the meritorious award from the Society of Competitive Intelligence Professionals for outstanding contributions to the field of competitive intelligence. He was a founder and former president of the Society of Competitive Intelligence Professionals.

CHARLES W. TAYLOR, a recently retired faculty member of the US Army War College, where he was a strategic futurist with the Strategic Studies Institute and occupied the General Douglas MacArthur Academic Chair of Research. His futures research extends over 25 years. He is known internationally for his strategic forecasts and for his contributions of methods and designs. He is the author of a number of futures studies including *A World 2010: A New Order of Nations and Alternative World Scenarios for a New Order of Nations*. He is a member of the American Academy of Political and Social Sciences, World Future Society, Population Reference Bureau, Association of Electronic Defense, Fellow of the Inter-University Seminar on Armed Forces and Society, Military Operations Research Society and the Planning Forum.

INTRODUCTION

This book examines some of the recent and new thinking about strategic management, with particular reference to competitive performance. It begins with a chapter which gives a thought-provoking view of the future of strategic management. I was fortunate in being able to persuade Bob Mockler to write this key chapter. Bob's contribution to strategic management has been consistent and significant, and he is well placed to give a view on its future evolution.

This is followed by a selection of chapters on the theme of improving competitive performance, which begins with a scene-setting chapter by Charles Taylor, who offers a scenario of the world in 2015. I first met Charles at a conference in Hungary, and was impressed by the depth and thoroughness of his work. Later he sent me one of the books in which his forecasts for the US Army had been published. It seemed to me that any discussion of ways of improving competitive positions should be in the context of the likely state of the world in which we will operate. His thorough analysis provides such a context.

In Chapter 3, John Prescott traces the evolution of competitive intelligence. He is well placed to write this chapter, as, among many other achievements, he was a founder and past president of the Society of Competitive Intelligence Professionals, and is editor of the *Competitive Intelligence Review.*

Graham Beaver and Peter Jennings write on a completely different aspect. The chapter is called *The Art of Identifying Successful Small Firms*, and deals with the issue of how to identify success potential at the pre-start-up stage, by concentrating on the significant factors which should be available at the outset of the entrepreneurial venture.

The theme of competitors as engaged in economic warfare is taken up in the chapter by Hans Hinterhuber and Boris Levin. These authors explore whether viewing competitors as enemies can contribute to corporate success. Professor Hinterhuber is another good friend and is on the editorial board of this book, and the *Journal of Strategic Change* which I also edit.

There are three case examples in this part of the book. Chapter 5 by Dolores O'Reilly looks at the airline industry, to determine whether classical competitive strategy applies in newly deregulated industries. My own Chapter 10 gives an example of the application of competitor analysis by one firm operating in a fragmented industry. The purposes of these two chapters are very different. Dolores seeks to take the concepts of competitive strategy further forward, while my own contribution is to show how competitor analysis can be applied. The third case study (Chapter 12) is by Dianne Lewis, and deals with researching strategic change in an Australian educational organisation.

One reason for choosing the theme of competitive performance rather than competitor analysis was that I wanted to include some chapters on benchmarking. Certainly benchmarking can have a role in competitive strategies, but is most likely to be successful when it is used as one step on a path to world-class performance. This often means that the most relevant organisations to benchmark are not competitors but organisations in other industries from whom much can be learned. Bengt Karlöf is a leading contributor to strategic thinking, and his short chapter moves from benchmarking to what he terms benchlearning. Jean Hiltrop and Charles Despres describe approaches to benchmarking human resources practices.

These two chapters are separated by another of my own which shows how to conduct a strategic audit of human resource management within the organisation. This underlines my belief that linkage between HR management and the corporate vision and strategy is essential for long-term competitive advantage. This is a practical chapter giving guidance on how to conduct such an audit.

I was familiar with the work of Marie McHugh and was pleased when she discussed the theme of her chapter with me. It deals with stress in strategic change, and is an area which is not as extensively covered in the strategic management literature as it deserves. Marie's chapter helps to fill this gap.

My thanks go not only to those who have contributed papers but also to the many who have given support and lent their reputation to this book and my previous series, the *International Review of Strategic Management*. Between us we have tried to encourage the development of the subject.

1

STRATEGIC MANAGEMENT: THE BEGINNING OF A NEW ERA

Robert J. Mockler

Professor of Management, St John's University Graduate School of Business

1.1
STRATEGIC MANAGEMENT IN THE 1990s:
A MORE NARROWLY DEFINED FIELD OF STUDY

This section discusses the evolving concept of the strategic management process, the growing breadth of the field, and its lack of definition.

AN OVERALL PERSPECTIVE: THE STRATEGIC MANAGEMENT PROCESS

When asked what strategic management means to him as Chairman of a $4.5 billion international corporation, the Gillette Company, Colman Mockler, shortly before his death in 1991, replied: "I knew precisely what kind of company I envisioned; I just didn't know exactly what it would look like." For him, formulating the overriding strategic concept (a synthesizing strategic vision, direction, or objective) of the kind of enterprise envisioned for the future was a relatively easy initial task when he was promoted to CEO in the mid-1970s. He knew intimately and so had thoroughly analyzed the industry/competitive market and was by nature and

Rethinking Strategic Management
Edited by D. E. Hussey. © 1995 John Wiley & Sons Ltd

training an exceptionally intelligent, conceptual thinker.

The most difficult aspect of strategic management for him was the *organizational dynamics* necessary to shape the specifics of the vision and to make it work. For example, it took him several years to put in place the kind of key entrepreneurial managers (staff) he knew could create the organizational environment and structure needed to carry out his strategic vision within a very turbulent competitive market. He was also determined to do it while maintaining Gillette's corporate culture which placed a high premium on preserving and fostering human values. Fortunately, he also possessed the natural and acquired *leadership* skills needed to develop and foster the strategic thinking, policy framework, entrepreneurial organizational culture and structure, and controls needed for the precise definition of his strategic vision to emerge and be carried out over time.

His definition of strategic management then was:

(1) Formulating *enterprise-wide* strategy, that is, strategy which identifies longer-term objectives and plans that enable an enterprise to interact effectively and efficiently with its competitive environment. This is often an emergent process, depending on the situation, as the detailed definitions of strategies are developed in stages over time, where possible and appropriate with participation of operating management.

(2) Creating an organizational environment or *framework* which fosters this emergent development process and enables effective plan implementation through organizational culture and structure re-engineering, staffing, leadership, integrated computer information systems, and well-defined general policy guidelines. The actual implementation work through which a strategic vision is given specific definition and carried out is often best done by operating managers and personnel (from "the bottom up" in Colman Mockler's words or "doing whatever is necessary to get the job done within well-defined legal, moral, ethical, and policy guidelines") and so goes beyond and is not included in the descriptive concept "enterprise-wide strategic management". Actual implementation, therefore, is basically just management.

(3) Using specific tools (such as advanced information systems, strategic alliances, organizational re-engineering, scenario-based planning) selectively, where they directly support specific tasks outlined in (1) and (2).

In a sense this definition of strategic management is new from the

following viewpoints:
- It differs from the original concept of strategic management he encountered at Harvard Business School over 35 years ago, which seemed to overly emphasize corporate management's role in actually doing strategy formulation.
- It differs from the view prevailing in the 1980s that is described in the following section, which extended the concept of strategic management implementation so far into operating areas that the concept "strategic management" became almost synonymous with management in general.
- It differs from the "schools of management" approach in that it focuses on context-specific *contingency* processes used by individual managers in specific companies, and so encompasses a wide range of rational, chaotic and even paradoxical processes within a confined contingency theory concept.

It is my judgment, as explained in this chapter, that a more limited and applications-oriented vision of strategic management will prevail over the coming decade as a working definition to guide and give focus to work in a field called "Strategic Management".

AN EVOLVING CONCEPT, LACKING IN CLEAR DEFINITION

Strategic management, a relatively new term covering enterprise-wide strategy formulation and strategy implementation, emerged during the 1980s as a major subject area—in business, at annual conferences, in doctoral programs at several major universities, and in professional societies and journals. For example, the Strategic Management Society only recently celebrated its 10th anniversary, and a recent bibliography lists 568 doctoral dissertations in strategic management and related fields in the last five years (Mockler, 1993a).

As planning efforts at major US corporations grew in the 1970s and early 1980s, their focus shifted from emphasizing financial planning to more issue-oriented planning (Mintzberg, 1994; Mockler, 1993b, Appendix B). At the same time, planning efforts became more formalized at the corporate or enterprise level. As the 1980s progressed, there was a further shift from focusing on plan development to focusing on plan implementation, and from centralized planning to decentralized planning (Early, 1990; Noyes, 1985; Prescott and Smith, 1989). With the shifts in emphasis, the term "strategic management", instead of "strategic planning", was used more and more in business to describe this evolving process, especially as greater attention was paid to implementation considerations.

A major contributor to the growing popularity of the term "strategic management" was its emerging role as the required American Association of Colleges and Schools of Business (AACSB) capstone course in graduate and undergraduate business programs world-wide. This provided a large captive market to advance the concept of strategic management. This also gave a major incentive to book publishers, journals, and conference organizers to pursue and profit from the widespread institutionally supported interest in strategic management. In fact, some pundits have whimsically referred to strategic management as an invention of academics, without any basis as a distinct discipline in reality.

The situation appears to be changing in the 1990s. First, in business, questions have been raised as to whether strategic management is a distinct and useful discipline. The range of subjects related to strategic management today includes: strategy formulation, industry and competitive market analysis, strategy implementation (individual and group behavior, organizational culture and structure, leadership, and staffing), enabling planning and action (marketing, computer systems, finance, accounting, control, production/operations management), managing technology, international management, entrepreneurial management, ethics and social values (and their influence on strategic management), strategic alliances, and case study and development. These subjects, which appear in strategic management texts and bibliographies, span a wide range of general business subject areas (Mockler, 1993a). As a result, as the field grew in the 1980s, strategic management emerged as an eclectic collection of essays and ideas involving all areas of business management which were only very loosely associated under a vague umbrella process concept, strategic management. This has been pointed out by many writers, including Henry Mintzberg (1994) in his *The Rise and Fall of Strategic Planning*.

Problems with defining the term *strategic management* also arose in part because, as the subject grew in popularity and was more and more absorbed into operating management, it began to lose its primary focus. Instead of focusing on just *enterprise-wide strategy formulation and on policy organization and systems framework development* (the original concept of business policy), the focus shifted to managing strategically at any level of management where enterprise-wide strategies are implemented. Since different levels of management are involved in managing strategically, as shown in

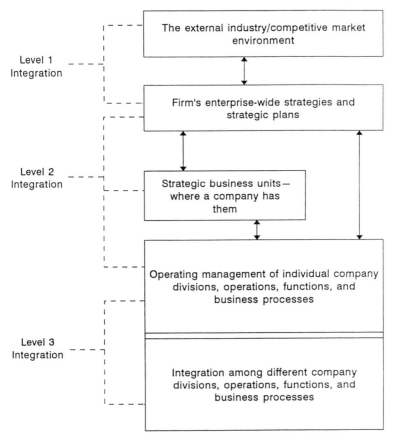

Figure 1.1   Integrative enterprise management: different levels of integration

Figure 1.1, in essence the concept has become *integrative enterprise management*, that is, management at any level within the context of overall enterprise (business firm or not-for-profit organization) strategies. In this sense the concept of strategic management has become almost synonymous with business management. This has seriously diminished its usefulness as a distinct controlling concept.

1.2
ATTEMPTS AT CREATING A UNIFIED DISCIPLINE CALLED STRATEGIC MANAGEMENT: A MICRO CONTINGENCY SYSTEMS ORIENTATION

This section discusses the emerging positions of *macro* and *micro* viewpoints, as well as other specific contingency theories and applications, in defining core strategic management processes.

LINKING THEORY TO PRACTICE THROUGH MACRO INDUSTRY/COMPETITIVE MARKET RESEARCH

Since management in business is context-specific—what works in a specific manager's business or market (long and short term) is the focal point—contingency theory and processes are significant strategic management research areas. The work done at the economy, industry, and general competitive market level is sometimes referred to as *macro* contingency theory research. Econometric models are examples at the economy/industry level. First, studies are made of how a selected economy works. A mathematical model of the interrelationships of key factors (the process) is developed and then used to simulate the impact of changes in variables (such as inflation) on outcomes. Such mathematical models are also extended to include the input of economic/industry/competitive market factors on a firm (Rosenkranz, 1979; Mockler, 1992). A second, more specific level of macro contingency theory involves studies of industry/competitive markets of varying scope. The following discussion of macro contingency theory focuses on this more specific macro level.

Macro research at any level focuses on explaining and exploring a general industry/competitive market, a necessary step in developing macro contingency models. For this reason, the focus is basically on explaining how things work (macro content research) rather than on developing contingency models that can be used to guide individual managers in getting their jobs done in a specific company and related industry/competitive market situations. Many research studies related to contingency research described in the major academic research journals, such as *Strategic Management Journal, Academy of Management Review, Academy of Management Journal, Management Science* and *Sloan Business Review*, focus on this macro approach. For example, all five articles and notes in the November 1993 *Strategic Management Journal* fall into this category.

While their explanations of how industries and competitive markets work are very useful, macro contingency models arising from this research have been widely criticized for failing accurately

STRATEGIC MANAGEMENT: THE BEGINNING OF A NEW ERA   7

to replicate real world complexities (for example, Dess and Rasheed, 1991). As explained in these criticisms, these macro models very often do not fully explain reality; nor are they directly useful to individual planners in domain-specific situations, except for those involving very large companies. Unfortunately, they are all too often academic exercises designed to help the researcher become familiar with business dynamics and to compensate for the researcher's lack of business experience. The benefits for the knowledgeable and experienced business manager are negligible.

For example, Sharfman and Dean (1991) formulated a model that builds on work by Aldrich (1979) and by Dess and Beard (1984). The model was designed to measure performance and other characteristics of major firms in an industry/competitive market in relation to three factors: complexity (geographic concentration, product diversity, and technical intricacy), dynamism (market instability and technological instability), and competitive threat (resource availability and competition). Reality, however, is much more complex than the three factors used in the model. For instance, the factor market instability should also take into consideration: the difficulty of market entry (the easier it is, the more naturally unstable the market will be), the level of maturity, and the nature of the product (the fashion industry is highly unstable, while the electric utility industry usually remains relatively stabilized). Each of these sub-factors will affect a firm's measure of success differently. Because they do not accurately represent reality and lack relevance, such *macro* research and the models it developed have not had a major impact on the field.

Another potentially useful macro contingency research area focuses on techniques or possible solutions. For example, there are studies of different kinds of turnaround strategies and of market and company situations in which these strategies do and do not work (Hofer, 1980, 1991; Pearce and Robbins, 1991; Schendel and Patton, 1976; Schendel *et al.*, 1975). This is again useful basic research that helps researchers in particular to understand how things work. Business managers are generally familiar with these tools and concepts. However, what they seek and need is a sense of how these concepts and tools can be used in individual firms like their own. Unless the focus is directly on usefulness or application to individual managers, which it rarely is as presented in the *macro* research studies, it does not fulfil the basic need of an application discipline such as strategic management.

The underlying concept of the macro contingency approach described in this section is given in Table 1.1.

Many researchers cited above recognize that a *micro* orientation is

Table 1.1   Macro top-down contingency approach: technical orientation

Situation:	For example, a competitive market
Task:	Identify what does or doesn't work and why
Reconceptualization:	Picture how a situation works including what factors and interrelationships lead to success or failure (for example, Ansoff's Turbulence Theory)
	Approaches defined and related to factors affecting their unity. For example, turnaround strategies of organization structures
	Advantages and disadvantages of each approach are identified—a start at developing contingency framework
Application:	Situations in which they can be successful or unsuccessful—an illusory contingency framework
	The exceptions usually include a very large number of enterprises and so render the model valueless, reducing it to an academic exercise

not only more useful to managers but also better explains how business actually works. For example, David Jemison (1987) in his "Risk and the Relationship Among Strategy, Organizational Processes and Performance" and Jay Barney (1986) in his "Strategic Factor Markets: Expectations, Luck, and Business Strategy" found that individual firms' management and organization processes have a greater impact on success than critical competitive market factors. Jemison and Sitkin (1986), Wensley (1990), Priem and Harrison (1994), Hart and Baubury (1994), and Dierickx and Cool (1989) have drawn similar conclusions. This work illustrates another of the interesting paradoxes of strategic management. While it is indispensable to have a thorough knowledge of a company's industry and competitive market environment, in many situations the ultimate strategy chosen is dictated more by the core competencies and personal characteristics of the CEO involved.

A REFOCUSED APPROACH TO STRATEGIC MANAGEMENT CONTINGENCY THEORY: A MICRO ORIENTATION

Working managers do not so much need to be lectured about market dynamics. They need to know what to do about them, given their own resources. For example, a study of how Procter & Gamble successfully responded to the declining interest in brands on the market and creatively overcame problems dramatically made the point that what you do with what you've got is very often the essence of successful strategic management (Laing, 1993).

For these reasons, other current research being done explores ways to develop more individual manager-focused (that is, applications-oriented) contingency models by going beyond the basic macro research studies explaining phenomena cited above to develop micro contingency guidelines for use by managers.

When making complex decisions, managers often first formulate some kind of decision-making approach or concept of a solution. This general process, which in essence is a model of the process described in the "Overall Perspective" section at the beginning of this chapter, is illustrated in Figure 1.2. Both the nature of the business (left box of Figure 1.2) and the strategic management task under study (right box of Figure 1.2), as perceived by the manager, affect the kinds of cognitive models developed and the resulting decision solution.

(1) *The situation.* The kind of situation will affect the kind of model formulated and the way it is used. For example, these models can differ in relation to the kind of industry, size of company under study, and the nature of the consumer, competitors, and competitive market conditions. Additional

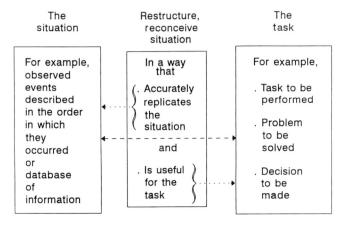

Figure 1.2 Decision making involves reorganizing reality in a way that enables effective decision making

situation factors which can influence the kind of model developed include factors relating to available resources and possible actions, as well as factors relating to the decision maker including:

- Amount of information available—imperfect information can lead to tentative solutions.
- Past experience—a manager can have a perception about buyer motivation based on specific incidents he or she encountered.
- Personal bias—some favor emphasizing people factors, others emphasize rational aspects.
- Personality traits—some are naturally more aggressive than others.
- Even physical and emotional wellbeing—people think differently when tired or unhappy.

(2) *The task.* The reconceptualization process is influenced in part by the aspect of strategy formulation and strategy implementation under study.

(3) *Reconceiving or reconceptualizing.* Managers reconceptualize situations and develop solutions in a wide range of ways when managing strategically. Such diversity is not surprising, since enterprise-wide strategies can be formulated in many ways. In addition, the best way to reconceptualize is very situation-context-dependent, and so far there are very few contingency/ situational guidelines for what are the best ways to formulate strategies and implement them in different kinds of situations. These realities of strategic management in practice are among the many reasons why no fully formed discipline of strategic management has yet been developed.

ADAPTIVE CONTINGENCY MODELS OF STRATEGIC MANAGEMENT PROCESSES

Three kinds of strategic management processes and models are discussed in this section: general strategic management processes; strategy formulation processes; and strategy implementation processes. The discussions describe an incipient major strategic management research area which is expected to experience significant development over the next decade.

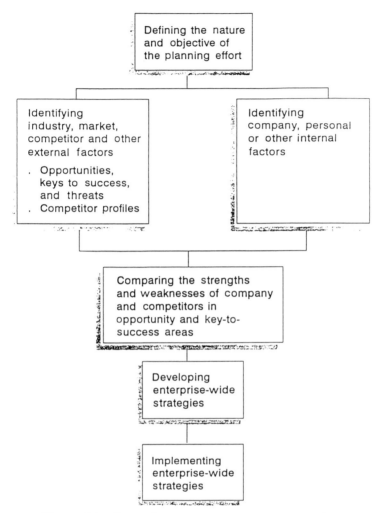

Figure 1.3   Strategic management process overview

General Strategic Management Processes

A frequently cited familiar general process outline for strategic management is shown in Figure 1.3 (Mockler, 1993c). While accurate, it is much too general to be anything more than an overview/framework for the subject. In many situations, a considerable amount of analysis goes into examining the wide array of company and competitive market factors, and it is difficult to identify all influencing factors and their impact on strategy decisions. Complex reconceptualizations are also needed to synthesize this information in order to formulate and implement strategies. Personal heuristics are involved in making associations among, and drawing inferences from, situation factors when formulating strategic concepts. Further, a sense of real-world limitations is needed to create workable solutions and considerable interpersonal skills are needed to make solutions work.

Figure 1.4 gives a limited version of the general models shown in Figures 1.2 and 1.3. This model, which is limited to strategy formulation, was based in part on Michael Porter's work (Porter, 1980, 1990) and was used to develop experimental knowledge-based systems in 1986 and 1987 (Mockler, 1989a,b). These early studies and the process models resulting from them demonstrated that *general overall* strategic management thought processes are simply too complex to be accurately replicated, given the limited existing knowledge of them (Mockler, 1993b).

As a result, research was refocused to concentrate on modelling lower-level, more domain-specific, strategy formulation and implementation processes. Feigenbaum and Dennett were among the many other experts working in the artificial intelligence and psychology areas who advised refocusing research in this way at that time (Dennett, 1981, 1987, 1988; Feigenbaum, 1987). Their premise was that a decade or more of defining the thousands of specific expert strategic management decisions and actions was needed to build a firmly documented research base upon which more general process models could be built.

The following sections discuss several kinds of narrowly defined processes modelled over the past six years as part of ongoing research projects which focus on developing contingency models of specific strategic management processes. These models build on the general ones shown in Figures 1.2–1.4 and prior research cited elsewhere in this chapter.

Strategy-formulation Processes

The general strategy-formulation process involving the examination of both industry/competitive market (external) and company (internal) situation factors is outlined in Figures 1.3 and 1.4. The actual process in action is difficult to identify and describe, as well as to generalize about.

For example, in some situations an enterprise-wide strategy may initially be no more than a CEO's vision of a company's future,

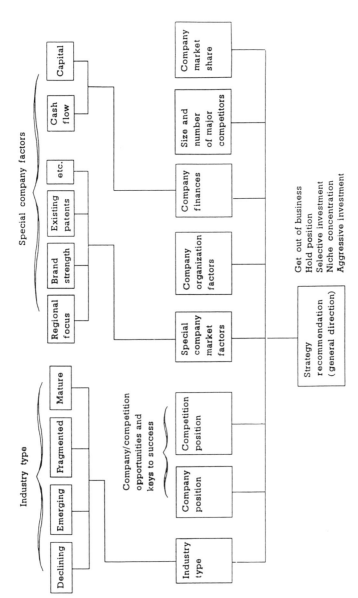

Figure 1.4 Diagram of situation to be prototyped for general strategy direction (initial prototype)

based on experienced-based knowledge of the company and its industry/competitive market. Technically, the processes outlined in Figures 1.3 and 1.4 are at work here, but in practice the actual process is often informal and almost intuitive. In addition, that strategic vision may not yet be a fully formed idea. While planning was proceeding, this was the late Colman Mockler's vision of Gillette, when he became CEO in 1974 after the company's rapid diversification under the prior CEO. Mockler's vision was shaped, defined, made specific and translated into action over a period of time in a cooperative way, in his words "from the bottom up" (McKibben, 1990). The vision had considerable flexibility during its implementation, as the company expanded rapidly into growing foreign markets, as complex joint ventures became needed, and as new technology enabled faster new-product development in the company's well-defined major business areas: razor blades, personal-care products, and writing instruments. The essence of Mockler's vision was maintained even though its realization was dynamic and adaptive.

What is clear from such studies of business practices is that the strategy-formulation process is not always explicit, and both the strategy itself and the process through which it is formulated can vary considerably from situation to situation. For example, Mintzberg, among others, has on several occasions pointed out that there are at least ten different definable kinds (or "schools") of planning processes (Mintzberg, 1990, 1994).

Strategic planning is often a paradoxical process, which is contingent on each situation's characteristics. If a planner is familiar with the company and industry involved, for example, the analytical or decomposing aspects of the process may be done quickly and the focus be on synthesizing them into initial general strategy statements, as was the case with Colman Mockler at Gillette. Planners less familiar with a situation may initially become more involved in the analytical phase of planning. What is important at one point in the process, therefore, may be less important at a later time, depending on the situation. Further, circumstances change, creating an environment which can range from stable to turbulent to chaotic (Gleick, 1987).

In addition, clear distinctions between strategy formulation and implementation cannot always be made; strategies are not always written down; and the role of strategy in affecting the company's future is not always the same. This was true long before Mintzberg mentioned it in his doctoral studies. While general strategic management process models, such as those shown in Figures 1.3 and

1.4, are useful, therefore, the realization of these concepts in day to day business operations can be a complex process which is hard to define and put into a systematic body of knowledge—that is, into a discipline or science called strategic management.

In spite of these difficulties, progress is being made on identifying and structuring individual manager-oriented strategic management processes. Figure 1.5, for example, outlines one such strategy-formulation process. This situation involves the development of a strategy for introducing a new product into a foreign affiliate of a multinational company, a familiar strategy-formulation task. External factors (customer, market, and competitor) and company factors (local and corporate) are examined. Well-defined expert heuristics are then used to reason with data gathered about the situation to reach a strategy conclusion. The data used is situation-specific, as seen in Figure 1.6, a model (dependency diagram) of the computerized knowledge-based system replicating the process. The question marks at the top of Figure 1.6 are used to solicit (and input into the system) information on a wide range of external and internal factors specific to the situation under study. This is why such models are called "situation-specific". They are personal constructs based on experience and training since they replicate human expert planners' reasoning processes. They are the basis for developing gradually expanded, more generalized, models of strategy-formulation processes.

In contrast to macro contingency research, research in the micro area begins with expert planners and the specific situations they face. Scenarios are developed of decisions made in specific situations. Incremental prototyping involves working with additional experts, testing developed models of expert thinking processes with other experts, consulting written sources (including available general market studies and macro contingency studies such as Michael Porter's), and so inductively creating new models of gradually broader scope and increasing complexity. Modifications, expansions, and refinements can be made piecemeal since the models are modular and the technology adaptive. In this sense, the incremental model prototypes are looked on only as successive approximations of reality, not final versions of sophisticated expert strategic management reasoning processes.

In addition to the process models already discussed, many other strategic management contingency models have been developed. Researchers at the University of Michigan (Kochen and Min, 1987) and at Carnegie Mellon (Hidding, 1989) have developed theoretical models designed to evaluate competitor strengths and weaknesses,

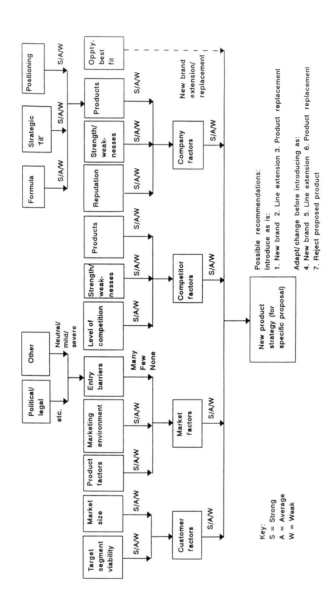

Figure 1.5 Diagram of decision area to be prototyped: new product strategy for local country product proposal

technological trends in the market, and an individual firm's position within a market (Humpert and Holley, 1988). Goul has developed a formal decision-making model, and extended it into the strategy-formulation area (Goul, 1985, 1987; Goul *et al.*, 1986). A number of university researchers are also defining and modelling specific strategy-formulation processes, many in conjunction with developing knowledge-based computer systems which replicate the strategy formulation processes. For example, a University of Massachusetts' project focuses on product planning processes (Abraham, 1990). Another product, at Stanford Research Institute (SRI), focuses on analyzing company, market and technological factors, and on recommending competitive market strategies in the polyfins (a special kind of plastic) industry (Syed and Tse, 1987). Conceptual structures used in competitive market analysis in the banking industry are studied by Reger (1988) at the University of Illinois. Companies such as IBM (Benson, 1989; Krcmar, 1985) and Andersen Consulting (Hidding, 1989) are also working on modelling and replicating in expert knowledge-based systems specific strategy-formulation processes useful to individual managers (Rowe, 1989).

Similar cognitive models and related knowledge-based systems are being developed worldwide: in Finland, Russia, the Czech Republic, Slovakia, and Poland, in England and France, in Tokyo, in India, and in Beijing, to name just those of which the author is personally aware (for example, Arunkumar and Jamakiram, 1992; Walden, 1992). The work described in this section, therefore, is only one small project in a very large field, designed to help refocus contingency theory in particular and strategic management research in general on individual managers' needs. All this work, which is admittedly only a beginning, is needed to build a base for developing broader, more generalized adaptive *micro contingency* models of individual manager-oriented strategic management processes, that is, process models that can help individual managers more effectively and strategically manage their own enterprises.

As seen from the following discussions, these process models are only a small beginning at defining one aspect of strategic management theory. There is a long way to go before an adequate base for theory can be built using this inductive micro approach. This is nonetheless an important part of strategic management theory building. Curiously, this work has to date been almost totally ignored in current mainstream strategic management research literature.

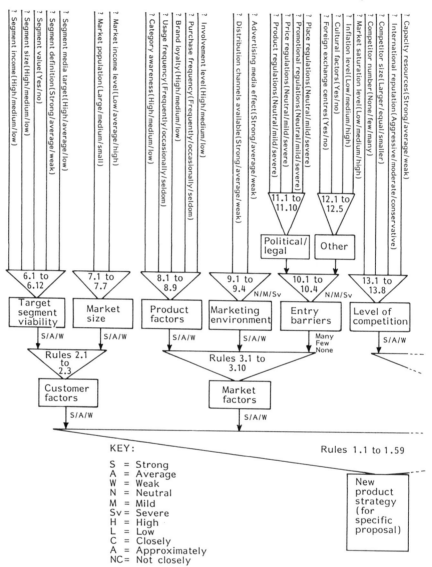

Strategy-implementation Processes

In practice, identifying and structuring strategy-implementation processes is even more difficult than identifying strategy-formulation processes. This is because they involve individual and group behavioral, as well as cognitive, processes. Work is nonetheless proceeding in this area, though much more slowly than

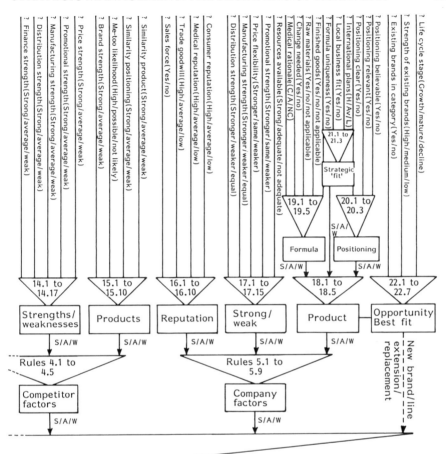

Figure 1.6 Dependency diagram: new product strategy selection for local country product proposal (initial prototype). (© 1994 R. J. Mockler)

in the strategy-formulation area.

Figure 1.7 models a system being developed for organization design and strategy implementation. At this time, a series of more detailed structured models is being developed by researchers within this framework for strategic management of the computer information systems function (Mockler, 1993b). Knowledge-based

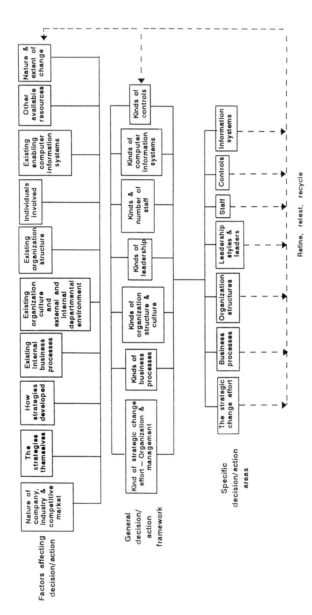

Figure 1.7   Strategy implementation. (© 1994 R. J. Mockler)

systems based on these models have been created and used. These systems are being developed and expanded in the same way as the strategy formulation ones described above.

The problem from a discipline definition viewpoint is that actual implementation, while the key to translating strategies into successful action, is outside the scope of a useful concept definition of strategic management, which has been defined here as encompassing only developing organizational/behavioral *frameworks* for action. In addition, the variety and complexity of implementation processes make them almost impossible to define in terms of meaningful and useful discipline generalities, a limitation which has been noted in the behavioral area where very few universals can be validated (Cronbach, 1986; Kast and Rosenzweig, 1985; Lorsch, 1980; Lorsch and Morse, 1974; Osigweh, 1989).

If implementation was that easy to define in a way useful to individual managers, why did it take six years for Ann and Tim Coleman and Ann and Bill Schlatter to get their candy toy to market? After all, it was an overall product concept which had been popularized long before in such movies as *Chitty Chitty Bang Bang* in 1968 in which a candy toy whistle "tootsweet", was the basis of a major musical number during which a candy factory was nearly destroyed (Lawson, 1994).

Reality is, of course, that, on average, fewer than 1% of inventions make it to market. The first two candy toy products invented by the Colemans and Schlatters had over $50 million in annual retail sales in 1993/4, so the work was worth it in their case.

OTHER DISCIPLINES AND AREAS MICRO CONTINGENCY THEORY DRAWS UPON

Strategic management contingency theory goes beyond what is described in the preceding sections. It draws upon a wide range of other areas and disciplines, especially systems theory, cognitive science, and organizational and behavioral sciences.

Systems Theory: Working within Broader Business Contexts

When examining a strategic management situation, the focus is on the total contingent context. That perspective is called the total business process or system context. Figure 1.8 gives a summary outline of an integrated business systems context.

For the enterprise as a whole, this system context would be the

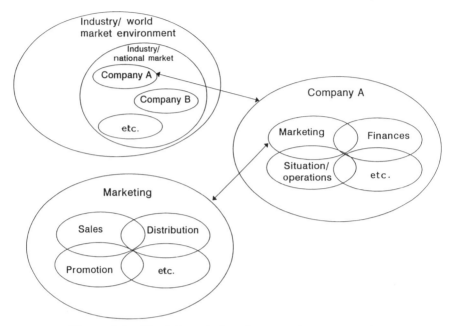

Figure 1.8   The integrated systems context perspective

industry and competitive market—that is, the business system that serves the customer or market. Michael Walsh had this broad perspective at Union Pacific Railroad in 1986. He quickly established an overall vision of customer accommodation to meet the competitive requirements of the turbulent domestic transportation industry. In keeping with this vision, success depended on the company's ability to respond quickly to customer's changing shipping needs at the point of customer contact. This was almost impossible under the existing conditions, since decisions passed through many management layers. In addition, Walsh faced an intransigent bureaucracy (Hayes, 1992; Machalaba, 1991).

Confronted with these problems, Walsh changed the corporate structure by reducing management layers from nine to three. This both simplified and speeded up decision making and sent a signal that change was coming, with or without the cooperation of middle managers. A new computer information system was introduced to enable operating personnel at the customer level to get a quick response to proposed scheduling changes from an integrated, company-wide traffic control center. By focusing on the total system context—the customer needs and the total system required to fulfil those needs—Walsh was able to make changes in a way that strategically improved overall company operations and profitability.

Effective management of the many different operating levels within an enterprise also requires consideration of broader contexts—enterprise-wide strategies, as well as the operations of other units, divisions, functions, and operations within an enterprise—in many different ways, as shown in Figures 1.1 and 1.9. For example, marketing management decisions must be, at times, made with reference to other areas supporting them, such as manufacturing; on another level, marketing and manufacturing would strive to integrate their operations with enterprise-wide strategies.

Viewing a total business or specific business operating segment within a company from a total systems context viewpoint is not a new concept. Such studies have a long history (Forester, 1965; Mockler, 1968, 1974). Peter Senge (1990) is one of the people who has more recently written on the subject of the total systems thinking

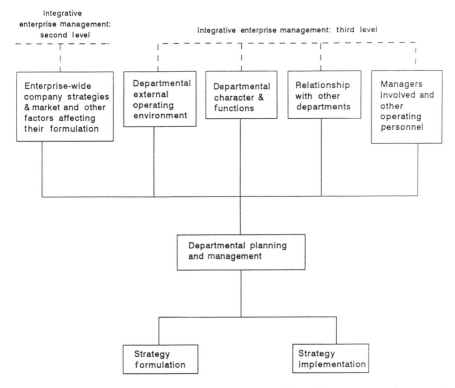

Figure 1.9 Factors affecting integrating overall and departmental strategic plans: second- and third-level integrative enterprise management

approach to strategic management and to creating "learning" organizations. All the work discussed in this section relates directly or indirectly to the work done by Jay Forester at MIT over the past 30 years.

Cognitive Science

The work and research involving cognitive modelling of individual decision-making processes is based largely on cognitive psychology studies concerning the various ways people, particularly business managers, reconceive situations in order to simplify and handle them effectively. For example, there is substantial evidence that people formulate mental pictures—sometimes called models (Porac and Thomas, 1990) or constructs (Reger, 1988)—of a decision situation they face. The flow diagram shown in Figure 1.2, as well as substantial portions of the work discussed in the micro contingency section above, originated in part from this work. Such influencing decision factors and their impact on strategic management is an exciting area of future contingency research in which extensive background work has already been done (Adams-Webber, 1978; Bannister, 1970; Bannister and Mair, 1968; Bukszar, 1990; Fransella and Bannister, 1977—bibliography studies based on personal construct theory; Haiss, 1990; Kelly, 1955; Porac and Thomas, 1987; Senge, 1990, 1992).

Organization and Behavioral Sciences

The success of strategy development and implementation depends to a large extent on the individuals and groups involved in a systems development project. Contingency theory studies in the behavioral area have had a long history (Lawrence, 1967).

Early studies by Fiedler (1967) and later by Rowe (1987, 1992) (among many) have identified contingent guidelines for selecting *leadership* styles appropriate for different change management situations. For example, studies have shown how certain leadership styles (for instance, autocratic) or leader personality types (for instance, sensing/intuitive) are best suited for managing different types of strategic change situations.

Individuals can be apprehensive when confronted with change. Change itself, as well as any new strategic directions, can be threatening and create *resistance to change*. Many factors can affect an individual's reaction to change. Different individuals interpret change differently; not all individuals resist change. Personality variables may also be related to one's propensity to resist change (Stone and Kemmerer, 1984). *Managing change* when introducing new strategic directions, therefore, involves balancing many factors, and the behavioral sciences can provide considerable support and guidance in doing this.

Communication skills and *training* in all areas related to managing change are also important behavioral study areas which provide a rich resource when approaching a change management situation (Gordon, 1987; Stewart, 1985). Building step by step through continuing small success stories is another identified way to move a change initiative forward (Leonard-Barton, 1987; Mahler, 1986; McConahey, 1992).

Re-engineering organizations, a subject which has been studied from both organizational behavioral and systems theory viewpoints, is often directly related to strategy implementation as is seen in later discussions in this chapter.

In addition to studies of re-engineering, leadership, and barriers to change, *organization structure* studies of group dynamics and the move from hierarchical towards flat organizations are particularly useful in working through computer information systems deployment situations (Byrne, 1993).

It is rare that crises do not arise and quick action is not needed to improvise solutions to them. A growing body of research into *crisis management, improvisation, chaos theory*, and what is termed "situated action", i.e. action designed to meet a specific situation's immediate needs, has proven very useful in strategic management projects (Barton, 1993; Gleick, 1987; Lave and Wenger, 1991; Perry, 1993; Suchman, 1987).

Chance and luck can also play a role in strategic management. For example, opportunities are at times stumbled upon accidentally. Alias Research Inc., a young software company, was originally founded to provide computer software animation for the movie industry (it worked on movies such as *Terminator* 2). Other applications of the company's technology, to product design, were stumbled on by the president during a chance meeting at General Motors. It turned out that Alias's three-dimensional mathematically accurate images helped engineers to simulate future products and work out bugs more quickly than did the traditional manual methods, such as physical mock-ups (Farnsworth, 1991).

Stimulating Creativity

Other, less-structured processes useful in strategy formulation have also been studied. For example, taking contrarian views—sometimes in conjunction with brainstorming sessions—can simulate opportunity identification. Richard E. Rainwater, a consummate contrarian like many investors who have amassed huge fortunes, buys troubled properties and businesses when they are out of favor, hoping to cash in when they become popular. In 1991 he bought Sun Belt hospitals, a depressed business. While eventual success is far from certain, one of his early efforts—with American Medical—yielded him $56 million on an investment of $26 million (Freudenheim, 1993; Jones, 1993). Ruth Owades did what others said could not be done and sold flowers by mail. Started in 1989, her Sun Petals company sales were $5 million in 1990, $10 million in 1991, and $13 million in 1992 (Strom, 1992). In spite of the extraordinarily difficult competitive conditions in the airline industry in 1993, there were 15 new airlines which had identified niche markets in which they hoped they would survive and prosper (Bryant, 1993a; Salpukas, 1993; Rothman, 1993).

Well-defined Specific Strategic Management Application Areas of Study

Strategic management research findings, and underlying process and tool definitions, have broad applications among *multinational companies*. In these situations a balance is struck between context-specific situation requirements which can vary from country to country and common processes and tools which travel easily from one culture to another. Good examples of this balance are found in the unique combination of free-market controlled economy approaches used in China, Japan, and the four big and four little dragons/tigers in Asia. The special problems encountered in planning for small companies and new ventures, as well as planning for not-for-profit organizations, are other major valid strategic management application areas of study.

THE FUTURE

Based on a study of the work discussed in this section, there clearly exists a good beginning for developing a body of unifying strategic management theory based on *context-specific, application-oriented, individual manager-focused, micro contingency theory* using a variety of approaches and drawing upon a variety of scientific and other research and application areas. At present it may be more an orientation than a disciplined scientific body of theory. But by narrowing its focus to a more useful realistic individual manager focus, this micro contingency work shows promise of being the basis for a more scientific and useful discipline called strategic management that will emerge over the next decade.

1.3
EMERGING WELL-DEFINED SPECIALIZED ADVANCED STRATEGIC MANAGEMENT AREAS OF STUDY

In addition to the redefinition of strategic management (Section 1.1) and the contingency research and theory work on strategic management process definition and redefinition (Section 1.2), other specific areas are emerging as potentially part of the well-focused but narrowly defined concept of strategic management for the next decade.

COMPUTER INFORMATION SYSTEMS

For example, advanced database and data processing systems have enabled life insurance companies to handle claims effectively and efficiently 24 hours a day (Marciniec, 1993), airlines to provide total customer service 24 hours a day, mail order companies to service millions of customers in a personalized way (Ambrosio, 1992), baked goods companies and large retailers, to automate restocking orders, control inventories and reduce turnaround time dramatically (Forsythe, 1989), and express mail companies to monitor package delivery (Ramirez, 1993). These are only a few of hundreds of examples of strategic computer information systems which have enabled companies to compete effectively and at times gain competitive advantages.

Sophisticated management information systems and executive information systems can provide major competitive advantages, as they have at Banc One, where such systems enable managing customer accounts in ways that promote increased product sales activities (Lohr, 1991). Such systems help in providing not only management planning information but also information for strategic control. Advanced computerized decision-support systems enable improved evaluation through simulation of financial impacts resulting from proposed strategic alternatives (financial modelling), of economic trends (econometric models), and of a wide range of other strategic management decisions (computer software involving decision matrices, pairwise comparisons, sensitivity analysis, decision trees, linear programming, and risk assessment). Computer systems are also available to foster more effective group decision making (Mockler, 1991) and to replicate a variety of expert decisions. A new computer software package, *The Solution Machine*, introduced in 1993, even guides users effectively through a number of creative thinking approaches (Gemini, 1993).

COMPETITIVE INTELLIGENCE SYSTEMS

Since the mid-1980s, large companies have made significant investments in competitive information gathering, analysis, dissemination, and use in strategic planning. These moves have been stimulated both by computer information systems and telecommunication technology advances and by growing business problems arising from rapidly changing and intensely competitive market environments. For example, a 1989 study (Prescott and Smith, 1989) indicated that at the 95 large companies surveyed, the competitive intelligence programs were, on average, only four years old. The programs were evenly divided between doing strategic planning and helping to implement strategic plans. Of the programs, half were project-oriented, half were on-going programs. The third variable studied showed an even division between programs that were run by corporate or division planning departments, and those run by functional departments, such as marketing. Their average annual budget was $550000. Further supporting this trend, another survey in 1989 showed that the more control that user departments had of information systems technology, the more aggressive the company's competitive strategy was (Tavakolian, 1989).

SCENARIO-BASED PLANNING

Scenario development is a useful way to develop information for planning studies and to evaluate alternatives (Bonnett, 1994; Duncan, 1994; *Planning Review*, 1992; Schwartz, 1991; Wack, 1985a,b). When doing customer-focused strategic management, for example, the saying is "When in doubt start with the buyer", that is, pick a point in the business process, preferably the customer's, and trace how the buying decision and actual purchase are made. This is called a *competency chain analysis*—an analysis of the competencies needed to get people to buy a product, in other words, the critical factors affecting success and failure. Next, focus on another point, and trace the business process flow, from the purchase of raw materials, through production, distribution, and sale. This is called a *value-added chain analysis*. Then check this scenario (or any other reconceptualizations of the industry) against the initial impressions or against available descriptions of how the business works. Surprisingly, they do not always match. At this point, another scenario might be constructed. Often the scenario is more useful or accurate than the initial or generally accepted descriptions. This is called the *third alternative approach* in innovative decision making. Applications using this technique exist in almost every strategic management area.

ORGANIZATIONAL RE-ENGINEERING

The process involved in redesigning or re-engineering internal business processes to meet strategic customer needs and other enterprise-wide strategic objectives and then reorganizing operations to meet the needs of these newly designed processes is not new (Rigby, 1993a). In the early days of computer systems development in the 1960s, for example, there were methods analysts whose job was to study work flows and recommend changes in the business process to improve efficiency and effectiveness as a first step in developing and introducing computer information systems. The author worked on such business systems re-engineering efforts. The common wisdom then was that the major benefits of any computer systems development effort was not in the computer's contribution but in the improvements in operations which arose from the business process study. In fact, the improvements from the study were sometimes put into place without introduction of computer systems.

Many business process re-engineering studies being done today, while often more complex and elaborate, are fundamentally the same as those done 30 years ago. For example, Henk Sol of Delft University (Belgium) described how, when working on a computer systems project, the preliminary business process analysis done in 1991 for Heineken Breweries led to major improvements in the transportation system itself at the port of Rotterdam. This benefit ($500 million annual cost saving) resulted from organization/

business process changes made based on the preliminary study, prior to any benefits which came from installing new computer systems (Sol, 1992; Sol and Streng, 1992).

Many companies studied have moved towards creating more strategically adaptive organizations through business process re-engineering (Hammer and Jampy, 1993; Treece *et al.*, 1992). Among those companies are Aetna Life Insurance (Marciniec, 1993), Pepperidge Farms (Forsythe, 1989), Banc One (Lohr, 1991; Quint, 1989) and Wal-Mart, Southwest Airlines, and Compaq Computer (Furey, 1994). These and other companies are among examples of how using computer systems led to major changes in internal organization environments that made them more responsive to changing market needs, that is, changes that made the organizations more adaptive (Gleckman, 1993). It is not necessary to do organizational re-engineering as part of a computer information systems development effort, however. AT&T's credit division, for example, installed an adaptive new organization structure that was based in systems thinking but did not involve consideration of computerized competitive information systems (Deutsch, 1991). Total quality management studies are also done using business re-engineering techniques.

BENCHMARKING

Benchmarking, which involves studying best industry practices and performance and then re-engineering to adapt or surpass these benchmarks in one's own company, is used in strategic management to improve business processes and better exploit core competencies. Pratt and Whitney, American Express, SunHealth, Chevron Oil Company, Xerox, and Coopers & Lybrand are among the many companies who have used it (Davis and Patrick, 1993; Krause and Liu, 1993; Prairie, 1993; Pryor and Katz, 1993; Ransley, 1993; Watson, 1993).

LEADERSHIP AND MANAGING STRATEGIC CHANGE

The effectiveness of putting strategies to work in a business depends, to a large extent, on skilfully directing and managing changes. For example, one of the major reasons cited for a successful turnaround of Salomon Brothers brokerage firm after the 1991 trading scandal was the appointment of Warren Buffet as CEO. Buffet, an Omaha investor noted for his conservative management style and ethical philosophy, implanted a very conservative, risk-aversive culture at Salomon and so enabled it to regain customer confidence. This was the same style Buffet exhibited when successfully managing Berkshire Hathaway Inc., another of his investments (Faison, 1992; Fisher, 1993; Norris, 1991; Tilsner, 1993). It was a style that enabled him to win the trust of managers and customers at Salomon, an important leadership success factor.

Determining which leadership style or combination of styles might be most effective in a manager's own situation will depend on situation factors such as those shown in Figure 1.7. Such a factor analysis may lead to the conclusion that a single leadership style will best suit the situation under study, or that a combination of leadership styles is more appropriate. For example, Thomas Murphy and Daniel Burke, who were credited with turning the merged Capital Cities and ABC Communication Company into a money machine, used a mixed style characterized as "prudence, management autonomy, and meddling when it is called for" (Auletta, 1991; Kneale, 1990). At other times, the leadership style needed will change over time as situation requirements change. At AM International a tough analytical leadership style was needed initially to take the company out of bankruptcy; later a style oriented towards people was needed (Johnson, 1987).

A body of work generally categorized as "Learning Organizations" (Senge, 1990), which also evolved under the guidance of Jay Forester at MIT, provides techniques for re-engineering organizations in a way that enables them to adapt to change more easily in the future.

STRATEGIC ALLIANCES

Many domestic US corporations, as well as global firms, are finding that collaborative arrangements between firms can be effective. For example, Ford and Mazda have an alliance that has lasted over ten years (Treece *et al.*, 1992). AT&T has entered into an astonishingly wide array of alliances which has enabled it to obtain positions in almost every corner of the communication business (Andrews, 1993a–c; Keller, 1993; Kirkpatrick, 1993; Markoff, 1993; Zielgler *et al.*,

1992). Four major US airlines moved (or were studying moves) to create permanent alliances with unions in 1993 by giving the unions a percentage of ownership in the companies (Bryant, 1993a; Kelly and Bernstein, 1993; McDowell, 1993a,b). Also, all three major US auto makers were discussing risk-reducing cooperative programs for developing electric cars in mid-1993 (Wald, 1993). Many such *strategic alliances*, both successes and failures, are described by Badaracco (1990) and Kanter (1989). Because of the growth of business development initiatives in this area, strategic management theory studies have again followed business practice, as they have in many other areas, so that strategic alliances have become and should continue to be a significant research and application area over the next decade.

ECONOMIC, FINANCIAL, AND OTHER PLANNING TOOLS

The planning tools with the longest history involve economic planning and financial planning. Prior to the 1970s, for the most part, strategic planning was mainly enterprise-level financial planning. At first, the plan was the equivalent of a budget, a financial projection of results planned for in all operating areas. Strategic planning, especially for large corporations, also involved studying the environment and industry context and projecting possible outcomes. As the 1970s progressed, computer tools were developed and improved, especially in financial simulation and modelling and in statistical and econometric analysis software. A complete review of these is given elsewhere (Mockler, 1993a).

   Few, if any, of the areas covered in this section are the exclusive province of strategic management; strategic management draws upon the economic, mathematical modelling, cognitive psychology, and group and individual organizational behavior areas for much of its substance. This section has selectively described several old and new strategic management tools and techniques. Over the next decade these and other specialized areas will presumably continue to be part of a distinct, well-defined strategic management subject area of study—as it develops niches of specialized knowledge.

   The above is only a partial review of strategic management tools and techniques. A 1993 study in *The Planning Review* (Rigby, 1993b), David Hussey's "Glossary of Management Techniques" (Hussey, 1992), and Mockler's *Computer Software to Support Strategic Management Decision Making* (Mockler, 1992) all cover more complete lists of tools and techniques useful in strategic management. *The Planning Review* every other month continually reviews new tools and techniques. At one time or another all of them can be useful in strategic management. Seldom are they a "major" cure for problems, even though some managers treat them as such. Rather, the approach used is a situational contingency one, through which appropriateness of a tool for a specific situation is determined, adaptations made where feasible, and new tools and techniques created/developed where needed for an individual manager's situation (Rigby, 1993b). Often many of these tools and techniques are fads or simply new names wrapped around older familiar concepts (Bleakley, 1993).

1.4
CONCLUSION

In discussing the future of strategic management, three aspects have been identified in this chapter. All these are areas on which strategic management will focus, in my judgment, over the next decade:

(1) A narrowing of the focus of the strategic management field to the definition described in the "Overall Perspective" section of Section 1.1, based on the lessons learned from the experiences of many corporate executives, such as Colman Mockler at Gillette.
(2) Increasing research interest in different areas of micro contingency (situation application) theory as an underlying core concept for identifying and describing basic strategic management processes, as described in Section 1.2.
(3) Development of an increasingly sophisticated array of strategic management tools and techniques, ranging from traditional econometric and financial planning models to more advanced computer information tools—which, while useful, nonetheless have well-defined limited applications to a very selected range of actual business situations, as described in Section 1.3.

Hopefully this well-defined focus will provide a basis for strategic management to develop into a systematically organized body of knowledge and so move toward becoming a scientific discipline. This sense that a new era for a more well-defined and circumscribed field of study called strategic management is believed to be beginning.

34   ROBERT J. MOCKLER

The general term "strategic management" will continue to be used to refer to integrative management processes and continue to be promoted in strategic management textbooks, unfortunately. I say unfortunately, since such usage serves to create confusion and so inhibit progress in developing a more narrowly defined discipline of strategic management as defined in this chapter.

REFERENCES

Abraham, T. (1990) *Market Advisor: An Expert System for Product Development*, Doctoral dissertation, University of Massachusetts, Amherst.
Adams-Webber, J. R. (1978) *Personal Construct Theory: Concepts and Applications*, Chichester, Wiley.
Aldrich, H. E. (1979) *Organizations and Environments*, Englewood Cliffs, NJ, Prentice Hall.
Ambrosio, J. (1992) Honing in on target customers. *Computerworld*, 10 February, 97–8.
Andrews, E. L. (1993a) AT&T paying $12.6 billion for cellular giant. *The New York Times*, 17 August, A1, D18.
Andrews, E. L. (1993b) AT&T plans died in Europe. *The New York Times*. 8 November, D1–D2.
Andrews, E. L. (1993c) AT&T reaches out (and grabs everyone). *The New York Times*, 8 August, 1, 6.
Ansoff, H. I. (1984) *Implanting Strategic Management*, Englewood Cliffs, NJ, Prentice Hall.
Ansoff, H. I. (1991) Critique of Henry Mintzberg's 'The Design School: reconsidering the basic premises of strategic management'. *Strategic Management Journal*, September, 449–61.
Arunkumar, S. and Jamakiram, N. (1992) ESP: Knowledge-based expert strategy planner. *Expert Systems with Applications*, January–March, 99–115.
Auletta, K. (1991) *Three Blind Mice: How the TV Networks Lost Their Way*, New York, Random House.
Badaracco, J. L. (1990) *The Knowledge Link: How Companies Compete Through Strategic Alliances*, Boston, MA, Harvard Business School Press.
Bannister, D. (ed.) (1970) *Perspectives in Personal Construct Theory*, New York, Academic Press.
Bannister, D. and Mair, J. M. (1968) *The Evaluation of Personal Constructs*, London, Academic Press.
Barney, J. B. (1986) Strategic factor markets: expectations, luck and business strategy. *Management Science*, October, 1231–41.
Barton, L. (1993) *Crisis in Organizations: Managing and Communicating in the Heat of Chaos*, Cincinnati, OH, South-Western Publishing Company.

Bedeian, A. G. (1989) Totems and taboos: undercurrents in the management discipline. Presidential Address at 1989 Annual Academy of Management Meeting, *Academy of Management News*, October, 1–6.
Benson, R. (1989) *KBS for Strategic Planning at IBM*, Seminar, Decision Sciences Institute Meeting, New Orleans, LA.
Bettis, R. A. (1991) Strategic management and the straightjacket: an editorial essay. *Organizational Science*, August, 315–19.
Bleakley, F. R. (1993) Many companies try management fads, only to see them flop. *Wall Street Journal*, 6 July, A1, A6.
Bonnett, T. W. and Olson, R. L. (1994) Four scenarios of state government services and regulations in the year 2010. *Planning Review*, July/August, 26–34.
Bryant, A. (1993a) On the cheap, yet flying high. *The New York Times*, 15 July, D1, D5.
Bryant, A. (1993b) T.W.A. gets court approval to end time in bankruptcy. *The New York Times*, 12 August, D1, D20.
Bukszar, E. W., Jr (1990) *Strategic Management and the Perception of Order*, doctoral dissertation, University of Arizona, Tucson.
Byrne, J. A. (1993) The horizontal corporation: it's about managing across, not up and down. *Business Week*, 20 December, 76–81.
Cronbach, L. J. (1986) Social inquiry by and for earthlings. In Fiske, D. W. and Shweder, R. A. (eds), *Metatheory in Social Science*, Chicago, University of Chicago Press, pp. 83–107.
Davis, T. R. V. and Patrick, M. S. (1993) Benchmarking at the SunHealth Alliance. *Planning Review*, January/February, 28–31, 56.
Dennett, D. C. (1981) *Brainstorms*, Boston, MA, MIT Press.
Dennett, D. C. (1987) *International Stance*, Boston, MA, MIT Press.
Dennett, D. C. quoted in Linden, E. (1988) Putting knowledge to work. *Time Magazine*, 28 March, 60–63.
Dess, G. G. and Beard, D. (1984) Dimensions of organizational task environments. *Administrative Science Quarterly*, **29**, 52–73.
Dess, G. G. and Rasheed, A. (1991) Conceptualizing and measuring organizational environment: a critique and suggestions. *The Journal of Management*, December, 701–10.
Deutsch, C. H. (1991) Workers' get to redesign organization's structure. *International Herald Tribune*, 4 July, 11.
Dierickx, I. and Cool, K. (1989) Asset stock accumulation and sustainability of competitive advantage. *Management Science*, December, 1504–14.
Duncan, N. E. and Wack, P. (1994) Scenarios designed to improve decision making. *Planning Review*, July/August, 18–25, 46.
Dyer, W. G. Jr and Wilkins, A. (1991) Better stories, not better constructs, to generate better theory: a rejoinder to Eisenhardt. *Academy of Management Review*, July, 613–19.
Early, S. (1990) Issues and alternatives: key to FMC's strategic planning system. *Planning Review*, May/June, 26–33.
Eisenhardt, K. M. (1989) Building theories from case study research. *Academy of Management Review*, October, 532–50.

Eisenhardt, K. M. (1991) Better stories and better constructs: the case for rigor and comparative logic. *Academy of Management Review*, July, 620–27.

Faison, S. (1992) At Salomon, new focus, new attitude. *The New York Times*, 15 February, 37, 50.

Farnsworth, C. H. (1991) Software star on a roller coaster. *The New York Times*, 19 September, F15.

Feigenbaum, E. (1987) Roundtable, *Proceedings: Texas Instruments Third AI Satellite Symposium*, New York, 8 April, pp. 1-1–1-75.

Fiedler, F. E. (1967) *A Theory of Leadership Effectiveness*, New York, McGraw-Hill.

Fisher, A. B. (1993) Buffet's school of management. *Fortune*, 116–17.

Forester, J. (1965) A new corporate design. *Sloan Management Review*, Fall.

Forsythe, J. (1989) Systems give Pepperidge Farm freshness. *InformationWeek*, 20 March, 29–31.

Fransella, F. and Bannister, D. (1977) *A Manual for Repertory Grid Technique*, New York, Academic Press.

Freudenheim, M. (1993) Cashing in on health care's troubles. *The New York Times*, 21 July, Business Section. 1, 6.

Furey, T. R. and Diorio, S. G. (1994) Making re-engineering strategic. *Planning Review*, July/August, 6–11, 43.

Gemini Group (1993) *The Solution Machine*, Problem Solving Software, RD#2 Box 117, Bedford, NY 10506, USA.

Gleckman, H. (1993) The technology payoff. *Business Week*, 14 June, 57–72.

Gleick, J. (1987) *Chaos: Making a New Science*, New York, Penguin Books.

Gordon, T. (1987) *Leadership Effectiveness Training*, Ridgefield, CT, Wyden Books.

Goul, M. (1985) *The Inclusion of Expertise in a Decision Support System for Strategic Management Decision Making*, doctoral dissertation, Oregon State University, Eugene, OR.

Goul, M. (1987) On building expert systems for strategic planners: a knowledge engineer's experiences. *Information and Management*, March, 131–41.

Goul, M., Shane, B. and Tonge, F. M. (1986) Knowledge-based decision support systems in strategic planning decisions: an empirical study. *Journal of Management Information Systems*, Spring, 70–84.

Haiss, P. R. (1990) *Cultural Influences on Strategic Planning*, New York, Springer-Verlag.

Hammer, M. and Jampy, J. (1993) *Re-engineering the Corporation*, New York, Harper Collins.

Hart, S. (1992) An integrative framework for strategy making processes. *Academy of Management Journal*, April, 328–57.

Hart, S. and Baubury, C. (1994) How strategy-making processes can make a difference. *Strategic Management Journal*, May, 251–70.

Hayes, T. C. (1992) Behind the iron hand at Tenneco. *The New York Times*, 6 January, D1, D5.

Hidding, G. (1989) *KBS for Strategic Planning at Coopers and Lybrand*, Seminar, Decision Sciences Institute, New Orleans.

Hofer, C. W. (1980) Turnaround strategies. *Journal of Business Strategy*, 1:1, 19–31.

Hofer, C. W. (1991) Turnaround strategy research: the next generation. Paper presented at Decision Sciences Annual Meeting, Miami Beach, FL, DSI, 24–26 November.

Huber, G. (1992) New organizational forms from new information technology. *Hawaii International Conference on Systems Sciences (HICSS)*, 25th Annual Meeting, Kauai, Hawaii, 7–10 January.

Humpert, B. and Holley, P. (1988) Expert systems in financial planning. *Expert Systems*, May, 78–100.

Hussey, D. E. (1992) Glossary of management techniques. In Hussey, D. (ed.), *International Review of Strategic Management*, Chichester, John Wiley, pp. 47–75.

Jemison, D. B. (1987) Risk and the relationship among strategy, organizational processes, and performance. *Management Science*, September, 1087–1101.

Jemison, D. B. and Sitkin, S. B. (1986) Acquisitions: the process can be a problem. *Harvard Business Review*, March/April, 107–16.

Johnson, R. (1987) AM International's ex-chief Freeman tells how his success got him fired. *The Wall Street Journal*, 24 August, A1, A14.

Jones, K. (1993) A hospital giant comes to town, bringing change. *The New York Times*, 16 September, D1, D5.

Kanter, R. M. (1989) *When Giants Learned to Dance*, New York, Simon & Schuster.

Kast, F. E. and Rosenzweig, J. E. (1985) *Organization and Management: A System and Contingency Approach*, 4th edn, New York, McGraw-Hill.

Keller, J. J. (1993) AT&T rivals face off in wireless wars: players boast deep pockets, technology. *The Wall Street Journal*, 19 August, B1, B5.

Kelly, G. A. (1955) *The Psychology of Personal Constructs*, Vols 1 and 2, New York, Norton.

Kelly, K. and Bernstein, A. (1993) United's unions would rather buy than strike. *Business Week*, 23 August, 71.

Kirkpatrick, D. (1993) Could AT&T rule the world? *Fortune*, 17 May, 55–66.

Kneale, D. (1990) Murphy and Burke: duo at Capital Cities scores a hit, but can network be part of it? *The Wall Street Journal*, 2 February, A1, A6.

Kochen, M. and Min, M. K. (1987) *Proceedings*, 7th Annual Workshop on Expert Systems and Their Applications, Avignon, 13–15 May, p. 41.

Krause, I. and Liu, J. (1993) Benchmarking R & D productivity. *Planning Review*, January/February, 16–21, 52.

Krcmar, H. (1985) *Enterprise-Wide Information Management*, Los Angeles, IBM Los Angeles Scientific Center.

Laing, J. R. (1993) New and improved Procter & Gamble fights to keep its place on the top shelf. *Barron's*, 29 November, 8–9, 22, 24, 26.

Lave, J. and Wenger, E. (1991) *Situated Learning*, New York, Cambridge University Press.

Lawrence, P. R. and Lorsch, J. W. (1967) Towards a contingency theory of organization. In *Organizations and Environment*, Boston, MA, Harvard University, Division of Research, Chapter VIII, pp. 185–210.

Lawson, C. (1994) A tricky path to market for a simple candy toy. *The New York Times*, 4 July, 35, 38.

Leonard-Barton, D. (1987) Technology implementation as integrative innovation. *Sloan Management Review*, October–November, 84–109.

Lohr, S. (1991) The best little bank in America. *The New York Times*, 7 July, Business Section, 1, 4.

Lorsch, J. W. (1980) Organization design: a situational perspective. In Koontz, H., O'Donnell, C. and Welhrich, H. (eds), *Management: A Book of Readings*, New York, McGraw-Hill, pp. 50–58.

Lorsch, J. W. and Morse, J. J. (1974) *Organizations and Their Members*, New York, Harper and Row.

Machalaba, D. (1991) Tenneco, recruiting new chairman, gets ready for a shakeup. *The Wall Street Journal*, 8 August, A1, A4.

Mahler, E. (1986) The business needs approach. In *Knowledge-Based Systems: A Step-by-Step Guide to Getting Started (The Second Artificial Intelligence Symposium)*, Austin, Texas, Texas Instruments Company, pp. 1-18–1-25.

Marciniec, J. (1993) Reengineering: from strategy to results. Presentation, Distinguished Speaker's Series, The Planning Forum, New York, 23 September.

Markoff, J. (1993a) A free and simple computer link. *The New York Times*, 8 December, D1, D9.

Markoff, J. (1993b) Pen-machine move made by AT&T. *The New York Times*, 16 August, D1, D2.

McDowell, E. (1993a) American stems tide of losses. *The New York Times*, 22 July, D1, D5.

McDowell, E. (1993b) Northwest signs last pacts needed to avert bankruptcy. *The New York Times*, 7 August, 37, 46.

McKibben, G. (1990) Gillette's Mockler: going out on top. *The Boston Sunday Globe*, 18 November, Business Section, A1, A7.

McConahey, S. (1992) *The Emerging Role of the Strategic Planner in the 1990s: Key Elements*, New York, Planning Forum's Strategic Planning Special Interest Group, 8 April.

Mintzberg, H. (1989) *Mintzberg on Management*, New York, The Free Press.

Mintzberg, H. (1990) The Design School: reconsidering the basic premises of strategic management. *Strategic Management Journal*, March–April, 171–95.

Mintzberg, H. (1994) *The Rise and Fall of Strategic Planning*, New York, The Free Press.

Mockler, R. J. (1968) *Circulation Planning and Development for The National Observer: A Research Study on Business Applications of Management Planning and Control Principles*, Bureau of Business and Economic Research, Georgia State College.

Mockler, R. J. (1970) Theory and practice of planning. *Harvard Business Review*, March–April.

Mockler, R. J. (1974) *Developing Information Systems for Management*, Columbus, OH, Charles E. Merrill.

Mockler, R. J. (1989a) *Knowledge-based Systems for Strategic Planning*, Englewood Cliffs, NJ, Prentice Hall.

Mockler, R. J. (1989b) *Knowledge-based Systems for Management Decisions*, Englewood Cliffs, NJ, Prentice Hall.

Mockler, R. J. (1991) Integrative groupware useful in strategic management. Co-author, *Long Range Planning*, The Journal of the Strategic Planning Society and European Planning Federation, August, 44–57.

Mockler, R. J. (1992) *Computer Software to Support Strategic Management Decision Making*. New York, Macmillan.

Mockler, R. J. (1993a) *Strategic Management: A Research Guide with Comprehensive Bibliographies*, The Planning Forum, Oxford, OH, and Strategic Management Research Group, New York.

Mockler, R. J. (1993b) *Strategic Management: An Integrative Context-Specific Process*, Harrisburg, PA, Idea Group Publishing.

Mockler, R. J. (1993c) Why strategic management is no longer an appropriate course for the AASCB Capstone course. Working Paper 93–5, Strategic Management Research Institute, New York.

Mockler, R. J. (1994) Re-engineering strategic management research. Working Paper, New York, Strategic Management Research Group, December.

Montgomery, C. A., Wernerfelt, B. and Balakrishnan, S. (1991) Strategy and the research process: a reply. *Strategic Management Journal*, January, 83–4.

Norris, F. (1991) Forcing Salomon into Buffet's conservative mold. *The New York Times*, 29 September, Business Section, 8.

Noyes, T. E. (1985) The evolution of strategic planning at Signode. *Planning Review*, September, 10–13.

Osigweh, C. A. B. (1989) Concept fallibility in organizational science. *Academy of Management Review*, October, 579–94.

Pearce, J. A., II and Robbins, D. K. (1991) An empirically-driven conceptual model of organizational turnaround. Paper delivered at the Eastern Academy of Management Conference, Hartford, CT, March.

Pepper, J. (1991) The battle for the skies. *Information Week*, 11 February, 44–9.

Perry, L. T., Scott, R. G. and Smallwood, W. N. (1993) *Real-Time Strategy: Improvising Team-Based Planning for a Fast-Changing World*. New York, John Wiley.

Planning Review (1992) Special issues on scenario writing and use. March/April and May/June.

Porac, J. F. and Thomas, H. (1987) Cognitive taxonomies and cognitive systematics. Paper presented at the meeting of the Academy of Management, New Orleans.

Porac, J. F. and Thomas, H. (1990) Taxonomic mental models in competitor definition. *Academy of Management Review*, April, 224–40.

Porter, M. (1980) *Competitive Strategy*. New York, The Free Press.

Porter, M. (1990) *The Competitive Advantage of Nations*, New York, The Free Press.

Prairie, P. (1993) An American Express/IBM consortium benchmarks information technology. *Planning Review*, January/February, 22–7.

Prescott, J. E. and Smith, D. C. (1989) The largest survey of the 'leading edge' competitor intelligence managers. *Planning Review*, May/June, 6–13.

Priem, R. L. and Harrison, D. A. (1994) Exploring strategic judgment: methods for testing the assumptions of prescriptive contingency theories. *Strategic Management Journal*, May, 311–24.

Pryor, L. S. and Katz, S. J. (1993) How benchmarking goes wrong (and how to do it right). *Planning Review*, January/February, 6–11, 53.

Quint, M. (1989) A bank that's riding technology to the top. *The New York Times*, 31 March, D7.

Ramirez, A. (1993) Teller machines inspire a new kiosk business. *The New York Times*, 31 March, D7.

Ransley, D. L. (1993) Training managers to benchmark. *Planning Review*, January/February, 32–5.

Reger, R. K. (1988) *Competitive Positioning in the Chicago Banking Market: Mapping the Mind of the Strategist*, doctoral dissertation, University of Illinois, Urbana, IL.

Rigby, D. (1993a) The secret history of process reengineering. *Planning Review*, March/April, 24–7.

Rigby, D. (1993b) How to manage the management tools. *Planning Review*, November/December, 8–13.

Rosenkranz, F. (1979) *An Introduction to Corporate Modelling*, Durham, NC, Duke University Press.

Rothman, A. (1993) Little airlines, big opportunities. *Business Week*, 5 July, 90.

Rowe, A. J. (1989) Expert systems in strategic management. Paper presented at Decision Sciences Institute 20th Annual Meeting, New Orleans.

Rowe, A. J. and Mason, R. O. (1987) *Managing With Style*, San Francisco, CA, Jossey-Bass.

Rowe, A. J. and Boulgarides, J. D. (1992) *Managerial Decision Making*, New York, Macmillan.

Salpukas, A. (1993) Newest airlines find conditions ripe to succeed. *The New York Times*, 19 May, A1, D5.

Schendel, D. E. and Patton, G. R. (1976) Corporate strategies and turnaround. *Journal of Economics and Business*, 236–41.

Schendel, D. E., Patton, G. R. and Riggs, J. (1975) Corporate turnaround strategies. *Journal of General Management*, Spring, 3–11.

Schwartz, P. (1991) *The Art of the Long View*, New York, Doubleday.

Senge, P. M. (1990) *The Fifth Discipline*, New York, Doubleday.

Senge, P. M. (1992) Mental models. *Planning Review*, March/April, 4–10, 44.

Sharfman, M. P. and Dean, J. W., Jr (1991) Conceptualizing and measuring the organizational environment: a multidimensional approach. *Journal of Management*, December, 681–700.

Sol, H. (1992) Dynamics in information intensive organizations. With Streng, R. J. A dynamic modelling approach to analyze chain dynamics on the inter-organizational level. *Research Project*, Delft University of Technology

(Belgium), presented at *Hawaii International Conference on Systems Sciences (HICSS)*, 25th Annual Meeting, Kauai, Hawaii, 7–10 January.

Stewart, C. and Case, W. B. (1985) *Interviewing: Principles and Practices*, 4th edn, DuBuque, IA, William Brown Publishers.

Stone, D. L. and Kemmerer, B. (1984) Relationship between rigidity, self-esteem, and attitudes about computer-based information systems. *Psychological Reports*, December, 991–98.

Strom, S. (1992) In the mailbox, roses and profits. *The New York Times*, 14 February, D1, D5.

Suchman, L. A. (1987) *Plans and Situated Actions: The Problem of Human Machine Communication*, New York, Cambridge University Press.

Syed, J. R. and Tse, E. (1987) *Proceedings*, 7th International Workshop on Expert Systems and Their Applications, Avignon, p. 689.

Tavakolian, H. (1989) Linking the information technology structure with organizational competitive strategy: a survey. *MIS Quarterly*, September, 309–17.

Thain, D. H. (1990) Strategic management: the state of the art. *Business Quarterly*, Autumn, 95–102.

Tilsner, J. (1993) Warren's world. *Business Week*, 10 May, 30–32.

Treece, J. B. *et al.* (1992) The partners. *Business Week*, 10 February, 102–7.

Vesper, V. D. (1979) Strategic mapping—a tool for corporate planners. *Long Range Planning*, December, 75–92.

Wack, P. (1985a) Scenarios: unchartered waters ahead. *Harvard Business Review*, September–October, 73–89.

Wack, P. (1985b) Scenarios: shooting the rapids. *Harvard Business Review*, November–December, 139–50.

Wald, M. L. (1993) Clean-air laws push big 3 to cooperate on electric car. *The New York Times*, 12 April, A1, D13.

Walden, P. (1992) Rule-based expert systems in strategic management. *25th Annual Hawaii International Conference on Systems Sciences (HICCS)*, Kauai, Hawaii, 7–10 January, and *Expert Systems in Strategic Market Management*, Turko, Poland, Abo Academy Press.

Watson, G. H. (1993) How process benchmarking supports corporate strategy. *Planning Review*, January/February, 12–15.

Wensley, R. (1990) The voice of the consumer? Speculations on the limits to the marketing analogy. *European Journal of Marketing*, July, 49–60.

Zielgler, B. *et al.* (1992) AT&T's bold bet. *Business Week*, 30 August, 26–32.

2

A GLOBAL ENVIRONMENT
CIRCA AD 2015

Charles W. Taylor

US Army War College
(Retired faculty member)

INTRODUCTION

A large number of potential future world environments can emerge from the world's societies as they exist today. Political, economic, sociological, scientific and technological trends and events rebound in heavy activity on a global scale. The concepts and realities of peace and war, rich and poor, love and hate, life and death confront all nations, especially the emerging free and independent nations of the late twentieth and early twenty-first centuries. These nations seek new self-identities and destinies of their own. They do so in a world situation that is dominated increasingly by global and regional economic powers and less in a world dominated by political ideological and military forces.

I believe that a common framework or background environment is essential to develop alternative future scenarios against which nations, such as those above, can plan their future and their destinies. A description of a basic environment that would be suitable for projections from midrange futures (10–20 years) to longer range futures (20–30 years or more) would be appropriate. *A World 2010: A New Order of Nations* (Taylor, 1992;[1] hereafter referred to as *A World 2010*), provides a plausible future world scene for planners wishing to build alternative planning scenarios.

Rethinking Strategic Management
Edited by D. E. Hussey. © 1995 John Wiley & Sons Ltd

A World 2010 is an estimate of the global environment as it might be around the years 2010–20. I have derived my estimates of the future based on projections of the probabilities of the consequences of twentieth-century trends and events and new trends as they came into being in an holistic setting. The projections take into account the most current strategic changes in the world's international environment and then forecasts the probability of strategic outcomes that could occur from about 2000 to 2020. The forecasts in *A World 2010* provide an adequate starting point for planners and policy makers. More importantly, they also provide a basis for constructing the architecture for future national policies and security strategies, defense and security forces, or organizational strategy and policy. *A World 2010* is summarized in this chapter. Detailed data that are less strategic or are needed for specific usage for the scenarios, e.g. projected technological advances or demographic data, can be compiled from data found in documents in the open literature.

A NEW ORDER OF NATIONS

In *A World of 2010* future environments for the early decades of the twenty-first century are built upon an evolving hierarchy of nations as they might exist around the years 2005 to 2020 and beyond. The reader should keep in mind that the new order of nations in *A World 2010* is describing an arrangement or hierarchy of the world's nations by loose categories of industrialization and modernization.

A World 2010 is not a new world order. It is an ordering or ranking of nations. A new world order describes a change such as in sovereignty, i.e. advancing from a city state to a nation state to a one world government. A result of this new arrangement is that it tends to create status for each nation in the world community or family of nations.

Essentially, in the context of these projections and in twenty-first century terms, there are no superpowers, nor are there nations called Third World. The notion of the term *superpower* basically is of cold war vintage, as is the concept of the *Third World* that evolved during that same era; the terms are twentieth-century creations. They were used to describe, on the one hand, the superpowers—those nations (there were only two) that either had wealth or power or both (e.g. the former Soviet Union that had more power than wealth and the United States that had both), and on the other, those nations of the world that had little wealth and little or no power and were easily exploited and manipulated into regional wars or revolutions. *Superpower*, moreover, connotes competitive economic and political ideology and military strength on a global scale among other nations with theoretically comparable power.

In an era where only a single superpower exists, flaunting that position serves little use internationally. Since the fall of the Soviet empire, the United States remains the only nation of the world recognized by all other nations as a superpower. The rising of any other nation of the world to challenge this US position over the next 20–30 or more years is unlikely.

The notions behind the term *Third World* are demeaning. The term *Third World* connotes a group of nations that are backward, unsophisticated, low in literacy, lacking in resources or having only one—often a strategic resource—and are unable or unlikely, despite their struggles to improve themselves, to be any better. Some of these nations are financially unable to build the infrastructures needed for modern industrial statehood; while still others are unwilling to make the sacrifices necessary to do so. These latter nations are more willing to demand and take advantage of the benefits they believe poor Third World states should receive from the wealthier nations of the world.

Many of these nations today are becoming industrialized and are now referred to as newly industrialized countries (NICs). Most of the NICs, once given status, very likely will increase their self-worth, will be encouraged to plan and set national goals, and, more importantly, will take the opportunity to pursue more self-directed destinies. Not all NICs, however, will be able to do these things by themselves and will look for help from supranational world agencies and from the world's wealthier leader nations (e.g. Europe,[2] Japan, and the United States). Chances are likely that once the NICs begin to adjust to the benefits derived from the combinations of modern industries and agro-technology, to experience new and independent political horizons and to enter into free-market economies, they likely will begin to rise to their new status. (The making of basic changes, of course, is unlikely to occur without struggle and sacrifice on the part of the people of the NICs.) I believe that the traditional twentieth-century descriptive modifiers for nations (e.g. more developed, developing, less developed countries, and the like) have not encouraged nations to reach their potential. Such modifiers for nations are now and will be inappropriate constructs to describe the nations of the twenty-first-century world.

Nations of the world are aligning in the direction of a new order.

This is happening primarily because of new economic and trade relationships and the cultural exchanges in which nations have been engaging increasingly in the early decades of the twenty-first century. Additionally, the decline of the international power positions of the twentieth-century superpowers—capped by the fall of the Soviet Union and the decline of the Soviet Communist Party—has encouraged many nations of the world to assert their individual concerns for and interests in developing their own futures. Imperialism and colonialism, as they have been known in the past, are unlikely to rise again. Further, during the period under consideration in this forecast, I believe that it is unlikely that there will be any nation of the world that will demonstratively seek to fill the world power gaps created by the decline of the superpowers. There are few nations that by mid-twenty-first century would be likely to have a political, military, and economic infrastructure to do this. All nations of the world, however, will continue to recognize that the United States most certainly will remain the foremost leader of the world's nations throughout the early decades of the twenty-first century. It would be diplomatically prudent and advisable for the United States to downplay its position as the world's only superpower and to deal with other nations as a quiet counselor and defender.

The new order of nations in the twenty-first century described in this chapter can be classified into five categories or groups according to their progress and potential in industrialization and modernization in the 2010–20 period (Taylor, 1986, 1988, 1992). The categories are post-industrial, advanced industrial, transitioning industrial, industrial and pre-industrial. Nations in each category are listed in Table 2.1. This chapter also includes a brief description of each category.[3]

The arrangement of nations in Table 2.1 was developed to substantiate the trend that the world is drifting away from political ideological bipolarity to economic multipolarity. The broad latitude created in a devolution of world power allows new economic agreements, alliances, and partnerships to form. It also allows states to achieve new levels of economic statehood; even to be carried along by the other nations within a category. For example, all of Europe is categorized as post-industrial, including Albania, Bulgaria, and most of the East European nations—states that are unlikely to achieve such a status on their own. They are symbolically carried along, while being helped by the other European nations to complete the general notion of European union and a twenty-first-century arrangement of nations.

Table 2.1   An arrangement of nations in 2010–20 by industrialization and modernization

Post-industrial	*Industrial*
Australia (including New Zealand)	China
Canada	Cuba
Europe	India
Japan	Korea
United States	Malaysia
Union of Social Democratic Republics	Pakistan
	Philippines
Advanced Industrial	Turkey
Hong Kong	Union of Sovereign Republics
Israel	Venezuela
Singapore	Vietnam
South Africa	
Taiwan	
Transitioning industrial	*Pre-industrial*
Argentina	All other nations of
Brazil	Africa, Asia, Latin
Chile	America, and Oceania
Costa Rica	not listed elsewhere
Mexico	

New Nations

Two new nations appear in Table 2.1 that must be identified. I believe that in order for the republics of the former Soviet Union to survive in a highly competitive twenty-first-century economic world, republics with common or like interests and needs will have to group together as new nations. There exists a possibility that of the original fifteen former republics, eleven of the former Soviet Union (excluding Estonia, Latvia, Lithuania, and Moldavia) will form three new national confederated entities that will be tied loosely together by a new commonwealth created around 2005 that will replace the Commonwealth of Independent States (CIS). For the purposes of this work I have created and named three hypothetical combinations. The number of former republics in each of these unions is not important nor whether there are four or five new nations. What is important is that there is a balance of power in the region.

The first nation, a confederation, is the largest in population and geographic area and is classified as an industrial country. It is the Union of Sovereign Republics (USR). The common bond that will

48 CHARLES W. TAYLOR

bring some of the former republics together in this new democratic confederation is primarily the retention of much of each republic's sovereignty. This is something like the relationship of states of the United States to the Federal government, but less like the Europe where the affairs of sovereignty of individual European states continue to be a background issue.

Another new nation, also a confederation, in Table 2.1 is called the Union of Social Democratic Republics (USDR).[4] The USDR is about half the size of the USR in population and geography. It is accepted marginally as a post-industrial country by the other nations of that category. The USDR includes former Soviet republics that believe they would like to continue some of the former socialist/Communist welfare programs within a new democratic government.

The third new nation, another confederation, is formed from most of the remainder of the former Soviet republics and includes some of the former autonomous areas and ethnic groups. This group likely will come together as free and independent states. This arrangement collectively is called the Union of Independent States (UIS). The UIS is classified as a pre-industrial country.

I believe that by 2010 there is a very good chance that the USDR will be an independent confederacy, loosely separated from the predominantly industrial to pre-industrial confederacy of the Union of Sovereign Republics (USR). I also believe that chances are better than even that the USDR and the USR will have close economic ties with one another as well as with the UIS. These three will be part of the new temporary commonwealth arrangement centered in Moscow. This type of arrangement will allow the USDR to provide the USR and the UIS with economic assistance and agricultural products in exchange for essential items. This will especially help the USDR and USR leadership to raise their nations to a higher status in the new order of nations and the UIS in building a national infrastructure to unite its peoples.

Other likely configurations of the former Soviet Union, e.g. an economic community, could come into being if the members of any of the former republics join together to form other new nations. Regardless of the number of new nations formed, the logic remains that the republics must join together because individually they all cannot survive economically or politically in the highly competitive world that will exist in the early decades of the twenty-first century. The EC and the rest of the free world must put forth a concerted effort through economic, scientific, and cultural exchange to assure that these new nations never resort to a configuration dominated by a military regime again as was the former Soviet Union.

THE CATEGORIES OF NATIONS[5]

Post-industrial

Post-industrial countries have sociopolitical infrastructures that support predominantly information, service, and knowledge societies. These societies have highly developed and efficient communication networks by way of earth and space systems. Their industries are predominantly science-based and technology oriented, using electronics, computers, optics, and robotics, as well as the intellectual technology of models and simulations. The largest single class of workers, about 80% of the workforce (Masuda, 1981), is composed of highly innovative and creative, multilingual, scientifically oriented professionals and their supporting staffs. Post-industrial economies produce information, services, and knowledge for export as well as for internal use. Their economies also support an abundance of automated and robotic, light fabricating specialty enterprises that encompass about 18% of the workforce, as well as techno-agricultural industries composed of a mere 2% of the workforce.

The post-industrial nations include the United States and Canada; the European countries; Japan, Australia and New Zealand, and the Union of Social Democratic Republics (USDR). Most of these countries or regions support small, high-tech, sophisticated defensive armed forces with comparable or near-comparable weapon systems and capabilities. Almost all the post-industrial countries are considered politically free,[6] while others in Eastern Europe (Albania, Bulgaria and Romania) that have made progress toward freedom can be considered partly free by 2010. The post-industrial nations assume responsibility for the peace of the world. The United States is the recognized leader.

Advanced Industrial

Advanced industrial countries have sociopolitical economic infrastructures that support highly modernized industrial and manufacturing societies. They are goods oriented and produce high-tech products and sophisticated automated and robotic manufacturing equipment. Their primary workers, about 60% of the workforce, are innovative and creative technologists but are not necessarily scientific professionals. Their products are predominantly for export. This group includes Hong Kong, Israel, Singapore, South Africa, and Taiwan. External difficulties of both

Israel and South Africa with neighboring countries continue to slow their progress toward developing into post-industrial countries. Moreover, twentieth-century South African internal issues have continued to hold back its economic advancement, despite continuing efforts by the government to guarantee freedom to all its citizens.

Except for Hong Kong, the advanced industrial countries support highly sophisticated, technologically oriented armed forces. Hong Kong has no armed forces except domestic police, nor does it have Chinese or any foreign forces on its territory. Hong Kong is a special administrative zone of China since the late 1990s.[7] Although China likely will declare Taiwan a special administrative zone with very special privileges for retaining a semi-autonomous status as a compromise to full reunification, Taiwan very likely will ignore the declaration. Israel is the only country of this group considered politically free; the others remain partly free.

Transitioning Industrial

Transitioning industrial countries have sociopolitical economic infrastructures that support advanced industrial, manufacturing, and agricultural societies. They are products oriented and primarily produce advanced, state-of-the-art machinery and machine parts and natural and synthetic food products, clothing, and chemicals, largely for export. People in their workforce are about evenly divided (about 30%) among manufacturing and industry, agriculture, and extractive processes. The workforce, in general, is lacking both intellectual ability and personal incentive for creativeness and innovation, except for the artistic talents expressed in their products.

This group includes Argentina, Brazil, Chile, Costa Rica, and Mexico. Within the next several decades (i.e. beyond 2010), one or two of the countries in this group (e.g. Brazil and Argentina) very likely will progress to advanced industrial status. They likely will shift more to automated and robotic systems. Their educational systems also will advance to produce a greater number of creative and innovative, scientifically oriented graduates. There is a very good chance that in 2010, Argentina, Brazil, Chile, and Costa Rica will be considered politically free. Mexico, whose preference is to remain oriented toward the south, will remain partly free in 2010, but within a decade could be expected to be politically free also. These transitioning industrial countries support well-trained armed forces that are equipped with advanced and sophisticated weaponry.

Industrial

Industrial countries have sociopolitical economic infrastructures that support modernized industrial, manufacturing, and agricultural societies. They produce industrial products of all kinds but are predominantly heavy-industry oriented. Their agricultural products are largely for internal consumption but agricultural exports are significant, especially by China. In general, the industrial nations are a mix of centralized governments supported by massive administrative bureaucracies and representative democracies. Government workers, generally, are poorly educated and are managed by an elite managerial corps. Blue- and white-collar unions permeate many of these societies with varying success, as have attempts to unionize labor in others. An estimate of their workforce would place about 60% in industry and manufacturing; 30% in agriculture and extractive processes; and about 10% in services.

This group includes China, Cuba, India, Korea,[8] Malaysia, Pakistan, the Philippines, Turkey, the USR, Venezuela, and Vietnam. Of these countries, only India, Venezuela, and the USR are clearly sovereign nations that can be classed as politically free; only Vietnam remains "not free"; and the others, partly free. The politically free industrial nations, almost certainly, may require a decade or more before they can develop infrastructures that will enable them to progress to transitioning industrial status. The remaining nations very likely will require an even longer time to reach that level. For countries such as India, upward progress almost certainly will continue to be constrained by growing population, social class structure, and religious practices.

The USR, however, has the potential to become a transitioning industrial country if: (1) it develops economic ties and favored- and friendly-nation status with the United States, Europe, and Japan; (2) it receives long-term economic support from the more advanced USDR; and (3) it maintains close political relations with the European community of nations. Of more importance and the greater task, the USR almost certainly will need to modernize all members of its Union. This, however, will take time. The advancement of the USR very likely will be hampered by imbalances in population growth as well as by ethnic, religious, and other social problems. The decline of international political influence, created by its past affiliation with the Soviet Union, very likely will also slow USR progress in modernization throughout its country. Other obstacles to progress very likely will be (1) the reluctance of the populace to change or adapt to modernization and (2) adherence to outmoded industrial and agricultural methods that require a large percentage of the USR workforce for manual labor. The populace and leadership also will be faced with understanding and accepting a new political ideology, i.e. democracy. Finally, progress in the USR will be impeded by its inability to provide the necessary energy needs throughout its vast populated territory unless it receives considerable foreign assistance.

The industrial countries support large armed forces, most of which are highly trained and equipped with a mixture of advanced, sophisticated, and modernized weaponry along with aging weapon systems of the twentieth century. The USR and China, however, have weapon systems with near-comparability to those of the post-industrial countries. For the USR (and the USDR), these weapons are a legacy of the former Soviet Union after arms-reduction agreements with the United States. In theory, the nuclear weapons and missiles remaining in the USR (and the USDR) territories are under the temporary command authority of the commonwealth center of the USDR, USR, and the UIS. Since the mid-1990s, much of the Soviet arsenal has been reduced through the arms-reduction agreements but around 2000 they will be controlled largely by the USR and the USDR. The USDR and USR, almost certainly, will remain formidable nuclear powers, as will France, the UK, and China.

Pre-industrial

Pre-industrial countries have a mixture of sociopolitical and economic infrastructure that range from partly industrial to almost completely agricultural. They also include the least developed nations of the world, many of which require significant economic, food, and humanitarian aid from other nations and world organizations merely to survive. The wealth of the pre-industrial countries, for the most part, continues to be lopsided in distribution, where the poor are getting poorer and the rich, richer. The populations of most of these countries are disproportionately large when compared to other countries of the world (except for China and India) and they are continuing to grow at rates significantly above replacement levels. The pre-industrial societies include those countries that have taken least advantage of the opportunities for industrialization or modernization of existing industries. Some have declined to advance by choice, others have declined because of their impoverished economies or because their countries lack natural resources as a source of national income.

The workforces of the pre-industrial nations are divided among various industries, including tourism (about 30%); agriculture and extractive processes (about 65%); and the remainder in services. They comprise the resource-rich countries that are involved mostly in extraction. They can be sub-divided further into nonindustrial countries desperately poor economically (such as Bangladesh and the poor countries of Africa) and those almost devoid of any natural resource base. There is a good chance that many of these nations will not survive through the twenty-first century without massive long-term infusions of external aid.

The pre-industrial countries include the remaining countries (not previously mentioned) of Africa, Asia, Latin America, Oceania, and the UIS. Within this group of countries, about two-thirds are rated as politically or partly free. The wealthier, pre-industrial countries support trained armed forces—generally, disproportionate in number to their needs—that are equipped with a mixture of antiquated twentieth-century weapons and advanced defensive weapon systems according to their ability to pay or obtain credit for arms.

To the extent financially possible and as a status symbol, the poorer pre-industrial (including the nonindustrial) countries also support small, poorly trained and ineffective armed forces that are mostly equipped with twentieth-century and earlier defensive weapons. There are still others that have no focus or weapons at all and very likely depend on protection from beneficent patron nations. Chances are good that a few of these nations, as a last resort for economic survival, will lease part of their territories for training areas to disbanded renegade armed forces, guerrillas, terrorists, or even to the US military.[9]

TRENDS

The characteristics of the world environment that are likely to span the period over the next 30 or 40 years are derived, for the most part, from trends of the last half of the twentieth century. The environment described in *A World 2010* addresses a period around the year 2010. It is derived from an aggregation of the plausible outcomes of seven basic trends selected for their universal and worldwide influence on almost all nations. These trends, generally recognized by futurists as important to the development of future world environments, are described briefly in this chapter. They are basic strategic trends that can be used by futurists and planners in government and industry. These trends very likely will continue to impact mankind for at least most of the next century. Moreover, these trends and their consequences create the framework needed to support the common background for the development of this chapter. The trends are described in the following paragraphs.

A New Arrangement of Nations

Nations of the world continue to align themselves in a new pattern of international political and economic order. In the absence of a bipolar superpower dominance based on political ideology, the world's nations very likely will continue to experience a devolution of power in the new century, i.e. a more multipolar world and one that emphasizes economic ideology. The devolution of global power that likely will evolve will shift increasingly from the twentieth-century superpower profile to the new order of nations. By 2010–20 the centers of international economic power structure will very likely swing variably from Washington to Berlin, Paris, Singapore, Tokyo, Kiev, Beijing, and Moscow. All nations of the world will remain nation states, but very likely will also be members of multinational economic organizations. By 2005 new confederacy groups of the former Soviet republics will have come together and will have established their right to sovereignty and statehood. By 2010 they will have organized new economic markets. Although the United Nations remains active, no nation has relinquished its sovereignty to that supranational body. The distribution of the new order of nations within each category is displayed in Table 2.2.

Global Population

Global population continues to increase. Demographers estimate that by the year 2020 world population will have increased by greater than 35% over the 1990s. Many nations will have slowed their rate of population growth by the year 2005 while some others very likely

Table 2.2 Distribution of nations by category, 2010–20

Approximate no. of nations	Nation status	Percentage of all nations
115	Pre-industrial	68
32	Post-industrial	19
11	Industrial	7
5	Advanced industrial	3
5	Transitioning industrial	3

Table 2.3   Distribution of population by category in 2010

Percentage of world population	Nation status	Population (in billions)
48	Industrial	3.36
30	Pre-industrial	2.10
16	Post-industrial	1.10
5	Transitioning industrial	0.37
1	Advanced industrial	0.10
100	World population	7.03

will be approaching zero growth by 2020 or sooner. Still others, where starvation had been prevalent before the turn of the century, will have gone bankrupt; others will have failed in nationhood and no longer exist, despite international aid from the UN and others. The population growth of others, however, although slightly reduced from that during most of the twentieth century, will continue at a high rate. The increasing population growth in urban areas is significantly adding to societal change as well as to new urban crime and social strife, much of which very likely will involve international crime syndicates. The population distribution for 2010–15 is displayed by category in Table 2.3. The distribution in 2020 throughout the new order of nations of an estimated 8.0 billion world population is displayed in Table 2.4.[10]

Interdependence

Interdependence among the world's nations continues to increase but in new patterns of political, economic, and cultural arrangements and competition. The growth of interdependence along with new economic treaties and trade arrangements among nations between 2005 and 2015 very likely will have caused: (1) a general abandonment of twentieth century trade agreements; (2) increases in the adoption of the free market and enterprise systems; (3) creation of an acceptable common currency throughout Europe; and (4) rises in economic growth for most nations of the world.

The new order of nations almost certainly will evolve gradually into a world economy that, for most nations, will generate greater wealth. The resulting redistribution of the world's wealth will especially benefit the transitioning industrial and industrial countries, while simultaneously lessening the economic influence of the twenty-first-century post-industrial countries. Inequality in the

Table 2.4   Projected population estimates by new order classification
(in millions)

	1986	1993	2010	2025
World	4948.0	5506.0	7041.0	8425.0
Post-industrial	*994.7*	*1046.1*	*1101.3*	*1133.8*
North America	267.0	287.0	331.0	371.0
Europe	493.0	513.0	523.0	516.0
Japan	121.5	124.8	130.4	125.8
Australia and New Zealand	19.1	21.2	24.8	27.1
Union of Social Democratic Republics	94.1	100.1	92.1	93.9
% of world population:	*20.1*	*19.0*	*15.6*	*13.5*
Advanced industrial	*65.3*	*73.8*	*96.1*	*112.7*
Hong Kong	5.7	5.8	6.3	6.2
Israel	4.2	5.3	6.9	8.0
Singapore	2.6	2.8	3.2	3.3
South Africa	33.2	39.0	55.9	70.0
Taiwan	19.6	20.9	23.8	25.2
% of world population:	*1.3*	*1.3*	*1.4*	*1.3*
Transitioning industrial	*271.2*	*292.3*	*365.5*	*412.8*
Argentina	31.2	33.5	39.9	44.6
Brazil	143.3	152.0	185.6	205.3
Chile	12.3	13.5	17.0	19.8
Costa Rica	2.7	3.3	4.5	5.6
Mexico	81.7	90.0	118.5	137.5
% of world population:	*5.5*	*5.3*	*5.2*	*4.9*
Industrial	*2397.1*	*2717.7*	*3362.1*	*3887.3*
China	1050.0	1178.5	1397.8	1546.3
Cuba	10.2	11.0	12.3	12.9
India	785.0	897.4	1166.2	1379.6
Korea	63.8	67.2	80.2	86.9
Malaysia	15.8	18.4	26.0	33.5
Pakistan	101.9	122.4	190.7	275.1
Philippines	58.1	64.1	85.5	100.8
Union of Sovereign Republics	180.2	185.0	202.3	213.6
Turkey	52.3	60.7	81.8	98.7
Venezuela	17.8	20.7	27.6	32.7
Vietnam	62.0	71.8	91.7	107.2
% of world population:	*48.5*	*49.4*	*47.8*	*46.1*
Pre-industrial	*1219.7*	*1397.2*	*2102.4*	*2866.9*
Africa	549.8	638.0	1025.1	1482.0
Asia	560.5	616.4	884.5	1149.4
Latin America	119.8	136.0	183.6	223.6
Oceania	5.9	6.8	9.2	11.9
% of world population:	*24.7*	*25.4*	*29.9*	*34.0*

redistribution, however, likely will increase in the resource-rich pre-industrial countries—with the rich becoming richer faster than the poor become rich. Foreign capital investments will be sought by the transitioning industrial and industrial states from the post-industrial and advanced industrial countries. Such arrangements will become increasingly more acceptable, will create a new capital flow, and will be a positive step toward increasing free enterprise in these countries. World-wide economic stagnation is unlikely in the 2015 scenario.

The resource-rich pre-industrial countries very likely will require economic assistance by 2010 due to poor financial management, new sources of competition, and because they believe their resources are beginning to show signs of depletion. Such economic aid most likely will be provided, in part, competitively by the industrial countries in return for bilateral, preferential access agreements and, in part, by the post-industrial nations, especially the United States, to sustain some vestige of economic influence. This intense competition for scarce natural resources, needed by almost all the modernized countries, will keep the cost of these resources high. The uneven natural distribution of these resources, found mostly in the single-industry, pre-industrial countries, makes the resource-poor pre-industrial countries even poorer. Without continued economic aid (emergency and survival) from the International Monetary Fund, the World Bank, UN agencies, and charitable organizations in the form of money, credit, food and other goods, many of the poorer pre-industrial countries will face the prospects of internal upheaval, bankruptcy and complete collapse and, eventually, disappearance as nations.[11]

These nations likely could survive their increasingly dire situations provided supportive, long-term economic aid, once given, is continued. The application of agro-technology likely could provide both food and employment for their people as well as their survival as nations. The destiny of these countries will lie more in the elimination of war and strife than it will in the unavailability of food as a source of famine and extinction (see Holden, 1983).

Social Change

Sociopolitical changes increasingly are affecting all nations of the world. Between 2000 and 2005, most of the world's nations can be expected to have experienced a sociopolitical reorientation. These changes or experiences very likely will reflect the new status in the international order of nations as well as a general relaxation of world tensions.

Nations and their leadership very likely will form new views of and make modifications to political processes and social structures as new industrial, economic, and technological infrastructures come into being within most nations. The spread of free enterprise on a world-wide scale increasingly will promote a rise in capitalism along with an increase in privately owned and controlled industries. Moreover, the influence of a free-market system[12] very likely will encourage a growing preference by many people for representative government and the recognition of human rights and social justice.[13] Such changes in political and economic systems that increasingly are occurring in nations of the world can be described as they relate to each nation's political and civil freedoms (see Table 2.5).

Nations increasingly will be rated by other nations for political and civil freedoms: where a political free baseline is a fully competitive electoral process and those elected clearly rule; where the baseline of civil liberties is where freedom of public expression for political change is not closed, and where courts protect individual expression. Also included in Table 2.5 is a partly-free category where there is overlapping of either political or civil freedoms, and a not-free category where governments are authoritarian and individual rights and freedoms are denied. The projections for the years 2005–20 in this study are those of the author and are based on his estimates of the economic and political potential of nations. There is a good chance that by 2010 even China will become partly free as it begins to recognize individual freedoms and blend free enterprise within a controlled economy and social democracy with Communism after the turn of the century. Through the early decades of the new century, most of the nations of the world can expect cultural and philosophical changes that most likely will continue to alter their societies profoundly. Unless technology can provide remedies, however, ignorance and apathy are likely to

Table 2.5 An estimate of political freedom around 2005–20

Category	Nations		Free		Partly free		Not free	
	No.	%	No.	%	No.	%	No.	%
Post-industrial	32	19.0	29	17.3	3	1.8	0	0.0
Advanced industrial	5	3.0	1	0.6	4	2.4	0	0.0
Transitioning industrial	5	3.0	4	2.4	1	0.6	0	0.0
Industrial	11	6.5	3	1.8	7	4.2	1	0.6
Pre-industrial	115	68.5	37	22.0	37	22.0	41	24.4
Totals:	168	100	74	44.0	52	31.0	42	25.0

result in new geographical patterns of pollution in and around the NICs. Paradoxically, a new growth of nationalism can be expected also to arise in most nations, which very likely will weaken twentieth-century world cooperative movements, international organizations, and alliances. On the upside, the spread of free enterprise worldwide increasingly will promote a continuing rise of capitalism and freedom, while on the downside, there is a good chance of a rise in terroristic acts (mostly by hoodlums, some by small international terrorist groups, but few or none by nation-sponsored terrorists) that will alter the progress of some nations.

Energy Sources

Reserves of petroleum, primarily, and gases continue to decrease as sources of energy while the use of coal, nuclear, and alternative energy sources rises. Some time before the end of the twenty-first century, barring any major discoveries of oil in China, in the former Soviet Union, or from offshore drilling, there is an even chance that conventional oil reserves of the world could be moving toward depletion.[14] If this trend is valid, then, around the year 2010, nations of the world can expect that the cost of pure oil and oil with added extenders very likely will become increasingly prohibitive for any practical use. The new order of nations with more industrial countries probably will continue to remain dependent on oil at least through the early decades of the new century. The source of oil during this period most likely will be from several suppliers, such as the twentieth-century Organization of Petroleum Exporting Countries (OPEC), if it remains in existence; an OPEC-like cartel and splinter cartels; or independent oil-rich countries. To replace oil as a source of energy production, the use of coal, gas, nuclear and renewable energy sources almost certainly will increase substantially over the long term—especially coal (US Department of Energy, 1983).

Toward the year 2010, most of the post-industrial, advanced industrial, transitioning industrial, some of the industrial, and a few pre-industrial countries increasingly will expand or begin their use of nuclear power as an energy source. Despite legal, technical, high-cost setbacks, a few plants shut down because of age and notable accidents (e.g. the US "Three Mile Island" incident, the Soviet Chernobyl catastrophe, and others), there is little likelihood that nations will abandon existing operational or planned nuclear power plants as the primary source of energy in the new century. As gas and fuel prices increasingly rise, nearly all nations will become aware that fossil fuels (oil and gas supplies) very likely will be approaching depletion during the latter half of the twenty-first century, leaving many nations dependent on coal and nuclear power for energy sources. By 2020, about 40 nations (as displayed in Table 2.6) may have acquired or restored nuclear power plants to satisfy their energy needs (Taylor, 1992).

Science, Technology, and Space

Science and technology continue to advance rapidly as do space exploration and use. Most nations of the world by 2010 will be benefiting from the continuing great strides in the advancements of science and the achievements of technology. All nations will be sharing in this progress; even the poorest of the pre-industrial states, despite cultural barriers. However, they will continue to receive the most advanced appropriate technology. By the turn of the century, the

Table 2.6   An estimate of nations possessing nuclear power plants in 2020

Post-industrial	Transitioning industrial
Austria	Argentina
Belgium	Brazil
Bulgaria	Chile
Canada	Mexico
Czech Republic	
Finland	*Industrial*
France	China
Germany	Cuba
Hungary	India
Italy	Korea
Japan	Pakistan
Netherlands	Philippines
Poland	Union of Sovereign Republics
Romania	Vietnam
Spain	
Sweden	
Switzerland	
Union of Social Democratic Republics	
United Kingdom	
United States	
Advanced Industrial	*Pre-industrial*
Israel	Egypt
Singapore	Iran
South Africa	Iraq
Taiwan	Saudi Arabia

transfer of technology, including technical information and equipment, is very likely to be unimpeded to all states that have the economic and societal infrastructures to afford its costs, understand its complexity, and absorb the societal changes it causes.

There is a good chance that many nations that could not afford the benefits of space in the twentieth century will be able to buy portions of satellite and shuttle activities after the turn of the century. Almost all nations increasingly will profit from the peaceful commercial and exploratory use of space. Several exploratory space programs will be shared in the joint efforts of the United States and the USR (e.g. a manned Mars expedition). The cost-benefits of such developments and activities by 2005–20 most likely will outweigh the uncertainties and risks of military weapon systems or missile defense systems in space.

Weapons Proliferation

Proliferation of conventional arms (including chemical and biological) and nuclear weapons continues. Despite the reduction of world tensions, almost every industrial nation will be armed with a range of conventional weapons, most of which will have been supplied to them by several of the former Soviet republics before and after their reorganization as new states, by the EC and the United States before the year 2005, and by new weapons-manufacturing nations. Many nations will continue to purchase or barter for the latest conventional high-tech weapons and exotic new chemical-like weapons, which will be available from new twenty-first-century arms suppliers.

Most nations, except the very poorest, very likely will demand the most advanced conventional systems they can afford to buy. They almost certainly will find a broader as well as different source of arms suppliers available than existed before the turn of the century. Hence the potential for conflict, almost certainly, will be high and continue to grow. Additionally and more importantly, by the end of the first decade of the century, nuclear proliferation will have increased (Manfredi *et al.*, 1986; see also discussion in Grimmett, 1986). There is a good chance that proliferation will continue despite the increased number of signatories to the Nuclear Non-proliferation Treaty.

The hypothetical table (Table 2.7) (Taylor, 1992) is based on the criteria that some nations perceive a need to have nuclear weapons in their arsenals and have the capability of producing their own or acquiring them surreptitiously. Their need might arise from a real or imagined threat, or a belief that possession of nuclear weapons raises their international status, or just because their neighbor has them.

Table 2.7   Estimates of nations possessing nuclear weapons and delivery means in 2010–20

Post-industrial	Industrial	Advanced industrial
France[a]	China[a]	Israel[b]
Germany[c]	India[b]	South Africa[b]
Japan[c]	Korea[c]	Taiwan[c]
USDR[a]	Pakistan[b]	
United Kingdom[a]	USR[a]	
United States[a]	Vietnam[d]	

Transitioning Industrial	Pre-industrial
Argentina[d]	Egypt[e]
Brazil[d]	Iran[e]
Chile[d]	Iraq[e]
	Libya[e]
	Saudi Arabia[e]
	UIS[?]

[a]substantial, 1000 or more; [b]significant, 1000 or less; [c]moderate, 500 or less; [d]modest, 100 or less; [e]very modest, 50 or less; [?]number unknown.

Chances are better than even that by 2010–20 the number of nations acquiring a military nuclear capability could approach 24 or more. Thus there is, at most, an even chance that a nuclear weapons accident, nuclear blackmail, or a limited nuclear conflict between small nations (e.g. pre-industrial and NICs) will occur within the early decades of the twenty-first century. Chances are almost certain that if proliferation of ballistic missiles and nuclear weapons is not halted in the very early years of the century, not only will the potential for accident or conflict increase, but so will the direct or indirect involvement of other nations (see Manfredi *et al.*, 1986). Chances are only slightly better than even that the proliferation of nuclear weapons alone will deter their use.

SUMMARY

This chapter has described a new order of nations that almost certainly will contribute toward a devolution of international power. The chapter also provides a base line world scenario in *circa* 2015 for the building of alternative scenarios. More importantly, new patterns of political and economic competition and cooperation among nations of the new order very likely will contribute toward a new intensity of competitiveness. Notwithstanding, many new international relationships and arrangements are likely to emerge in the early decades of the twenty-first century. Despite a period of relative peace and calm, collusion on the part of some nations, along with some international economic market chicanery on the part of others, likely will not be uncommon during the early years of the new century. For better or worse, the superpowers of the twentieth century were role models for many nations. Each had its followers. Each was sought by other nations for guidance and support: political, economic, or military. Even by 2010, many nations will not have as yet adjusted to the absence of the competitive leadership of the superpowers. The devolution of power has brought about new economic and political relationships among the six post-industrial and all other nations of the world.

By the turn of the century, the United States will be the accepted leader of the post-industrial states. And, although by 2010 it likely will find its twentieth-century international position of influence somewhat diminished, the United States will remain the pre-eminent world leader. However, other post-industrial states, many of which were once traditional US allies linked directly by security commitments, very likely will become even greater competitors for political influence and economic markets than they were in the past. Moreover, the United States might find its need for national and economic security occasionally challenged by these conscientious competitors who are bent on grasping the international industrial influence previously held over the past half-century by the United States. There is a very good chance that a few of the industrial countries and NICs will make a rigorous and substantial effort to fill that gap. The United States will retain its international position in political and economic influence through its status as the world's leader in services, information, and knowledge.

The world in the early decades of the twenty-first century, as described in this chapter, is a world of a new international order where many nations, formerly centrally controlled and Communist, have become free societies with free-market economies. Together, the world of 2010–20 might appear to be a relatively peaceful world. However, it is a world where political and economic stability is fragile; a world that is fraught with threats of crises, armed conflicts, and possibly wars among, between, and within nations, but almost all limited in nature.

There is a good chance that the USR will be ill content to remain an industrial country in the new order of nations; while the USDR and its twentieth-century rival the US advance beyond the USR's national capabilities. The USR leadership very likely will depend heavily on political and economic agreements with the European nations and the United States. Moreover, the USR leadership likely will depend on considerable assistance from the EC in the early years to help them develop sufficient economic capabilities to become a transitioning industrial nation. The USR very likely will continue national introspection to avoid what could be gradual national fragmentation, dissolution, or a return to state-controlled government. During the next ten or more years, the USR will be forced to devote more of its national assets toward creating and managing a new international image so that it can maintain a positive USR presence on the world scene. Moreover, the leadership very likely will reassess the late twentieth-century political and economic ideological decisions for a quick change to a free-market system. A self-imposed USR withdrawal from the international scene during this readjustment period very likely would exacerbate a steady decline of its perceived international image or prompt a resurgence of international aggressiveness.

Well within the first decade of the twenty-first century, all former Soviet Marxist support to governments and factions in the Middle East, Africa, and Latin America will have dried up. There is a likelihood that a small group of former Soviet Communist Party and military hardliners within the UIS will offer some support (but not substantial) to small nations unable to shake the yoke of the past and turn to democracy. Despite the fading interests in Communism, however, chances are good that Chinese hardliners will attempt the export of Chinese Communism at the turn of the century to fill this void in the ideological competition of democracy and Communism. Moreover, before 2005, arms sales of late twentieth-century high-tech conventional weapons in these same regions very likely will be replaced by the sale and transfer of twenty-first-century weaponry. While the USDR ar.d USR recognize a potential threat from China, internal political, social, and economic development within these two nations most likely will take priority over any external military investments or ventures.

To be realistic, futurists, planners, policy makers, and decision makers, whether they are optimistic or pessimistic about the world's economic, sociological, or political environments, must recognize that in all likelihood many changes in each of these elements will occur during the next 20–30 years. These changes very likely will direct and redirect the destiny of not only the United States and Europe but also every nation of the world and those that have yet to come into existence. Some of these changes have been described in this chapter and may be included by users in the development of long-range plans, policies, and decisions. These changes along with many others that may occur as a consequence of others will have some degree of influence, over time, as to what the world environment *circa* 2015 might be like.

NOTES

1. This chapter is adapted and summarized from *A World 2010: A New Order of Nations* (Taylor, 1992) and *Alternative World Scenarios for A New Order of Nations* (Taylor, 1993).
2. The European Community, as of November 1993, has become the European Union. It will, however, be referred to in this study as the single entity of the European Community (EC). This will give recognition to the different nations that likely will make up the EC in the twenty-first century. There is a good chance by 2005, and most likely by 2020, that the EC will include both the twentieth-century nations that made up Western Europe as well as almost all the East European nations of the former Soviet bloc. There is little likelihood that any of the republics of the former Soviet Union will be included in the EC by 2010 or 2020, except, perhaps, Estonia, Latvia, or Lithuania. It is also unlikely that any of the three confederacies, the USR, USDR, or UIS (as described in this study), will be members of the EC.
3. The descriptions of the categories of nations that appear in this chapter are composites of earlier descriptions found in the following documents: *A World 2010: A Decline of Superpower Influence* (Taylor, 1986, 2–5); *Alternative World Scenarios for Strategic Planning* (Taylor, 1988, 13–14, revised 1990, 14); and *A World 2010: A New Order of Nations* (Taylor, 1992, 16–21 and 27) and *Alternative World Scenarios for A New Order of Nations* (Taylor, 1993, 20–23).
4. The term "Union of Social Democratic Republics (USDR)", in this study, replaces the "Soviet European sector" used in the publication *A World 2010: A Decline in Superpower Influence* (Taylor, 1986, 4–5). The earlier document described this area as sufficiently advanced to be a near-equivalent of an advanced industrial or post-industrial and free-market country.
5. Notions for the development of the categories are adaptations from Molitor (1982, 85) and also from Masuda (1981, 29–33).
6. The notion of political freedom is an adaptation from a series published by Freedom House as a January–February annual report in *Freedom at Issue*, now, *Freedom Review*, entitled, "The Comparative Survey of Freedom". The survey was originated in 1973 and analyzed and reported by Raymond D. Gastil (now reported by McColm, 1993). In this survey nations are rated against comparative scales for political and civil freedoms. Neither Gastil nor McColm forecast the probability of freedom. The comparative surveys present only estimates of the

current year's situation and the progress made toward freedom in the previous year.

7. There is another possible projection regarding Hong Kong. Some Asian analysts believe that China does not and will not have the capability to manage the intricacies of the Hong Kong economic structure. They suggest that before 1997, when Hong Kong will reunify with China, most of the lucrative assets of Hong Kong will have departed the territory, and China will move in to expropriate an empty shell.

8. Bouvier (1984, 2a) forecasts that North and South Korea will be united by 2010 and that both China and Korea will be close to the service, information borderline before 2034.

9. It can be considered a fair likelihood that during the drawdown of US forces in the 1990s, US training areas will have been reduced (sold or leased for 99 years) in both size and number. The increasing need for training areas will benefit the poorer nations, but may be limited to their tropical climates.

10. Data adapted from Haub and Yanagishita (1993).

11. This is adapted from American Council of Life Insurance (1993, 15–18).

12. Bouvier (1984) believes that neither "capitalism as we have known it for the past 200 years and communism as it has developed over the past 65 years" will prevail through the twenty-first century and that the "developing nations" demand for a New International Economic Order will meet with some success during the next 50 years".

13. Bouvier (1984) projects "democracy, as distinct from capitalism, will survive and thrive as it ceases to be bound by capitalist ideology" and assumes the "democratic world's emerging social consciousness will spread to include a greater sharing of the wealth with less advanced nations". Additionally, Bouvier (1985, 35) suggests that both democracy and communism may be replaced by Ward's "Sociocracy". (Lester Frank Ward, *Applied Sociology*, New York, Arno, 1974, reprint of original published in 1906. The exact edition could not be located.)

14. Gordon (1981) and Gever *et al.* (1986) believe that world oil production will peak around the year 2000 and that substitutes cannot fully offset the decline in petroleum before 2025. They also believe that US oil and gas virtually will be exhausted by 2020. The actual date of the depletion of oil is not important; the reason for even mentioning it at all is to emphasize the point that one day there may not be oil to depend on. The substitutes and synthetics may not be efficient enough replacements unless science and technology are provided funds in the new century to discover and perfect these creations.

REFERENCES

Adamek, J. (1985) Centrally planned economics in Europe: economic overview 1985. Washington, The Conference Board.

Air National Guard (1993) *The 1993 Air National Guard Long Range Plan*, Vols 1 and 2, Washington, US Government Printing Office.
American Council of Life Insurance (1983) Collapse of the global financial superstructure. *Trend Analysis Program (TAP 23)*, Summer Issue.
American Council of Life Insurance (1986) New immigrants, new minorities (by Leon F. Bouvier). *Trend Analysis Program*, July.
Bell, D. (1961) *The End of Ideology*, New York, Crowell-Collier.
Bell, D. (1973) *The Coming of the Post-Industrial Society: A Venture in Social Forecasting*, New York, Basic Books.
Bouvier, L. F. (1984) Planet Earth 1984–2034: a demographic vision. *Population Bulletin*, Washington, DC, Population Reference Bureau, Inc., **39**, 1, whole issue.
Bouvier, L. F. (1991) *Peaceful Invasions: Immigration and Changing America*, Washington, DC, Center for Immigration Studies.
Didsbury, H. F. (ed.) (1983) *The World of Work*, Bethesda, MD, World Future Society.
Didsbury, H. F. (ed.) (1985) *The Global Economy*, Bethesda, MD, World Future Society.
Dizard, W. P., Jr (1985) *The Coming of the Information Age: An Overview of Technology, Economics, and Politics*, 2nd edn, New York, Longman.
Gever, J. et al. (1986) *Beyond Oil: The Threat to Food and Fuel in the Coming Decades*, Cambridge, MA, Ballinger.
Gordon, T. J. (1981) The year 2050: reflections of a futurist. *The Lamp* (an Exxon publication), **63**, Spring, 30.
Grimmett, R. F. (1986) *Trends in Conventional Arms Transfers to the Third World by Major Suppliers, 1975–1986*, Washington, DC, Congressional Research Service, The Library of Congress.
Etzold, Hon. T. H. (1990) *Strategy in the 21st Century: Alternative Futures for Strategic Planners*, Washington, DC, Center for Naval Warfare Studies and Naval Surface Warfare Center, co-sponsors.
Hall, L. (1982) Environmental Assessment. Preworkshop submission in *Public Issue Early Warning Systems: Legislation and Instructional Alternatives*. Hearing and Workshop by the Subcommittee on Oversight and Investigations and the Subcommittee on Energy Conservation and Power and the Committee on Energy and Commerce, US House of Representatives. 97th Congress, 2nd session, 1982, Washington, DC, US Government Printing Office, October, 235–66.
Haub, C. and Yanagishita, M. (1983) *1993 world population data sheet*. Population Reference Bureau, Inc., April.
Heller, C. E. (1993) *Twenty-First Century Force: A Federal Army and a Militia*, Carlisle Barracks, PA, US Army War College, Strategic Studies Institute.
Holden, C. (1983) Simon and Kahn versus Global 2000. *Science*, **221**, 4068, 2 July, 341–3.
Huss, W. R. and Honton, E. J. (1987) Alternative methods for developing business scenarios. *Technological Forecasting and Social Change*, **31**, 219–38.
Jones, T. E. (1980) *Options for the Future: A Comparative Analysis of Policy-Oriented Forecasts*, New York, Praeger.

68   CHARLES W. TAYLOR

Kahn, H. (1979) *World Economic Development: 1979 and Beyond*. Boulder, CO, Westview Press.
Kahn, H. (1983) Some comments on multipolarity and stability. *Discussion Paper*, HI-3662-DP, New York, Hudson Institute.
Kahn, H. and Wiener, A. J. (1967) *The Year 2000: A Framework for Speculation on the Next Thirty-Three Years*, New York, Macmillan.
Kahn, H. *et al.* (1976) *The Next 200 Years: A Scenario for America and the World*, New York, William Morrow.
Kennedy, P. (1987) *The Rise and Fall of the Great Powers, Economic Change and Military Conflict from 1500 to 2000*, New York, Random House.
Kennedy, P. (1993) *Preparing for the Twenty-First Century*, New York, Random House.
Lawson, H. A. (1992) *Beyond Tomorrow: A Look at 2050 AD*, Military Studies Program, Carlisle Barracks, PA, US Army War College.
Lepgold, J. (1990) *The Declining Hegemon: The United States and the European Defense*, Westport, CT, Greenwood Press.
Manfredi, A. F. *et al.* (1986) *Ballistic Missile Proliferation Potential in the Third World*, Washington, DC, Congressional Research Service, The Library of Congress.
Masuda, J. (1981) *The Information Society as Post-Industrial Society*, Washington, DC, World Future Society.
McColm, R. B. (1993) The comparative survey of freedom. *Freedom Review*, January–February, 5–21.
Meadows, D. H. *et al.* (1972) *The Limits to Growth, A Report for the Club of Rome's Project on the Predicament of Mankind*. New York, Universe Books.
Modelski, G. (ed.) (1987) *Exploring Long Cycles*, Boulder, CO, Lynne Rienner Publishers.
Molitor, G. T. T. (1982) The information society: the path to post-industrial growth. In Cornish, E. (ed.), *Communications Tomorrow: The Coming of the Information Society*, Bethesda, MD, World Future Society.
Murray, R. J. *et al.* (1987) Harvard University Seminar on US Army Long-Range Stationing Study, Cambridge, MA, John F. Kennedy School of Government, Harvard University (8–9 October, 1987). (Organized and conducted by Trinity International, Inc., a subcontractor to CACI, Inc-Federal, under contractor number MDA-903-87-C-0639, in support of the US Army Long-Range Stationing Study.)
Taylor, C. W. (1986) *A World 2010: A Decline of Superpower Influence*, Carlisle Barracks, PA, US Army War College, Strategic Studies Institute.
Taylor, C. W. (1988) *Alternative World Scenarios for Strategic Planning*, Carlisle Barracks, PA, US Army War College, Strategic Studies Institute (rev. edn 1990).
Taylor, C. W. (1992) *A World 2010: A New Order of Nations*, Carlisle Barracks, PA, US Army War College, Strategic Studies Institute.
Taylor, C. W. (1993) *Alternative World Scenarios for a New Order of Nations*, Carlisle Barracks, PA, US Army War College, Strategic Studies Institute.
Toffler, A. (1990) *Powershift: Knowledge, Wealth, and Violence at the Edge of the 21st Century*, New York, Bantam Books.

Toffler, A. and Toffler, H. (1993) *War and Anti-War: Survival at the Dawn of the 21st Century*, New York, Little, Brown.
US Department of Energy (1983) *The National Energy Policy Plan: A Report to the Congress*.

3

THE EVOLUTION OF COMPETITIVE INTELLIGENCE

John E. Prescott

University of Pittsburgh

The process of competitive intelligence (CI) is a core capability which firms need to develop if they are to succeed in the twenty-first century. CI programs and the processes which make it a core capability cannot be bought or developed in a short period of time. Rather, organizations must invest in CI and nurture its evolution. Managers, however, need to benchmark their CI efforts before they address the questions of how much to invest and in what areas. This chapter provides guidance in addressing the benchmarking question in two ways. First, a framework for examining the evolution of CI is developed. Second, by examining the stages of development and the issues facing organizations within a particular stage, firms can benchmark their current level of development. In this way, managers can make more informed decisions regarding where and how to evolve their CI efforts further.

The chapter is organized into several sections. First, the scope of the chapter is bounded and a definition of CI is presented. Next, explanations are developed as to why CI has grown so rapidly over the past 20 years. Then, a framework describing the evolution of the field and discussions of each stage follow. The chapter concludes with predictions related to the future development of CI.

Rethinking Strategic Management
Edited by D. E. Hussey. © 1995 John Wiley & Sons Ltd

SCOPE OF THE CHAPTER

The topic of intelligence is vast. In any one chapter it would be impossible to describe the history of the intelligence field. Intelligence has its roots in the military. One of the earliest sophisticated references is *The Art of War* by Sun Tzu (Griffith, 1971). The set of essays was written around 500 BC and has formed the basis for much of the developments in military intelligence. A second stream of intelligence activity concerns national security as a policy issue (Berkowitz and Goodman, 1989). This stream, particularly in the United States, has its roots in the Second World War era and is linked to political science.

A third stream that is the focus of this chapter places the business organization at center-stage (Ecells and Nehemkis, 1984). A systematic orientation towards business intelligence in organizations is a recent phenomenon. My focus is bounded in four ways. First, the historical analysis begins in the 1960–70 period. The choice of that date is admittedly judgmental. However, academic writing and practitioner activity were limited before 1970. A database search of citations on the topic of competitive intelligence confirms this assertion. Second, the analysis and discussion of the historical periods centers on "leading-edge" firms. Leading-edge firms were chosen because they represent the state of the art within a particular period. Since many firms are just beginning to implement competitive intelligence programs it is important to recognize that both the field of CI and a program within a particular firm follow an evolutionary path. Third, the historical analysis centers on North America and, to some extent, Western Europe and Australia. CI activities in Asia and developing countries are beyond the scope of this chapter (for discussions related to these areas see Prescott and Gibbons, 1993). Fourth, the academic literature rooted in organizational theory and strategic management, while important in its development of theoretical constructs, has had limited impact on the practice of competitive intelligence (for a useful classification framework and review see Lenz and Engledow, 1986). In this regard, I will draw on the literature only to the extent that it directly pertains to CI.

COMPETITIVE INTELLIGENCE PROGRAMS

An effective intelligence program (CIP) is an essential part of the foundation on which strategies and tactics are built, assessed and modified. Whenever the term CIP is mentioned, it elicits a wide set of images and perspectives. In this regard, it is important to briefly define my perspective on CIPs and describe their fundamental characteristics. I define CIPs in the following manner:

A competitive intelligence program entails a continuously evolving integration of both formalized and informal processes by which organizational members assess key trends, emerging discontinuities, the evolution of industry structure, and the capabilities and behaviors of current and potential competitors to assist in maintaining or developing a competitive advantage.

There are three aspects of this rather involved definition that warrant further explanation. First, a key component of CIPs is assessment. A central feature of assessment is the testing of hypotheses. A primary set of hypotheses that organizational members need to test are those related to *assumptions* regarding their theory of business, competitive moves, the evolving structure of their industry, their own firm's strengths and limitations and managerial motives. In many ways, one of the most important aspects of CI is to test assumptions based on data and the intelligence created from it. Second, CI efforts should focus on existing constraints and opportunities and how to exploit them. Only through the incorporation of intelligence into decision making does CIP have a *raison d'être*.

The third aspect of this definition is that all CIPs, regardless of the country in which they are located, have four commonalities: (1) a focus on the organizational and performance implications of industry evolution and the actions/reactions of competitors; (2) gathered data needs to be transformed into intelligence that is applicable to managerial needs; (3) the integration of formal and informal intelligence networks is essential; and (4) CIPs need to evolve over time to address current critical issues and to facilitate organizational renewal.

THE RISE OF COMPETITIVE INTELLIGENCE

A central question regarding the historical development of competitive intelligence concerns why it has blossomed over the past 20 years. While it would be attractive to suggest that the increased level of globalization, the expanding role of sophisticated technologies, and changing customer needs have been the root cause it would be an oversimplification. These and other trends have affected many aspects of business life. As a result, managers have searched for and implemented many theories, techniques, and approaches to address the fundamental issues of competitiveness (Krugman, 1994). Approaches such as the quality movement which have assisted managers in becoming more competitive have become institutionalized. Those theories, approaches, and techniques which do not produce "perceived" increased competitiveness become fads. Fads become footnotes in management textbooks. If CI has grown over the past two decades, what, then, has contributed to it not becoming another footnote?

The increasing acceptance of three basic assumptions or what I refer to as the "competitiveness test", has led to its growth. The first assumption is "that managers believe that CI is one piece of a puzzle which when constructed leads to sustainable competitive advantage". It is not clear what percentage of the puzzle involves CI. However, managers increasingly believe that a clear understanding of the competitive landscape is necessary for the design and implementation of strategy. It is interesting to note that the resource-based view of the firm (Barney, 1991) has challenged the percentage that CI and external analysis in general contributes to the puzzle. Carried to extremes, the resource-based view would place little, if any, emphasis on CI activity. However, unlike CI, the resource-based view has not been empirically subjected to the "competitiveness test".

The second assumption is that "a methodology exists for 'doing' and 'managing' CI that produces meaningful intelligence". It is very important to distinguish the "doing" of CI from its "management". The "doing" of CI relates to the processes of planning a study, collecting data, transforming data into intelligence, presenting and disseminating implications, and evaluating the effectiveness of the project. The management of CI involves the mission and structure of the CI unit and the characteristics of individuals assigned to the unit.

With respect to "doing", the field has benefited from related areas in the development of methodologies for collecting and analyzing data. The areas of marketing, library science, and strategic planning in particular have played important roles. Marketing played an early role since it was interested in better understanding customers. Both primary and secondary data collection techniques have had a long tradition in the marketing field. CI borrowed and modified many of the techniques and applied them to a wider array of topics including suppliers, competitors, technology, and alliance partners, to mention a few. Librarians as part of the discipline of library science have been used by managers to collect competitive data for decades. However, the decreasing costs of computing and the increasing availability of databases and networks have placed the field of library science at the center of CI.

One of the central tenets of strategic planning has been that relationships between a firm and its environment affect performance (Andrews, 1987). While there was some early strategic planning-oriented work in the area of CI (Aguilar, 1967; Fair, 1966), a substantial amount of it was not easily operationalized by those struggling to understand their competitors. Strategic planning, however, has played a major role in the areas of analysis where a range of techniques have been developed to assess competitive positions (see Oster, 1994; Prescott, 1986). It is important to note that most of the techniques of strategic planning assume away the data-collection issues. That is, they assume that the data are available or easily collected. This is a troublesome assumption.

CI has drawn from these three areas and developed methods on its own often through the assistance of consulting firms. There is a growing acceptance of the methodology. Practicing competitive analysts now have a broad set of books to draw on to both demonstrate the methodologies of the field to sceptical managers and to assist them in conducting a study. For example, Washington Researchers has developed a series of books on virtually every topic of information collection. One final topic related to "doing" CI relates to ethics (Paine, 1991). CI continues to emerge from the shroud of the "cloak and dagger" image. The spy image has been perpetuated to a large degree by the media industry. The media, interested in selling copy, continues (Caudron, 1994) to play up the role of spying. Yet, there has been no large-scale study to demonstrate that ethical issues are a major concern. In fact, the few empirical data that do exist (from the 1990 and 1994 surveys of competitive intelligence professionals) suggest that ethics are becoming less of a concern. Many firms have codes of conduct and practice the following advice: "Do not do anything that you would be embarrassed seeing on the front page of the *Wall Street Journal* or *Financial Times*".

The management of CI is less well developed than its counterpart "doing". Academics (Cox and Good, 1967; Cleland and King, 1975) played an early role in describing how monitoring systems should be designed. In recent years, other academics (Prescott and Smith, 1989b) and consultants (Bernhardt, 1994) have refined and extended the early prescriptions. In the section on the evolution of CI, management issues will be discussed in detail. In sum, the methodology of CI is becoming increasingly established and accepted as a normal part of conducting business. This acceptance has led to the growth of the field.

The third assumption is that "intelligence can impact the decision-making process". Currently, this is the most tenuously held assumption. One of the key tasks for any CI effort is to build a business case for its existence. To date, there has been little effort to investigate systematically the impact of CI on the decision-making processes and firm outcomes. The few attempts (Jaworski and Wee, 1993; Prescott and Fleisher, 1991) have been more directed in an effort to identify management processes that can be positively affected by CI. For example, both of the previously cited studies acknowledge that any direct connection between CI and bottom-line performance is not a particularly promising area to pursue at a systems level. Rather, examining indirect links related to outcomes such as information sharing, avoiding surprises, and sensitizing managers to the methodologies of CI may be a more fruitful direction to pursue. Of course, statements by executives such as Mr Flynn, Chairman of Nutrasweet, that CI has either produced or saved the company millions of dollars are testimonials that are extremely welcomed by CI professionals. What is needed is a study which evaluates the revenues generated and costs saved by companies as they implement individual CI projects. Thus, there are two types of evaluations that are necessary. One type should focus on the effectiveness of the overall CIP and the other on individual CI projects.

STAGES IN THE EVOLUTION OF COMPETITIVE INTELLIGENCE

The field of competitive intelligence has passed through three stages and is currently struggling to define its next stage of development. The first stage, "Competitive Intelligence Gathering" occurred through the 1960s and 1970s. Around 1980 the second stage, "Industry and Competitor Analysis", emerged and was most strong during the mid-to-late 1980s. Currently, the stage of development can be characterized as "Competitive Intelligence for Strategic Decision Making". The future rests on developing CI as a source of competitive advantage and is labelled "Competitive Intelligence as a Core Capability".

The stages portrayed in Table 3.1 and described below are based on the combination of five attributes: (1) the sophistication of the

Table 3.1 The evolution of competitive intelligence

Stages Characteristics	Competitive data gathering	Industry and competitor analysis	Competitive intelligence	Competitive intelligence as a core capability
Time period	Pre-1980	1980–1987	1988–Present	Future
Key defining event	Porter's 1980 book *Competitive Strategy*	The founding of the Society of Competitive Intelligence Professionals	The establishment of *The Competitive Intelligence Review*	CI courses taught in business schools across the world
Attributes:				
Degree of formality	Informal	Emerging formal units	Formal	Integration of formal and informal
Orientation	Tactical	Tactical	Mixed	Strategic
Analysis	Little or none	Limited quantitative	Both quantitative and qualitative	Qualitative emphasis
Link to decision-making processes	Little	Weak	Strong	Direct input
Top management attention	Low	Limited	Moderate	High
Principle location of CI personnel	Library/marketing	Planning/marketing	Marketing/planning/CI unit	CI units/marketing/planning
Key issues	• Development of skills in information acquisition	• Building a business case for CI • Spy image • Analytical skill development	• Demonstrating bottom-line input • Demand- versus supply-driven CI • Counter-intelligence • International CI • Technology CI • Role of information technology	• Managing the parallel process • Intelligence infrastructures for multinationals • CI as learning • Network analysis

formal and informal CI network, (2) the balance between intelligence oriented towards strategic versus tactical decisions, (3) the type and extent of analysis conducted on the data, (4) the degree of top management attention, and (5) the linking of CI into the decision-making process. Table 3.1 summarizes key characteristics of each stage with a focus on the key issues facing managers within a stage. In the discussion below, summary descriptions which encapsulate each of the five attributes for each stage are presented.

The movement between stages in the evolutionary framework is based on key defining events. In this section, the defining events will be overviewed followed by a detailed description of each stage of the evolutionary process of leading-edge firms. For each stage two topic areas will be explored: a description of CI practices and key topic areas/issues that were (are) of concern to researchers and practitioners.

Defining Events in the Evolution of CI

A defining event is one which fundamentally alters the direction, scope, and acceptance of CI in the business community. There are three defining events which have shaped and are currently shaping the field. The first event was the publication of Michael Porter's book *Competitive Strategy* in 1980. While the book has a broader scope than competitive intelligence, it brought to the attention of managers the manner in which industries and competitors can be analyzed. It took the better part of five years before the message of the book gained widespread acceptance. While the book did not provide a blueprint for the design of competitive intelligence systems within organizations it led to the framing of several key questions. Managers, consultants, and academics began asking questions such as "Why are we not currently doing CI?" "Where in the organization do we locate such a function?" "How do I get started?"

The second defining event was the establishment of The Society of Competitive Intelligence Professionals (SCIP). SCIP is a nonprofit professional association devoted to the art and science of competitive intelligence. A key function of SCIP was that it served to legitimize the field in a manner that was not possible through academic writings and consulting activity. With the establishment of SCIP, CI had a forum that was visible, oriented towards furthering the development of the professional skills of CI personnel, and establishing the boundaries of the field. SCIP acting on the behalf of its members could serve as a liaison between many different types of key stakeholders including governments, business leaders who funded CI jobs, vendors who supplied a wide variety of products/services, CI practitioners, and academics.

The third defining event was an agreement between John Wiley & Sons and SCIP jointly to publish *The Competitive Intelligence Review* (CIR). The CIR provides a vehicle for the inexpensive and broad distribution of practitioner and academic writings around the world. The scope of the journal is broad to include all aspects of the field. The peer-reviewed journal further legitimizes the field and serves as a memory for ongoing developments, debates and perspectives.

A fourth possible defining event is the establishment of competitive intelligence courses in business schools around the world. Currently there are a handful of CI classes being offered in both business and library science departments. If there is a widespread acceptance of CI in the curriculum several benefits will occur including: students receiving training in CI before they (re)enter the workforce; cooperation between business, suppliers of intelligence, governments and academics in the development of teaching materials; and academics directing more of their research efforts towards the topic. All these activities will further legitimize and institutionalize the field.

The discussion below describes each of the stages in the evolution of CI. I have drawn on empirical surveys to develop the stages and their descriptions (Sutton, 1988; Wall, 1974; and the Pittsburgh studies of 1987, 1990, and 1994).

COMPETITIVE DATA GATHERING

Prior to the end of the 1970s, CI can be classified as basically involving the collection of competitive data. Leading-edge firms could be described as follows:

> Competitive intelligence was primarily a library function although market research with an orientation towards customers was well established. There was little in the way of a formal CI process or network established throughout the firm. CI was done on an *ad hoc* basis involving limited (if any) analysis. Overall, there was a generally low level of top management involvement and relatively little input into the decision making process.

The above description characterizes a process that is informal and *ad hoc*. The firms collected data and created files on their competitors and industry structure. The analysis if conducted was static. The primary skills of CI personnel were oriented towards the "finding" of information. While this was not a particularly glamorous time for the field, it was important. Its significance centers on the establishment of firms such as Washington Researchers and on academic writing.

Firms such as Washington Researchers and Find/SVP concentrated their efforts on cataloging information, training, and information brokering. The underlying assumption of these firms was that intelligence is only as good as the data on which it was based. The cataloging of information was of two types. One type was the compilation of information sources on a variety of topic areas including how to find information on private companies, who to contact in the government concerning specific industries and organizations that had completed studies on specific topic areas. The second type of cataloging was related to databases. Database utilization was low during these years relative to today, but has its roots in the efforts exerted by the pioneering firms. Training was oriented towards "how to find information on topic X". There were few firms in this era which had the skills to conduct workshops to assist the business community. Information brokering, the third activity, is the collection of data on topic areas commissioned by another firm. Brokering was possible because firms did not have the skills in-house, they did not want to expose themselves to the sources from which they were attempting to collect data, or they felt it was more efficient to outsource the activity. Information brokering continues to be a very important part of the field.

During the formative years the academic literature was disjointed. A survey conducted by the Harvard Business School in 1959 focused on the current state of practice of intelligence. This study illustrated that the process was in its infancy and informal. Albaum's (1962, 1964) research was an important beginning in the sense that he not only developed arguments for the development of business intelligence but also empirically illustrated some of its consequences. He was interested in what would happen to the quantity, accuracy, and speed with which information travelled between a customer and one of its key suppliers. Critical information planted in the customer's organization was found to flow back to the supplier in small, distorted bits. The information was planted with individuals in the customer organization who had frequent contact with employees of the supplier firm.

Another significant set of research was produced by Pinkerton (1969). This set of five articles outlines in detail the steps undertaken by a company in the midwest that established a marketing intelligence system. This is the most detailed case study in the field. Other significant articles of this time period included Guyton (1962), Kelly (1965), Greene (1966), Aguilar (1967), Cox and Good (1967), Wall (1974), Cleland and King (1975), and Montgomery and Weinberg (1979).

There were two characteristics of this work. First, it was primarily oriented towards marketing intelligence. Thus, the scope of the material was narrower than today. Second, most of the work was conceptual or contained anecdotal evidence of leading-edge firms. Aguilar's (1967) work was an exception to both of these points. However, it took the publishing of Porter's (1980) book to bring CI to the next stage of its development.

INDUSTRY AND COMPETITOR ANALYSIS

The early 1980s saw the transition from an emerging field to one that was in a growth period. During this time there was a strong emphasis on the analysis of industry structure and competitors. Three challenges faced proponents of CI as they strove to make the transition from collection to analysis. First, the groundwork that was laid during the first stage regarding the collection of data gave employees in leading-edge firms an upper hand in their ability to "build a business case" for CI. Building a business case was centered on illustrating to management what CI was, why CI was important, how it could assist in decision making, where the process should be located in the organization, and the resources that should be devoted to CI. Line managers were particularly interested in CI personnel demonstrating the bottom-line outcomes of their efforts. One of the central debates is what I label the "vacuum cleaner" approach to CI. The vacuum cleaner approach is the establishment of a comprehensive system that attempts to collect as much information as possible. This approach surfaced as CI advocates searched for models of organizing their efforts. One such model was found in the government. The fatal flaw of designing a CI system based on the government model is that the resources governments have to spend on intelligence far exceed those of any business. For example, it is acknowledged that the CIA has a budget in excess of $30 billion. A second issue with the government model is the separation of analyst from decision makers. In many parts of government intelligence, analysts are expected to present intelligence findings, options and implications but not recommendations. In business organizations,

82   JOHN E. PRESCOTT

many line managers desire to have recommendations included. They may not follow the recommendations but they like to see them.

A second challenge facing in-house advocates was the spy image. Reporters working for newspapers and magazines such as *The Wall Street Journal, Fortune, Business Week,* and the *Financial Times* appear to be more interested in espionage and breaches in ethics than the methodology for doing CI. As a result, many managers were concerned that being involved with CI might result in their organizations being featured in articles in a manner that was not particularly attractive. In fact, this has occurred on several occasions. To this day, some firms are very reluctant to discuss their CI processes due to this concern.

A third challenge was developing skills in a variety of analytical techniques to transform data into intelligence. There were two outcomes of this challenge. First, the field of planning took center-stage. Planners had long been interested in relationships of a business to its environment. Now they had a set of frameworks (e.g. Porter's work and the early writings on the design of marketing intelligence systems) which allowed them to apply environmental analysis systematically in a manner line managers could relate to more easily. Second, a division of labor between those who specialized in collection and those who did the analysis/management of CI began to crystallize. Today, this division is even more entrenched with the increased availability of databases.

The leading-edge CI operation of this time is described below:

> The CI effort is in the process of developing and refining a formal structure and network. At least one person is responsible for CI activity. The collection of data includes a mix of general information and *ad hoc* projects related to industries and competitors. The analysis of the data is limited and involves primarily quantitative summaries. Emphasis is placed on tactical as opposed to strategic decisions. Top management's involvement in the process is limited to issues of high salience and as a result there is a relatively weak link into the decision-making process.

Many of the CI programs were located in planning and marketing departments. However, during this period there was an increasing number of CI units being established in firms such as AT&T. CI programs focused their attention on addressing five fundamental questions:

(1) What are the fundamental characteristics of my industry?

(2) Who are my competitors?
(3) What are the current positions of my competitors?
(4) What moves are my competitors most likely to make?
(5) What moves can we make to achieve a sustainable competitive advantage?

There was much more emphasis on the first three questions than the last two.

There was an explosion of writing during this stage. Practitioners (Sammon *et al.*, 1984) and consultants (Fuld, 1985; Kelly, 1987; Meyer, 1987; Tyson, 1986; Vella and McGonagle, 1987) were particularly active. These books primarily focused on how to collect information and techniques for analyzing data. The books were important because they further helped institutionalize and demystify CI (Smith and Prescott, 1987a). In addition, many seminars were being conducted both to teach the methodology of CI and for the consultants to learn about CI practices. However, there was limited attention through 1987 on the management aspect of CI.

Academic writing was beginning to appear but was scarce. There were a couple of articles that focused on the role of intelligence in industrial marketing (Smith and Prescott, 1987b; Zinkhan and Gelb, 1985). Both articles focused on the practices of practitioners. Prescott and Smith (1987), drawing on field research, formalized a project-based orientation to CI. This approach was developed as an alternative to the vacuum cleaner approach described earlier. A large group of academics primarily in the planning area were oriented during this time to developing and implementing a variety of analytical techniques for the assessment of competition. Their efforts related to CI were summarized in two articles (Prescott and Grant, 1988; Prescott, 1986) and books by authors such as Hax and Majluf (1984). These works summarized and illustrated the rich diversity of techniques available to the intelligence analyst. In Europe, the emphasis on CI was directed more towards security issues in general and national security in particular. A bulk of the work was organized by Steve Dedijer at Lund University. Unfortunately, much of his writing has not been widely distributed.

During this period SCIP played an important role in which the organization became more adept at organizing national and regional conferences, networking members, developing examples of CI practices, and experimenting with the beginnings of a journal. SCIP has always had difficulty in developing a marketing strategy and thus most of the increased awareness occurred through word of mouth.

COMPETITIVE INTELLIGENCE FOR STRATEGIC DECISION MAKING

Currently, the field has progressed to the point where an increasing emphasis is given to the strategic implications of CI efforts. Often, this involved the integration of CI efforts with other initiatives such as the quality movement. A much broader array of issues have surfaced in recent years as firms push the envelop of CI practices. The impetus occurred during the late 1980s when many organizations that had funded CI units were beginning seriously to question their contributions. While there was evidence that CI efforts assisted in the sharing of ideas, sensitized managers to the value of addressing competitive dynamics, identified new business opportunities, and avoided surprises, there was a lack of consensus on how it influenced the bottom line and whether it was user-oriented (Prescott and Fleisher, 1991; Barndt, 1994). One technique that addressed the issue was benchmarking. Benchmarking grew in popularity because it was a focused activity that had become an integral part of the quality movement and had a demand- as opposed to a supply-driven orientation. That is, benchmarking studies are commissioned by managers who want to address a particular issue. The user (demand-driven) directs what the CI analysts (suppliers) do. By focusing CI on benchmarking activity, CI analysts were able to address the bottom-line issue in a manner that was more tangible than other outcomes such as predicting the effects of industry evolution. In some ways CI took a step back. In those organizations where benchmarking became the central thrust, CI became very tactical. There were efforts by consulting firms such as Kaiser & Associates to promote benchmarking as a strategic tool, but they had mixed success.

A second issue that was emerging was the focus on counterintelligence. The downsizing that was occurring in the US armed forces and related intelligence activities resulted in many qualified intelligence officers looking to apply their skills in other arenas. One arena in which they found a home was business organizations. The Futures Group is one consulting organization that placed considerable emphasis in this area. Motorola and 3M were known to have implemented not only an excellent CI unit but also counterintelligence efforts. Related to this issue is the current debate on the role that governments should play in business intelligence operations (see the Fall 1994 issue of the *Competitive Intelligence Review*). The question is not whether governments should play a role, but rather what role they play in different countries and how it impacts competitiveness.

A third issue was to what degree would information systems play a role in CI. While information systems were available for many years, the question focused on the strategic use of those systems. For the CI unit, the emphasis was on how they could design, access, and interface with internal and external data in a manner that facilitated managerial decision making. Organizations such as Corning were leaders in this area as it related to CI. There also emerged a growing number of small consulting firms such as the HELICON Group which designed systems for organizations.

A fourth area was the role of technological CI (see the spring 1994 issue of the *Competitive Intelligence Review*). Again, many organizations had technology orientations as a central part of their strategic planning efforts. Part of the rise in the interest in technology and CI can be attributed to the type of organizations that were becoming more interested in CI. The computer, telecommunication, and pharmaceutical industries naturally wanted to explore how technological CI could assist them.

A fifth area that was ignored previously was international CI (Prescott and Gibbons, 1993). As firms increasingly competed across borders, regional trading groups emerged, and industries felt the sting of new foreign competitors, their interest in international CI grew. This interest provided another opportunity for the information specialists. How to collect data and how international CI is different from domestic CI became an opportunity for information brokers. For example, recently an organization, OPEN SOURCE SOLUTIONS, was formed to serve as an international public information clearing house. This interest also gave rise to a desire to understand better how to manage CI units that operated in different geographical areas of the world (Prescott and Gibbons, 1992b).

The leading-edge firms today can be characterized as follows:

The CI unit has a well-developed formalized process and network. There exists a strong link to the users of intelligence who primarily dictate and fund the types of projects undertaken. There is often sophisticated analysis involving a combination of both quantitative and qualitative data. A significant number of projects are oriented towards the strategic decisions. Top management explicitly recognizes the value of CI and links it directly into the decision-making process.

The writing during the third period has even further intensified. Practitioners and consultants (Fuld, 1988, 1994; Gilad and Gilad, 1988; Roukis *et al.*, 1990) have increasingly turned their attention to the management processes of competitive intelligence. A content analysis of 100 articles published in *The Competitive Intelligence Review* between 1990 and October of 1994 shows that 41 focused on management-related issues while 59 involved some type of data collection or analysis orientation. In this content analysis, it is interesting that only two articles focused exclusively on ethics and four on computer/software.

Academics have still not devoted much attention to the field of competitive intelligence. Some of the work during this time that is applicable to practitioners has focused on the management issues of CI (Ghoshal and Westney, 1991; Prescott, 1989; Prescott and Smith, 1989a; Prescott and Gibbons, 1992a, 1993; Zahra and Chaples, 1993). There are, however, three research streams that have the opportunity to make an impact on CI. First, the area of issue management holds the promise of bringing information-processing research more directly into CI (for a set of key references see Greening and Gray, 1994). This is particularly important as analysts focus on demand-side CI. A second area is encapsulated by the work of a group of colleagues at Maryland (Smith *et al.*, 1992). These researchers are examining how competitive dynamics can be studied with an orientation towards moves and countermoves. A third stream involves the learning literature (Senge, 1990). The development of learning principles and learning organizations rests heavily on competitive information and its conversion into intelligence. However, to date, none of these streams of research has been oriented towards the competitive intelligence professional.

COMPETITIVE INTELLIGENCE AS A CORE CAPABILITY

Having laid out the past and present state of competitive intelligence, I will develop some ideas related to the future of CI. A key assumption of this scenario is that CI will continue to become institutionalized in the business community. A description of the leading-edge firms of the future is as follows:

> The CI process within a multinational firm is institutionalized on a world-wide basis although there is local responsiveness. The vast majority of the employees appreciate the value of CI and participate in the process including counterintelligence efforts. Data analysis is extensive with qualitative input often dominating quantitative data. The intelligence is integrated directly into strategic decisions often

through sophisticated information systems. Top management uses CI as one of the ways in which it shapes the future of the organization and considers it an integral part of the "learning organization".

A key component of the above future is that managing behavioral dimensions of CI becomes critical. While collection and analysis are important, how organizations mobilize the informal CI process will determine their effectiveness. The process of integrating the formal and informal CI activities has been labelled the "parallel CI process" by Prescott and Gibbons (1992a). Their research identified reasons why the parallel process exists and actions organizations can take to integrate but not eliminate it. An important conclusion from their work is that organizations must harness the process and not try to subdue it.

The parallel process is closely linked to the integration of CI operations across geographical locations in multinationals. While the international business literature has grown rapidly, it has not adequately addressed how multinationals manage the flow of information across subsidiary–subsidiary and corporate–subsidiary relationships. This is a rich area for research and will be increasingly important in the coming years.

One set of analytical techniques that will gain wide acceptance is network analysis (Burt, 1992). Network analysis is concerned with the nature and type of relationships that firms establish. Competition, in this view, is less concerned with the power of a firm and more concerned with productive relationships that give the firm access to freedom. The field of network analysis has a rich tradition in sociology but is only beginning to emerge in the business arena.

Academics can contribute to the field in at least two ways. First, as mentioned earlier, they need to begin to teach the topic of CI in their curriculum. Second, I suspect that one reason why CI has not gained more attention in academics is the lack of a theoretical framework. Given the promotion requirements of most schools, publication in a select set of journals is required. Those journals require theoretical frameworks. When a theoretical framework is developed that is subject to empirical testing, academics will flock to the field.

CONCLUSION

In this chapter I have traced the evolutionary path of CI. It was my objective that practising managers can use the chapter to assess their organization's stage of development and then devise a plan for the challenges that lie ahead. The field has made great strides in the last 20–25 years. While there are several mountains to climb, it appears that CI will not become a footnote in the history of business but will be a central chapter.

REFERENCES

Aguilar, F. J. (1967) *Scanning the Business Environment*, New York, Macmillan.

Albaum, G. (1962) *A New Approach to the Information Function in Marketing*, unpublished PhD dissertation, Department of Commerce, University of Wisconsin, Madison, WI.

Albaum, G. (1964) Horizontal information flow: An exploratory study. *Academy of Management Journal*, **7**, 1–33.

Andrews, K. R. (1987) *The Concept of Corporate Strategy*, 3rd edn, Homewood, IL, Richard D. Irwin.

Barndt, W. D., Jr (1994) *User Directed Competitive Intelligence*, New York, Quorum Books.

Barney, J. B. (1991) Firm resources and sustained competitive advantage. *Journal of Management*, **17**, 1, 99–120.

Berkowitz, B. D. and Goodman, A. E. (1989) *Strategic Intelligence for American National Security*, Princeton, NJ, Princeton University Press.

Bernhardt, D. (1994) *Perfectly Legal Competitor Intelligence: How to Get It, Use It and Profit from It*, London, Financial Times/Pitman.

Burt, R. S. (1992) *Structural Holes: The Social Structure of Competition*, Cambridge, MA, Harvard University Press.

Caudron, S. (1994) I spy, you spy. *Industry Week*, October, **243**, 18, 35–40.

Cleland, D. I. and King, W. R. (1975) Competitive business intelligence systems. *Business Horizons*, December, 19–28.

Cox, D. F. and Good, R. E. (1967) How to build a marketing information system. *Harvard Business Review*, May–June, 145–54.

Ecells, R. and Nehemkis, P. (1984) *Corporate Intelligence and Espionage: A Blueprint for Executive Decision Making*, New York, Macmillan.

Fair, W. R. (1966) The corporate CIA—A prediction of things to come. *Management Science*, June, B489–503.

Fuld, L. M. (1985) *Competitor Intelligence: How to Get It; How to Use It*, New York, John Wiley.

Fuld, L. M. (1988) *Monitoring the Competition: Find Out What's Really Going On Over There*, New York, John Wiley.

Fuld, L. M. (1994) *The Competitor Intelligence*, New York, John Wiley.

Ghoshal, S. and Westney, E. (1991) Organizing competitor analysis systems. *Strategic Management Journal*, **12**, 17–31.

Gilad, B. and Gilad, T. (1988) *The Business Intelligence System: A New Tool for Competitive Advantage*, New York, AMACOM.

Greene, R. M., Jr (ed.) (1966) *Business Intelligence and Espionage*, Homewood, IL, Dow-Jones and Richard D. Irwin.
Greening, D. W. and Gray, B. (1994) Testing a model of organizational response to social and political issues. *Academy of Management Journal*, June, **37**, 3, 467–98.
Griffith, S. E. (1971) *Sun Tzu: The Art of War*, New York, Oxford University Press.
Guyton, W. J. (1962) A guide to gathering marketing intelligence. *Industrial Marketing*, March.
Hax, A. C. and Majlif, N. S. (1984) *Strategic Management: An Integrative Perspective*, Englewood Cliffs, NJ, Prentice Hall.
Jaworski, B. and Wee, L. C. (1992/1993) Competitive intelligence and bottom-line performance. *Competitive Intelligence Review*, Fall/Winter, **3**, 3/4, 23–7.
Kelley, W. T. (1965) *Marketing Intelligence: The Management of Marketing Information*. London, Staples Press.
Kelly, J. M. (1987) *How to Check Out Your Competition: A Complete Plan for Investigating Your Market*, New York, John Wiley.
Krugman, P. (1994) *Peddling Prosperity*, New York, Norton.
Lenz, R. T. and Engledow, J. L. (1986) Environmental analysis: The applicability of current theory. *Strategic Management Journal*, **7**, 329–46.
Meyer, H. E. (1987) *Real-World Intelligence: Organized Information for Executives*, New York, Weidenfeld & Nicholson.
Montgomery, D. B. and Weinberg, C. B. (1979) Toward strategic intelligence systems. *Journal of Marketing*, Fall, 41–52.
Oster, S. M. (1994) *Modern Competitive Analysis*, 2nd edn, New York, Oxford University Press.
Paine, L. S. (1991) Corporate policy and the ethics of competitive intelligence gathering. *Journal of Business Ethics*, **10**, 423–36.
Pinkerton, R. L. (1969) How to develop a marketing intelligence system. *Industrial Marketing* (series of five articles), April, May, June, July and August.
Porter, M. E. (1980) *Competitive Strategy: Techniques for Analyzing Industries and Competitors*, New York, The Free Press.
Prescott, J. E. (1986) A process for applying analytic models in competitive analysis. In King, W. R. and Cleland, D. L. (eds), *Strategic Planning and Management Handbook*, New York, Van Nostrand Reinhold, pp. 222–51.
Prescott, J. E. (ed.) (1989) *Advances in Competitive Intelligence*, Vienna, VA, The Society of Competitor Intelligence Professionals.
Prescott, J. E. and Fleisher, C. (1991) SCIP: Who we are, what we do. *Competitive Intelligence Review*, Spring, **2**, 1, 22–6.
Prescott, J. E. and Gibbons, P. T. (1992a) The parallel process of competitive intelligence: Why it exists and what can we do about it? *Competitive Intelligence Review*, Summer, **3**, 2, 11–13.
Prescott, J. E. and Gibbons, P. T. (1992b) Europe 1992: A new dimension for competitive intelligence. *The Journal of Business Strategy*, November–December, 20–6.

Prescott, J. E. and Gibbons, P. T. (eds) (1993) *Global Perspectives on Competitive Intelligence*, Alexandria, VA, The Society of Competitive Intelligence Professionals.

Prescott, J. E. and Grant, J. H. (1988) A manager's guide for evaluating competitive analysis techniques. *Interfaces*, May–June, **18**, 3, 10–22.

Prescott, J. E. and Smith, D. C. (1987) A project-based approach to competitive analysis. *Strategic Management Journal*, **8**, 411–23.

Prescott, J. E. and Smith, D. C. (1989a) The largest survey of leading-edge competitor intelligence managers. *The Planning Review*, May/June, **17**, 3, 6–13.

Prescott, J. E. and Smith, D. C. (1989b) A framework for the design and implementation of competitive intelligence systems. In Snow, C. C. (ed.), *Strategy, Organization Design, and Human Resource Management*, Greenwich, CT, JAI Press.

Roukis, G. S., Conway, H. and Charnov, B. H. (1990) *Global Corporate Intelligence: Opportunities, Technologies, and Threats in the 1990s*, New York, Quorum Books.

Sammon, W. L., Kurland, M. A. and Spitalnic, R. (1984) *Business Competitor Intelligence: Methods for Collecting, Organizing and Using Information*, New York, John Wiley.

Senge, P. M. (1990) The leader's new work: building learning organizations. *Sloan Management Review*, Fall, **32**, 1, 7–23.

Smith, D. C. and Prescott, J. E. (1987a) Demystifying competitive analysis. *The Planning Review*, September/October, 8–13.

Smith, D. C. and Prescott, J. E. (1987b) Couple competitive analysis to sales force decisions. *Industrial Marketing Management*, **16**, 55–61.

Smith, K. G., Grimm, C. M. and Gannon, M. J. (1992) *Dynamics of Competitive Strategy*, Newbury Park, CA, Sage.

Sutton, H., Jr (1988) Competitive intelligence. *Research Report 913*, New York, The Conference Board.

Tyson, K. W. M. (1986) *Business Intelligence: Putting It All Together*, Lombard, IL, Leading Edge Publications.

Vella, C. M. and McGonagle, J. J., Jr (1987) *Competitive Intelligence in the Computer Age*, New York, Quorum Books.

Wall, J. L. (1974) What competition is doing: You need to know. *Harvard Business Review*, November–December, 22.

Zahra, S. A. and Chaples, S. S. (1993) Blind spots in competitive analysis. *The Academy of Management Executive*, May, **7**, 2, 7–28.

Zinkham, G. M. and Gelb, B. D. (1985) Competitive intelligence practices of industrial marketers. *Industrial Marketing Management*, **14**, 4, 269–75.

4

PICKING WINNERS: THE ART OF IDENTIFYING SUCCESSFUL SMALL FIRMS

Graham Beaver
Nottingham Business School, The Nottingham Trent University

and Peter L. Jennings
Sheffield Business School, Sheffield Hallam University

INTRODUCTION

The principles and ingredients of successful entrepreneurial activity have been the subject of a great deal of academic research and debate over the past twenty years. Many researchers such as Storey *et al.* (1987), Burns and Dewhurst (1989), Foley and Green (1989), and Wood and Woodruff (1993) have invariably sought to produce, develop, and refine explanations, frequently presented as taxonomies, which describe criteria applicable to the successful entrepreneurial venture. Indeed, the majority of current national advertising, by leading support agencies, is developed around this theme.

A successful entrepreneur is seen to be someone who is able to establish and manage a new enterprise—successfully negotiating the 'credibility merry-go-round' (Birley, 1989). Such obstacles arise from the new business concept, through resource acquisition and deployment, to the problems and opportunities of business development, the transition from 'entrepreneurial to professional management' (Flamholtz, 1991), delegation and the fragmentation of the ownership/control relationship (Jennings and Beaver, 1993).

Rethinking Strategic Management
Edited by D. E. Hussey. © 1995 John Wiley & Sons Ltd

Despite the existence of numerous taxonomies which provide checklists specifying the principal influences upon small business development, the failure to success ratio of new enterprise start-ups, within their first two years, remains unacceptably high (SBRC, 1992).

This chapter introduces a longer-term study of the 'art' or 'science' of identifying success potential at the pre-start-up stage. It examines the arguments which link small business and/or entrepreneurial success with business performance. Attempts to identify those significant factors which should be visible at the outset of the entrepreneurial venture and the extent to which external agencies may use such factors as predictors of success are taken as the special themes. Given that such support agencies have limited resources at their disposal, every effort must be made to target such scarce resources upon those ventures with the greatest potential for long-term success.

The chapter begins by exploring the concept of business success and challenges the singular constructs of established success measures so prevalent among support agencies and policy agendas. This section concludes that such singular notions are inadequate in describing the diversity of success criteria and an alternative, pluralistic definition is provided.

The rationale for attempting to identify potentially successful entrepreneurial ventures, pre-start-up, is then discussed. This seeks to influence the attitudes and behaviours of both support agencies and the entrepreneurs themselves, in an effort to maximise the chances of success.

Given that the checklist approach appears to have provided such strong, clear guidance of the *theoretical* route to success, the question why failure rates are so high is then debated. Traditional notions of the symptoms and causes of business failure are described and their weaknesses highlighted. An alternative explanation is provided. The argument is then reversed to attempt to identify those characteristics which should be found if the new enterprise is to have a good chance of success in the long term.

Finally, the chapter concludes by discussing the relevance and implications of identifying and quantifying success potential, pre-start-up, for support agencies and policy makers. These conclusions are closely tied to the principal theme of contemporary government support for small businesses and specific suggestions for revised policy initiatives, support agency action and further academic research are given at the end of the chapter.

DEFINING BUSINESS SUCCESS

Existing studies commonly define success in narrow, accountancy terms using criteria based upon financial analyses and ratios such as sales growth, profitability, cash-flow and productivity. More crudely still, quantitative measures such as job creation are frequently regarded as primary evidence of success. Further traditional analyses assert that the assessment of success, for small business ventures, solely embraces explanations, reasons and motivations of why people start their ventures, what problems business ownership overcomes and generates for the owner(s) and specifically what the firm owner(s) actually wish to achieve for themselves (cf. Chaganti and Chaganti, 1983; Hornaday and Wheatley, 1986; Storey *et al.*, 1987; Thorpe, 1989; Kelmar 1990).

However, the attribution of success to small firms is complex, dynamic, and problematic. This chapter departs from the narrow considerations of traditional analyses but does *not* reject the individual criteria suggested. There is, instead, a need to think imaginatively about the construction and application of success criteria recognising the pluralistic nature of business by adopting a stakeholder perspective. *The ways in which success will be defined and measured are then dependent upon the stakeholder's orientation towards the enterprise and can be expected to change over time.* Furthermore, the relative positions of stakeholders will invariably reflect a wide variety of objectives and aspirations, with respect to the new venture, some of which will undoubtedly be mutually exclusive. Therefore, the new venture cannot possibly fulfil all criteria of success simultaneously.

Given the very nature of small business, it would seem appropriate to regard the entrepreneur or owner–manager as the primary stakeholder and to begin by considering how he or she might define success. Clearly, many of the criteria used will reflect the underlying motives and reasons which predispose people to enter self-employment. These will be influenced by characteristics such as gender (Jennings and Cohen, 1993; Marlow and Strange, 1993), ethnicity (Ward, 1991), social marginality (Curran and Stanworth, 1973) and so on. For example, Carter and Cannon (1992) in their study of female entrepreneurs sought to recognise the centrality of gender in defining success and rather than imposing externally defined criteria, canvassed the views and opinions of a sample of women owner–managers. Their research revealed eight principal, common criteria:

(1)   Independence

(2)   Customer service
(3)   Personal satisfaction
(4)   Employment for the owner
(5)   Quality of working life
(6)   Growth potential
(7)   Employment of staff
(8)   Finance/income.

Paradoxically, it would appear that these factors are not, in fact, gender-specific and other studies of mixed or male samples reveal similar measures (cf. Foley and Green, 1989; Stanworth and Gray, 1991; Wood and Woodruff, 1993).

Some of the criteria cited reflect the centrality of the entrepreneur and the recognition of their responsibility in facilitating the satisfaction of other stakeholders' aspirations. For example, financial measures such as cash-flow assume responsibility for loan repayments to financial institutions, payments to suppliers, wages for employees, and other working capital needs. Profitability assumes responsibility for venture capital returns and investor support, as well as being one of the justifications for venture development.

The reasons why other stakeholders would wish to see the new venture succeed are equally personalised and this results in narrow, particular criteria for judging performance. *No one single set of criteria are*, per-se, *any more or any less valid and important then any other set*. Each is equally appropriate, in the right circumstances. Examples of some of the typical stakeholder groupings and their likely success requirements are illustrated in Figure 4.1. (Note: this is *not* intended to be a comprehensive listing.)

An additional complicating consideration is that the relative weighting and importance of these measures will change over time as the business progresses from start-up through periods of transition and growth to maturity as an established, hopefully successful, corporate entity.

The above illustrates that there is no single criterion, label, or definition of success. The formulation, development, and implementation of policy initiatives is simplified by accepting singular notions since target objectives, accountability, and measureability are enhanced. However, the fundamental purpose of policy initiatives is to help and support the small business sector which must, therefore, accept a pluralistic understanding of success. Accordingly, a revised definition of small business success is: '*The sustained satisfaction of principal stakeholder aspirations*' (see Figure 4.1).

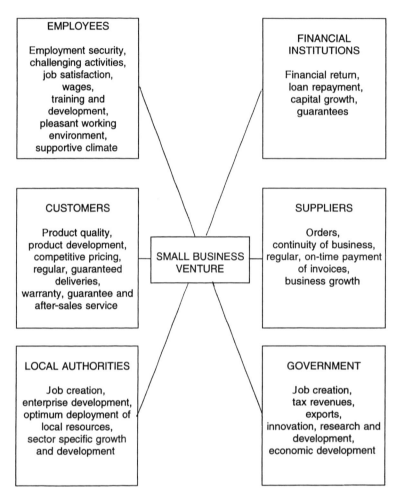

Figure 4.1   The stakeholder web of the small firm

WHY SHOULD WE 'PICK WINNERS'?

Why is this topic worth investigating?

The fundamental problem in accounting for the differing performance of small and large firms is that many small firms only exist for a very short period. Failure rates are more than ten times as high for new small firms as for larger well established firms . . . failure, in our view, is the central characteristic of the small business sector . . .

makers of public policy [should pursue] selective assistance, either
to prevent failure or to promote further growth . . . (Storey *et al.*,
1987).

As the above quotation contends, the failure rate among small firms,
especially new small firms, is inordinately high. This results not only
in high economic costs but also in high social costs and in lost
opportunities throughout the economy. Romantic economic theory
embraced the notion that for every small firm which fails there is a
redeployment of resources resulting in a new, more efficient business
which acts as a natural corrective. Current statistics do not support
this view and show a depletion of the UK small business stock.
Indeed, DTI statistics (ending December 1993) show that the failure
rate of small firms (i.e. those de-registering for VAT purposes) is at
an all-time high. *This has led to the 'bar-room' approach to small business
proprietorship of 'How do you obtain a small business in 1993? Buy a big
one and wait!'* This is not only a major loss to the British economy,
with decreased revenues for the exchequer, but also a significant
reduction in the competitive position of many large firms in their
search and desire for suppliers and collaborative partners—as well
as reducing competition and limiting consumer choice.

The majority of current small firm initiatives are non-
discriminatory and are aimed at all small firms irrespective of sector,
complexion, track record, financial profile, and so on. However,
according to Barber *et al.* (1989) approximately 4% of all small firms
account for 50% of real growth in the sector. The remainder of the
firms will either cease to trade in a relatively short time or will
experience only very modest growth. This seems to provide a
powerful argument for targeting policy initiatives upon those
businesses most likely to grow—since this appears to maximise the
chances of the sustained satisfaction of stakeholder aspirations—
but this presupposes that firms with growth potential can be
identified.

Targeting support activities upon high-potential ventures should
therefore maximise the probability of considerable benefits accruing
to the rest of society. These benefits would include:

(1) The creation of employment/reduction of unemployment.
    Fostering and nurturing high-potential ventures should lead,
    as quickly as possible, to the creation of a maximum number of
    jobs (Binks and Coyne, 1983; Birch, 1979).
(2) Addressing the disadvantaged competitive position of those
    small firms who could be in a position to compete effectively

with larger firms and who are thought to possess a generic advantage *vis-à-vis* their contemporaries (Stanworth and Gray, 1991).

(3) The more effective deployment of limited public resources by concentrating upon those most likely to succeed.

(4) The maximisation of returns from the use of public resources leading to income from taxation.

(5) The multiplier effect—successful firms need more resources from other firms and hence place more orders, generate more business and circulate more money in the economy.

(6) The provision of role models and mentors for other firms to copy and work with (e.g. Body Shop International, Derwent Valley Foods, Virgin Group plc).

(7) The promotion of innovation and the provision of help to cover risk, uncertainty, and higher costs.

(8) The prevention and check of monopoly positions and power by larger firms. This helps reduce industrial concentration and prevent market inefficiencies.

(9) The provision of a basis for policy interventions likely to benefit the wider small business community.

(10) The identification of the personal characteristics of entrepreneurs. This may highlight training and development needs in others and act as a vehicle for analysis.

(11) The facilitation of investment by private capital providers through the focusing of investment strategies upon the highest growth potential ventures.

Support agencies have limited resources and therefore these should be deployed on projects and ventures with the greatest success potential—measured by all our pluralistic definition criteria.

In order to predict success potential pre-start-up, there is a need to identify factors and features which contribute to success within the small firm environment, which assist owner–managers and which influence behaviour in starting, managing, and developing small firms.

SMALL BUSINESS SUCCESS AND FAILURE

Being able to define success, no matter how personalised or how generalised, is not the same as being able to explain it. The fundamental question remains therefore, why do some small businesses succeed while others fail? The quantity of research and publications which address this issue confirms that there are no easy

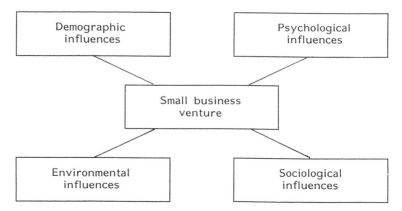

Figure 4.2   Influences upon success potential

answers and no consensus of agreement. A detailed review of the existing literature is beyond the scope of this chapter. However, an analysis of the major points may be summarised as shown in Figure 4.2.

The sociological influences paradigm focuses upon explaining success in terms of gender, age, social class, marital status, education, ethnicity, and so on (cf. Schumpeter, 1934; Birley and Norburn, 1986; Ward, 1991). As may be expected, there does not seem to be a given combination of these factors which leads to success. Men and women of all backgrounds create and manage both successful and unsuccessful businesses.

The psychological influences paradigm centres mainly upon personality traits and has several strands. These tend to equate the entrepreneur with the small business venture (cf. McLelland, 1961; Dunkleberg and Cooper, 1982; or Chell, 1985) and assume a successful entrepreneur equals a successful enterprise. Exceptions include Carland *et al.* (1984) and Stanworth and Curran (1976), who seek to differentiate not only the entrepreneur from the enterprise but also an entrepreneur from an owner–manager. The underlying premise of this paradigm is that success can be explained in terms of the psychological set of the principal actors.

The demographic paradigm concentrates upon the background and lifestyle of the business founder and seeks to explain success in terms of the trigger event which leads to self-employment (cf. Cooper, 1981; Shapero, 1975; Birley, 1989). The environmental paradigm focuses upon the physical and situational circumstances, in which the new enterprise is founded and seeks to explain success in terms of the networking of resources and support services and industrial/commercial sector (Carswell, 1990; Stanworth and Gray, 1991; Foley and Green, 1989; Porter, 1980).

Some studies have sought to combine all or most of the above in creating a integrated paradigm to explain success. These range from cursory, surface analysis to in-depth detailed research. For example, high-growth Japanese companies, according to the Nikkei Industrial Daily (reported in *Asiaweek*, Hongkong Bank, 12 May 1993), use MAGIC! The mnemonic describes Medium size, Agility, Garage-shop (entrepreneurial) mentality, Innovation, and Concentration (on a specific field). Ray and Hutchinson (1983) conducted a study of 'supergrowth companies'—i.e. companies which grew rapidly to a stock market quotation—compared to a matched sample of 'passive' small firms which did not grow to flotation. They found, among other issues, that the 'supergrowth companies' were considerably more focused in their objectives, with a strong emphasis on forecasting financial data on a regular basis; particularly cash-flow but also profit and sales. The changing style of management and organisational structure is also apparent as the companies develop.

Furthermore, the dynamics of the business environment suggest that the relative importance of influencing factors will ebb and flow in two key dimensions. First, over time, change in the general business environment will subtly alter the mix of dominant influences which impinge upon the overall level of success within the economy as a whole. Second, any situationally specific influences will alter as the organisation itself develops. For any firm to remain successful over a sustained period there *must* be a capability to adapt to changing circumstances. Indeed, Greiner (1972) shows that failure to adapt to a series of 'crises' caused by growth is one of the principal causes of failure for all organisations. Hence, one of the primary ingredients in small firm success must be the managerial competence of the owner–manager.

Further insight may be gained by examining reasons for failure since successful firms must, by definition, have avoided or better managed those events which have led to the demise of their counterparts. Many surveys of small business survival and growth have been undertaken both in the UK and the other developed economies (Ganguly, 1983; Hall and Stark, 1986; LBS, 1987; Robson Rhodes, 1984; Stanford, 1982; Storey *et al.*, 1987). It is interesting to note that, in many respects, the approach to researching small business failure has been very similar to the approach to researching entrepreneurs and entrepreneurship, thereby confirming an inextricable link between entrepreneurial activity and small firm performance (Jennings and Beaver, 1993). Most seem to have also investigated small business failure and suggest situational, operational or personality-driven causes. For example, according to Stanford (1982), the causes of small business failure may be:

(1)   Inadequate accounting systems
(2)   Poor location
(3)   Lack of marketing skills
(4)   Lack of a capital budget
(5)   Inadequate provision for contingencies
(6)   Lack of management skills
(7)   Excessive inventory
(8)   Incompetency
(9)   Lack of experience
(10) Neglect
(11) Fraud
(12) Disaster
(13) Poor record keeping
(14) Reckless money management
(15) Lack of formal planning
(16) Insufficient marketing talents
(17) Indifferent employees
(18) Inability to cope with growth.

Jennings et al. (1992) point out that Stanford (as with most others) has not attempted to distinguish between *symptoms* and *causes* and the occasional exogenous event which may force a small business into liquidation. For example, a natural disaster may not be foreseen, and although it can be argued that managers should make provision for such events, in reality such preparations are seldom adequate. Alternatively, a prime business location may be rendered less than attractive—either temporarily or permanently—by the actions of others beyond the control of the owner–manager. Paradoxically, while exogenous, relatively rare events may spell disaster for one small business, such circumstances often create opportunities, at least temporarily, for the astute entrepreneur. Generally it can be seen that while *symptoms* such as inadequate accounting systems, lack of capital budget, excessive inventory, poor record keeping, or demotivated employees may be the reason for a small business failure, the root *cause* may be ineffective management. This seems to confirm the basic notion of managerial competence as a significant influencing factor.

What are these managerial competencies which underpin the

successful small business? A useful guide may be to examine the contents of small business training and development programmes. There is a need to distinguish between training and development which might be necessary for employees within a small business and training and development which is focused upon the specific needs of the owner–manager(s) themselves. The small firm owner–manager requires specific, transferable, managerial skills directly related to entrepreneurship and professional management within the operating environment of the business. He or she needs to be able to initiate and implement change and improvement in services, products, and systems. This raises the question whether small businesses fail through lack of managerial skills, which let down otherwise good skill and competence in providing the product or service, or through lack of competence in providing the product or service demanded by the customer, despite otherwise competent management in the organisation.

It is very easy to note the obvious—that providing all the necessary skills and competencies are found across the whole team which makes up the small enterprise, the business should be capable of achieving success. However, adept management is still required to blend and bring out these abilities. As Jennings and Beaver (1993) illustrate, the personality and positional power of the entrepreneur often means that latent talent within the team goes unrecognised or underutilised.

A further difficulty concerns whether training and development programmes are focused upon an actual or a perceived need of owner–managers and entrepreneurs. The principal coordinator of education, training, and development services, offered by a wide variety of national and local government departments, private sector training, and consultancy companies and further and higher education providers, has been the Department of Employment via a semi-autonomous unit which has been known, over time, as The Training Services Agency, The Manpower Services Commission, The Training Commission, The Training Agency and The Training Education and Enterprise Department! While not all management training and support has been part of this initiative, during the period 1977–88 The Department of Employment offered fourteen different programmes or courses targeted on three separate categories of business practitioner. These included, for example, New Enterprise Programme (1977/8), Small Business Course (1980/81), Management Extension Programme (1982/3), Firmstart (1985/6) and Business Growth Training (1988). Initial emphasis was placed upon helping individuals start their own business and little or no help was available to the owner–manager seeking to grow, develop, or even simply survive. Later initiatives focused upon removing people from the unemployment statistics and were accompanied by financial incentives.

In October 1989 the central coordinating role of the Training Agency was abandoned and responsibility for small business training and development was decentralised, with the creation of 82 Training and Enterprise Councils (TECs) in England and Wales and 20 Local Enterprise Companies (LECs) in Scotland. The creation of LECs and TECs was intended to give the local business community a sense of ownership for local training services and to allow local needs to be reflected in the provision. Specific training and development programmes were divided into five categories each focused upon a slightly different target market.

The higher and further education sectors would argue that courses and programmes which benefit small businesses and small business owner–managers have always been available. However, it is only in the last five years that there have been serious attempts to customise provision specifically for the special needs of smaller enterprises. Modules and units which cover topics like entrepreneurship and small business management are increasingly finding their way into the curricula of 'standard programmes' such as undergraduate business studies and postgraduate management studies. The traditional and new universities are now making efforts to market their services as consultants and as training providers to small firms and cooperating with TECs and LECs to provide local training and development services.

Private sector involvement, which is often coordinated and supported by TECs and LECs, falls into two main categories:

(1) Companies (often small businesses themselves) whose principal activity is to provide support services on a fee-paying, profit-making basis.

(2) Companies (often medium to large enterprises) who offer staff secondments or other forms of help as an aside from their main business and who seek to, at best, cover cost and possibly provide services free of charge as part of their efforts to help the community (e.g. Business in the Community, which is a government-sponsored initiative).

However, each of these initiatives and programmes is targeted on a different segment of the small business sector. Similarly, each has different reasons or motivations for their *raison d'être*. Hence, the perceived needs which each seeks to satisfy will not be fully representative of the range of managerial competencies necessary to support a successful small business. Also, the take-up rate for programmes remains extremely poor (Stanworth and Gray, 1991; Jennings *et al.*, 1992). This is evidence of the low regard for such schemes within the sector and seems to confirm that the many initiatives do not target the *real* needs of owner–managers—catering for the needs *perceived* by the provider only.

To overcome this difficulty, for the purposes of 'picking winners', it is necessary to make use of training and development schemes which purport to cover the whole sector and identify competence requirements authoritatively and comprehensively. Such an attempt has recently been undertaken by the Small Firms Lead Body on behalf of the National Council for Vocational Qualifications (NCVQ). Their functional map and occupational standards will provide the basis for forthcoming National Vocational Qualifications (NVQs) in small business management. In common with other Lead Body standards, these provide an extremely detailed and pedantic listing of competence requirements which may be summarised in four key areas:

(1) Establishing and evaluating the business opportunity
(2) Managing the business to produce products and services which satisfy customer needs and generate revenue
(3) Monitoring business performance to sustain and improve profit
(4) Developing business operations to improve performance.

In attempting to identify success potential, pre-start-up, support agencies should seek confirmation of the possession of these competences. In the future, it is hoped that the award of an NVQ will provide satisfactory evidence.

CONCLUSIONS AND RECOMMENDATIONS

The singular notion of business success in 1990s is not only inappropriate but is also naive and dangerous. The complexity and dynamism of the business environment demands attention to a combination of demographic, sociological, environmental, and psychological factors which is tempered by astute, competent management if the venture is to prosper and provide the returns the wider public perceives and requires from successful small businesses.

It must be recognised that some entrepreneurs or owner–managers define success in much more narrow terms than external stakeholder groupings and the public in general. These owner–managers seem to be oblivious to the benefits which they can provide to the wider community. For them, success is internally defined and measured. Undoubtedly such enterprises can be regarded as successful in these terms but it is questionable whether in times of scarce resources and economic recession these firms should receive priority assistance from the public purse.

There is nothing automatic about the birth and development of a 'winning' small firm. It has to be planned and managed from the top against a seemingly endless array of internal and external constraints. This is an issue which has major implications and significance for both support agencies and local and regional development.

Our preliminary findings would suggest the policy implications which follow shortly. However, we are extending our research significantly in order to report in more detail in the future.

- The criteria which underpin policy agendas must be redefined to embrace a pluralistic notion of success.
- Future policy should be focused on those organisations that seek to maximise their returns to the wider stakeholder community.
- Decision makers should recognise that many prospective ventures are unlikely to possess all the suggested ingredients of success initially. Support and assistance will be required in developing the success potential, of many ventures, prior to supporting the actual venture itself.
- Policies which seek to encourage growth and development of 'winning' firms must be sustained, consistent, and focused on their actual needs.
- Policy makers should recognise that certain business sectors are more conducive to producing 'winning' firms.
- Policy should recognise that 'winning' small firms need to be supported financially, tactically, and strategically.
- Future policy must overcome the current problems of short-termism, fragmentation, and lack of relevance to real business needs in targeting 'winning' enterprises.
- Policy must address the personal needs, aspirations and motivation of the business proprietor.

REFERENCES

Barber, J., Metcalfe, J.S. and Porteous, M. (eds) (1989) *Barriers to Growth in Small Firms*, London, Routledge.

Beaver, G. (1984) The entrepreneurial ceiling: A discussion of the small Business Management Process. *7th National Small Firms Policy and Research Conference*, Nottingham.

Binks, M.R. and Coyne, J. (1983) *The Birth of Enterprise*, IEA Hobart Paper No. 98.

Birch, D.L. (1979) *The Job Generation Process*, Cambridge, MA, MIT Press.

Birley, S. (1989) The start-up. Chapter 2 in Burns, P. and Dewhurst, J. (eds), *Small Business and Entrepreneurship*, London, Macmillan.

Birley, S. and Norburn, D. (1986) Who are the high flyers? *Strategic Management Conference*. Singapore.

Burns, P. and Dewhurst, J. (1989) *Small Business and Entrepreneurship*, London, Macmillan.

Carland, J., Hoy, F., Boulton, W.R. and Carland, J.C. (1984) Differentiating entrepreneurs from small business owners. *Academy of Management Review*, 9, No. 2, 354–9.

Carswell, M. (1990) Networking and small firms. *13th UKEMRA National Small Firms Policy and Research Conference*, Harrogate.

Carter, S. and Cannon, T. (1992) *Women as Entrepreneurs*, London, Academic Press.

Chaganti R. and Chaganti, R. (1983) A profile of profitable and not-so-profitable small businesses. *Journal of Small Business Management*, 21 (3), 47–61.

Chell, E. (1985) The entrepreneurial personality: A few ghosts laid to rest? *International Small Business Journal*, 3, No. 3, 43–54.

Cooper, A.C. (1981) Strategic management: new ventures and small business. *Long Range Planning*, 14, No. 5, 39–45.

Curran, J. and Stanworth, J.S. (1973) *Management Motivation in the Small Business*, London, Gower Press.

Dunkleberg, W.C. and Cooper, A.C. (1982) Entrepreneurial typologies. In Vesper, E. (ed.), *Frontiers of Entrepreneurship Research*. London, Croom Helm.

Flamholtz, E.G. (1990) *Growing Pains: How to Make the Transition from an Entrepreneurial to a Professionally Managed Firm*, Oxford, Jossey-Bass.

Foley, P. and Green, H. (1989) *Small Business Success*, London, Paul Chapman Publishing.

Ganguly, P. (1983) Lifespan analysis of business in the UK, 1973-82. *British Business*, 12 August.

Greiner, L. (1972) Evolution and revolution as organisation grow. *Harvard Business Review*, July/August.

Hall, G. and Stark, A. (1986) The effects of the conservative government as reflected in the changing characteristics of bankrupt firms *International Journal of Industrial Organisation*, 4, No. 3.

Hornaday, R.W. and Wheatley, W.J. (1986) Managerial characteristics and the financial performance of small firms. *Journal of Small Business Management*, 24, No. 2, 53–67.

Jennings, P.L. and Beaver, G. (1993) The abuse of entrepreneurial power. *Small Business and Small Business Development Conference*, Leicester.

Jennings, P.L., Beaver, G. and Richardson, W. (1992) Improving the role of accreditation in the training and development of small business owner/managers. *15th National UKEMRA Small Firms Policy and Research Conference*, Southampton.

Jennings, P.L. and Cohen, L. (1993) Invisible entrepreneurs. *16th ISBA National Small Firms Policy and Research Conference*, Nottingham.

Kelmar, J.H. (1990) Measurement of success and failure in small business— a dichotomous anachronism. *13th UKEMRA Small Firms Policy and Research Conference*, Harrogate.

London Business School (1987) *A study to determine the reasons for failure of small businesses in the UK*. London, London Business School.

Marlow, S. and Strange, A. (1993) Female entrepreneurs: success by whose standards? *Occasional Paper No. 2*, De Montfort University, Leicester Business School.

McLelland, D.C. (1961) *The Achieving Society*, Princeton, NJ, Van Nostrand.

Porter, M.E. (1980) *Competitive Strategy*, New York, Free Press.

Ray, G.H. and Hutchinson, P.J. (1983) *The Financing and Financial Control of Small Enterprise Development*, Aldershot, Gower Press.

Robson Rhodes (1984) *A Study of Businesses Financed under the Small Business Loan Guarantee Scheme*, London, DTI.

SBRC (1992) *The State of British Enterprise*, Small Business Research Centre, University of Cambridge.

Schumpeter, J.A. (1934) *The Theory of Economic Development*, Cambridge, MA, Harvard University Press.

Shapero, A. (1975) The displaced uncomfortable entrepreneur. *Psychology Today*, November.

Stanford, M.J. (1982) *New Enterprise Management*, Reston, Reston Publishing Co.

Stanworth, M.J.K. and Curran, J. (1976) Growth and the small firm—an alternative view. *Journal of Management Studies*, 13, No. 2.

Stanworth, M.J.K. and Gray, C. (1991) *Bolton 20 Years On*, Small Business Research Trust, London, Paul Chapman Publishing.

Storey, D., Keasey, K., Watson, R. and Wynarczyk, P. (1987) *The Performance of Small Firms*, London, Croom Helm.

Thorpe, R. (1989) The performance of small firms: predicting success and failure. *10th UKEMRA National Small Firms Policy and Research Conference*.

Ward, R. (1991) Economic development and ethnic business. In Carran, J. and Blackburn, R.A. (eds), *Paths of Enterprise*, London, Routledge.

Wood, L. and Woodruff, N. (1993) Shattering the glass ceiling: barriers to growth within UK Enterprise Ltd. *Small Business and Small Business Development Conference*, Leicester.

5

MANAGEMENT BY WAR – A HELPFUL WAY TO VIEW THE COMPETITION?

Hans H. Hinterhuber and Boris M. Levin

University of Innsbruck, Austria

INTRODUCTION

'We are not talking about competition anymore. We are talking about economic warfare, where you cannot let any of your global competitors steal a march on you in any part of the chess board' (Roy Brown, Unilever).

Strategy is above all a practical discipline, giving those who try to implement it a possibility to express and develop themselves. Only in the real world can the strategists show what their theories are really worth. Japanese managers trying to enter the European markets talk about gaining a 'toehold' or implementing an 'offensive action plan'. The European managers are increasingly adopting a similar military strategists' vocabulary, giving the impression of an on-going brutal economic war where sheer survival is at stake. In light of these developments it seems of importance to research the question of what influence the way of viewing the competition by management has on corporate success. This will be discussed in three parts:

- Definition of strategy as an elastic and highly pragmatic discipline with its roots in the art of conducting warfare

Rethinking Strategic Management
Edited by D. E. Hussey. © 1995 John Wiley & Sons Ltd

- Comparison of military and business strategy, identifying those characteristics of military strategy readily adaptable by today's managers in their day-to-day operations
- Examination of the strategic options available to the market leaders, followers, and new entrants dependent on the state of the business segment and answering the question of the importance of viewing the competition as an enemy. An attempt will be made to observe whether such an attitude helps to mobilize the latent possibilities of focusing the energies of a firm and increasing the group solidarity of the employees involved.

STRATEGY AND STRATEGIC CUSTOMER MANAGEMENT

'Strategy is nothing else than the application of good common sense, and this cannot be taught.' (Moltke)

Etymologically, the word 'strategy' derives its roots from the Indo-European language (Hinterhuber, 1990):

ag: to drive, to put in motion, to lead (Greek ἄγφ)
ster: horde, group, later army (Greek στρατοσ)

The definition has its roots in the art of conducting a war and means the leading of an army on a grand scale. Looking at a Greek word στρατηγοσ (army leader) we translate the word as an art of leading a military troop. The practical conducting of warfare or of an actual battle is excluded from the definition of the word strategy and has much more to do with the short-term tactic adhering to the big picture defined by the accepted strategy.

There is not, and probably never will be, a full definition of the word strategy, since in the real world strategy and tactical action plans are often intertwined on different levels and influence each other. Strategy in its very root is not a theoretical, but very much a practical discipline. Strategy is implementation in light of a grand design. The German general von Moltke defined strategy as '… nothing more than the use of a healthy common sense', meaning the ability to see things in the right perspective, to think long term and achieve short-term goals at the same time (Hinterhuber, 1990).

For the shortest and most precise way to define strategy we turn to Moltke: 'Strategy is the evolvement of the originally guiding idea according to continuously changing circumstances'. The most important guiding idea of a business entity is to achieve a quasi-monopolistic position (or at least to become a leading competitor) in a chosen niche or market segment by applying a core competence for the solution of a problem for the customer in a unique, as well as in a long-term defendable (from the competitors) fashion.

A business entity which is the leading competitor in a certain market segment has its objective in defending its position in the long run—a defensive strategy. A firm that does not belong to the leading competitors in a chosen segment examines its weaknesses and develops a plan to overcome them and achieve the uniqueness described above—an offensive strategy. Should the barriers to achieving a leading position be unsurmountable, it is usually advisable to direct the available management and financial resources to another market segment following a retreat or a disinvestment strategy.

This elastic definition of strategy and strategic options available to a business entity includes the competition as a critical factor that must be considered in every strategic plan and tactical implementation. Strategy is thus nothing more than a constant adaptation of the own actions to the reactions of competition with an aim of offering the best possible product, return or relationship to the strategic architecture or network (Hinterhuber and Levin, 1994) existing around the particular business entity and including all the stakeholders (employees, vendors, equity holders, etc.) as well as the customers. Strategic customer management touches on the most important group of the stakeholders in the network—the end customers (Haedrich and Tomczak, 1990). Strategic customer management is satisfying the customers' needs in a way that goes beyond the current offer of the competition and thus solidifying the long-term customer loyalty—a cornerstone of existence of any firm.

Within the strategic customer management it is of paramount importance to continuously:

- Find out what the customer really wants, listen to the customer and to understand what are his or her real needs or problems that need to be solved
- Weigh the key criteria that would lead to customer satisfaction from the customers' point of view
- Compare the own performance in light of the customer-defined satisfaction criteria to that offered by the competition (benchmarking)
- Improve those criteria that weigh the most (prioritizing) to outperform the competition

COMPARISON OF MILITARY AND BUSINESS STRATEGIES

There is no real difference between the key fundamentals of the military and business strategies (Ungarelli, 1992):

(1) *All-encompassing knowledge of the own and enemy position within the battle environment.* Deep and detailed understanding of the geography, topology, and weather conditions find their counterparts in the business strategy, where the knowledge of the economic conditions, import/export laws, inflation, and the political climate is imperative for the right strategic goal-setting. The difficulty of setting up the supply lines or estimation of the size and the battle-readiness of the enemy correspond to the importance of sizing up the competitors' key strengths and weaknesses, their core competencies, assessing the distribution channels, and estimating the market shares.

(2) *Clear and precise definition of own strategy.* In both business and war strategy '...is the evolvement of the originally guiding idea according to continuously changing circumstances'. The overall aim in competition is to achieve a leading market position through changing the game (innovation, design), or the rules of the game (delivery times, product variety, price/quality relationship) to achieve a leading market position. Thus the ground rules of setting aims, actively pursuing them using the surprise and deceit tactics, maintaining flexibility and empowering the small units on-site, etc. are all of the same importance to the military and in the business world.

(3) *Clear and detailed action plans.* In war and business competition it is imperative to plan tactical conduct in detail, establishing clear responsibilities to achieve the set aims.

(4) *Establishment of quick and efficient communications and reporting systems.* In both areas communication must be simple, precise, and efficient. The key information must be delivered in time, so that tactics can be adjusted or corrected either to take advantage of the new opportunities or to avoid unforeseen risks.

(5) *Never putting off until tomorrow what can be done today.* Time is a critical competitive factor (Stalk and Hout, 1992). The ability to surprise an enemy corresponds in the business world to winning through being the fastest on the market with new products or services.

(6) *No compromises in the quality of the implementation.* Both military and business depend on a perfect implementation of the action plans for their success. To achieve their aims, generals and

managers must have resources and the 'empowerment' or flexibility to make decisions independently. Both rely on team morale to achieve perfect quality.

(7) *No compromises in the quality of personnel.* This principle, taken directly from the military strategy, means in the business world that:

– Each position must be filled with the best available person
– The best people get the responsibility for the key processes or tasks
– Rewards and promotions are given only on the basis of performance

Success in the implementation of the set strategy must not be hindered by the poor quality of personnel.

(8) *Concentration of the best available resources on a limited number of strategic aims.* Just as the successful generals have always attacked one army after another, avoiding a war on more than one front, good business strategists should not try to tackle too many important projects or processes at the same time, prioritizing their actions by attacking only the most attractive aims with available resources. The competition must never be underestimated and the ability to imagine oneself in the shoes of the competitor answering a key question 'how would I go about achieving the most for my stakeholders?' is one of the most important characteristics of a successful officer or manager.

(9) *The good example always comes from the top.* The best military leaders have always concerned themselves with the most important details in the action plans, never asking from their associates more than they themselves could deliver. In business competition, a good manager should not delegate the important details—a tendency of passing on unpleasant things to the subordinates must be avoided. A manager has to share in the difficulties and the frustrations in critical situations with his or her associates.

(10) *Excellent performance must be rewarded.* Just as the military commanders and soldiers receive decorations, honors, and promotions in the ranks, bonuses and making the success public are important to motivate the employees in the business world to continue trying to excel, innovate, and do things better. Furthermore, unsuccessful, but well-conceived efforts cannot and should not be reason for punishment.

The strategy concept has its root in the art of leading a war. How far do the parallels between the war-minded military commanders and today's business managers extend? The word *feindbild* is a German definition of a certain hostile attitude or worldview. Its meaning has to do with an image of something to be hated and therefore fought (Kurz, 1984). Is 'management by war' or an enemy view of the competition healthy for the development of a modern business entity? The following model, empirical cases, and secondary data examines this question in detail and try to give an answer(s).

MANAGEMENT BY WAR IN BUSINESS COMPETITION

'Strategy is a system of expedients' (Moltke)

Depending on the state of a particular market, the relationship between competitors can be classified into three general categories:

- Markets where all competitors win—there are usually new, fast-growing, very dynamic markets where prices afford fat margins and the market growth allows the competitors to be complacent about each other. The strategic management consultancy services market in Germany is a good example. No market ever stays this way forever—maturing into the two categories that follow.
- Markets where some competitors win and others lose. This is the usual state of a moderately mature market—most of the business segments fall into this category. Automobile, food retail, or building materials—these are all markets at different stages of maturation where market leaders are clear winners and there are well-defined losers as well.
- Markets where all competitors lose. This is the final stage of the status quo, normally followed either by a complete death of the business segment or by the arrival of someone who radically changes the rules of the game (see the Swiss watch industry before the creation of SMH) (Bentivogli *et al.*, 1994). The retail end of the houseware/tableware business in Germany finds itself in this stage at the moment. None of the fragmented standalone stores earn any money on a full-cost allocation basis and the category-killers like Crate & Barrel in the United States or Geneviève Lethu in France have not arrived yet. The current state of the machine-building industry in Germany is another good example of such a market.

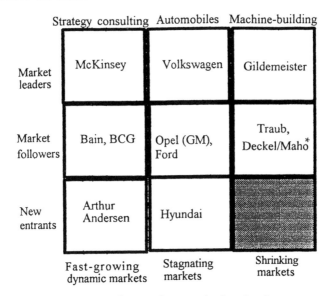

Figure 5.1 Segmentation and typology of the business competition landscape (with current examples in Germany) (*Bankruptcy in 1995)

Trying to group the possible types of competitors, we intentionally simplify the business landscape and generally observe three types of business entities—market leaders, market followers, and new entrants. Placing these firms into the three types of environments—growing, stagnating, or shrinking markets—we obtain a 3 × 3 matrix shown in Figure 5.1. The names of the firms placed in the matrix are current examples taken from some of the German industries mentioned above. Since the examples of new entrants into the shrinking markets are rare, the new entrants/shrinking markets position on the matrix has been left empty.

The field of strategic business management consulting in Germany was taken as an example of a fast-growing market (growth rates averaged some 20–40% per year in the past 5 years), with McKinsey being the undisputed leader, consultancies like Bain and BCG following, and large accounting firms like Arthur Andersen trying aggressively to break into the market in recent years.

Generally, in such dynamic markets, all the competitors 'win' with varying degrees of success. We speak therefore not of war but of 'enhancing' competition, where competitors learn from each other and take the best among themselves as role models for the others, just as athletes do in sports. There seems to be no particular need for management by war; all competitors observe each other, but there is no negative or emotional 'bogey man' image of the competition. As mentioned above, however, no markets stay in this high-growth phase for ever. This is a dynamic process of maturation, and as soon as the market segment enters the stagnation stage, competitors start behaving differently.

Automotive markets give a good idea of stagnating, saturated markets in any Western industrialized country. Volkswagen has the largest market share in Germany, with Opel (a subsidiary of General Motors) and Ford following. The Korean Hyundai is a newcomer in Germany, trying to establish itself on the market at considerable expense and with mixed success.

In these markets—and we are talking about the bulk of the existing market segments today—competition is more than a sporting exercise. 'We are talking about Feindbild where substantial amounts of jobs will be lost' (Rüssli, 1991). Management by war is a way of gathering the troops around a specific aim or target, giving the teams a focused 'we feeling'—sometimes with negative undertones. The usefulness of this almost ideological attitude depends on the strategic maturity of management (see case studies later in the chapter).

The 'mainstream' segment of the machine-building industry in Germany has gone through a horrible patch in the past 4 years, shrinking at double-digit annual rates. Gildemeister is the market-leader, eyeing-up the quickly dying merger of Deckel/Maho as an acquisition. As a rule, there are no new entrants into these markets apart from buy-out firms, attracted by asset-stripping possibilities, whose motivation is normally far from strategic competition and do not have to be considered for our purposes.

Shrinking markets, where in the long run all competitors lose, like the dynamic markets described above, do not stay this way for ever. Either these markets simply fade away, accompanied by asset-stripping exercises, or new technologies combined with new ideas change the rules of the game, thereby also changing the nature of the market.

In the long run, there is a normalizing force converging most of the markets to a more or less stable position; attractive, fast-growing markets see a great deal of entrants, making this particular business segment less attractive, while unattractive markets will be revolutionized, stabilize at a lower market volume, or disappear. Monopolistic positions, normally attained either as a result of governmental protection or by possession of long-term patents, are exceptions.

Having defined strategy as basically a military discipline, we observe two types of management attitudes towards its competition:

(1) A *feindbild* (a German word for an 'enemy image': like *blitzkrieg* or *Hauftragstaktik* (directives), not easily translatable) attitude where management mobilizes employees' emotions focusing on a particular competitor and using these emotions to achieve its strategic objectives
(2) A more placid approach where management disapproves of management by war, preferring a more gentlemanly attitude

The usefulness of a 'management by war' attitude depends on the position of a particular business entity in one of the eight possible fields of the simplified model presented in Figure 5.1. The firms therefore have an option whether they should be applying this strategic tool and how they should go about it depending on their current situation.

Strategic Options of a Market Leader (Lele, 1992)

● Market leaders, who find themselves in dynamic markets, are concerned with holding their leading position, trying to continue improving technologies and services needed to optimize customer satisfaction. The need to develop an enemy image of a particular competitor depends on how successful this business entity is in realizing these goals.
● Stable markets normally mean more severe competition from other competitors, who have assumed a number 2 or number 3 position in a market with a more or less oligopolistic structure. In this position, given a cool, non-emotional approach (see case studies), an 'enemy' attitude towards a competitor will mobilize the forces in the firm, giving the team a vitality and focus needed to fight off the assailants. Results of this 'management by war' attitude will be discussed later in this chapter.
● Being a market leader in a shrinking market, a firm will seek ways to use the weakness of the competition and will try to solidify its position by acquiring the other firms in the market, it will try to change the nature of the market by refocusing on what customers really want (see case studies), or it will try to exit the market by selling or liquidation. None of these options requires a 'management by war' attitude.

Strategic Options of a Follower

● A follower finding itself in a dynamic market will often try to assail the number 1 company or at least improve its position in the pecking order. Fixing its sights and energies on one particular firm (the leader) a relentless pursuit of this enemy in all critical market success determinants will mobilize the 'we against them feeling' in the firm, and—channelled correctly—can have a crucial impact on the position of the follower after an often-inevitable shake-out.

- A follower in a stagnating market looks for ways of holding the position reached and for opportunities of lessening the distance to the market leaders. A business entity in this situation either tries to find new niches to differentiate itself or forms strategic alliances (Hinterhuber and Levin, 1994) to sharpen its competitive advantage. *Feindbild* or an enemy view of the competitor does not always serve a particularly useful purpose in this position.
- A follower in a shrinking market can develop an extremely negative bitter attitude towards competition, looking for the scapegoats responsible for its troubles. Not only is this unhelpful, but in times where 'cool heads' and clever ideas are life-saving, this attitude can be dangerously destructive.

Strategic Options of the New Entrant

- New entrants entering a dynamic market find themselves in an unpredictable environment, where the image of the market leader provides a stable navigation tool. In pursuit of this aim it is both convenient and helpful to focus on a target and mobilize the 'hunting' instincts of the management.
- Entering the established, stagnating markets, the new arrivals normally seek a niche, where they can establish themselves quickly or try to find a way of entering into a strategic network in order to minimize entry costs. In both cases there does not seem to be a particular use for 'management by war'.

The usefulness of the *feindbild* attitude to different types of competitors positioned in the three types of market discussed above can be summarized in Figure 5.2.

FEINDBILD IMPACT ON BUSINESS PROFITABILITY AND INNOVATION SUCCESS

Kienbaum—a German consultancy—have conducted a comprehensive study of success factors among German firms (Berth, 1993). One

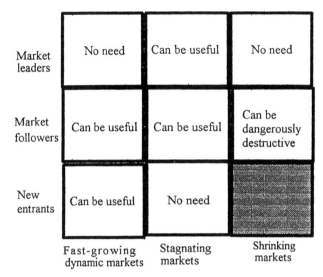

	Fast-growing dynamic markets	Stagnating markets	Shrinking markets
Market leaders	No need	Can be useful	No need
Market followers	Can be useful	Can be useful	Can be dangerously destructive
New entrants	Can be useful	No need	

Figure 5.2   The usefulness and dangers of a *feindbild* attitude

of the 27 key business success factors identified is a way of viewing competition as an enemy at war—having a *feindbild*. Over 430 managers were asked about their way of viewing competition. Some 15% viewed their competitors as an enemy at war with them—the rest found this attitude too aggressive. Interestingly enough, by segmenting the companies into 'outstanding' and 'others' Kienbaum has found that more than a quarter of the outstanding firms had the management by war attitude. For these firms the enemy is a very clearly defined market leader or someone of similar size and similar business mix, usually doing something 'irritable' in the market, i.e. being very aggressive on price, far more innovative, producing much higher quality, etc.

The results of the study were surprising to the Kienbaum consultants who considered this success factor as fairly unimportant and esoteric. Figure 5.3 shows the results relating to the financial performance. Firms with a *feindbild* are three times better at getting returns on their investment (ROI) and four times better in terms of both operating margins (ROS) and earning money on new launches (ROS new launches).

Overall innovation and the ability to manage innovation seem far better in the *feindbild* firms as Figure 5.4. testifies (scale is both per cent and months). Firms with a *feindbild* need about 2.5 years to achieve break-even on the new products launched compared to about 5 years in non-*feindbild* firms. Judged by a critical factor—

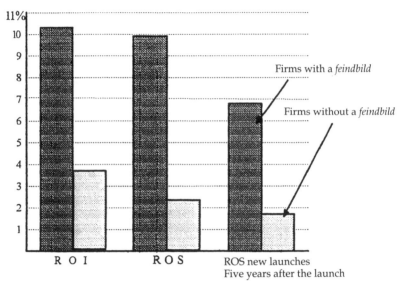

Figure 5.3   The performance of firms with and without a *feindbild*. (*Source:* Kienbaum)

share of new products as percentage of sales—the firms managing by war are far ahead—4.5 times more innovation share. *Feindbild* firms also seem to have a much better hit-rate with only 28% of total launches being classified as flops, whereas the more placid firms take half of their new launches from the market.

POSSIBLE TRAPS IN THE USE OF A *FEINDBILD*

There are, however, two sides to the *feindbild* attitude—some of the destructive characteristics of this view of competition include:

- Suspicion—'all that my competitor does is bad'
- Scapegoat search—'the competitor is responsible for our situation'
- Prejudice—'whatever they do, it can only hurt us'
- 'Bogey man' image—'they are the opposite of what we are and what we stand for'
- 'Zero-sum' thinking—'whatever is of use to him, hurts us, and vice versa'
- De-individualization—'whoever is with them is against us'
- No-mercy attitude—'empathy, sympathy or ethical criteria have no place in our relationship with the competition'

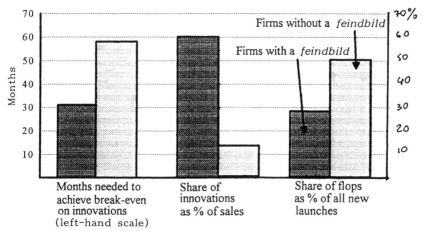

Figure 5.4 The management of innovations in firms with and without a *feindbild*. (*Source:* Kienbaum)

Henry Kissinger once said that 'there are no friends in politics, just temporary alliances'. Understanding the significance of this is just as important to a business strategist—the world of business is changing to a system full of more or less stable networks, some fleeting, some long-lasting. In today's increasingly complicated and confusing business landscape where the borders between competition and allies are blurred and the very boundaries of a corporation are increasingly difficult to define, use of the *feindbild* will be far more difficult in the future, evolving into a benchmarking exercise with some very delicate coordination of the emotional attitude of the employees towards the competition.

CHANGING THE GAME IN SHRINKING MARKETS

Along with the well-known success of SMH (Swatch), it is interesting to consider Yamaha's strategy (Ohmae, 1988) as a way of behavior in a shrinking market. Yamaha found itself a leader in a shrinking market for pianos. Instead of divesting itself out of this business, it tried and is succeeding in changing the game by giving its customers a completely new way of viewing and using the piano in their homes. Yamaha's inventors have taken the age-old idea of a player-piano and have adapted it for the computer-driven 1990s. By retrofitting their existing instruments, customers could buy 3.5-inch disks with recordings of well-known pianists and 'let' their piano perform these recordings in the privacy of their own home. Not only has this enlivened a shrinking market, it has given Yamaha an additional revenue source in the highly lucrative tuning market—since people now wanted their pianos to sound perfect and consequently used the tuners more often.

In this situation Yamaha has wisely ignored all the conventional wisdom of portfolio management by staying in a 'dog' business. Instead of trying to focus on a suffering competition the strategists of the firm have followed a 2,500-year old observation of Sun Tzu that 'the smartest strategy in war is the one that lets you achieve your objectives without having to fight'.

LEADERS WITH MISPLACED PRIORITIES

By following their self-created *feindbild* attitude towards their Japanese competition (chiefly Toyota) GM managers spent years in the 1980s talking about the Japanese competition and Pearl Harbor in the same breath. The result was a drastic loss in market share, an enormous sum of over $40 billion wasted on the wrong kinds of investments, and an unprecedented 'retirement' wave in recent months of senior managers.

Volkswagen has taken itself down a wrong path by having an easily avoidable fight with GM's German subsidiary, with VW's management trying to turn the squabble into an attack on German industry. Not only has this misfired badly, but the time spent (and being spent) on resolving the fight could have been far more valuably employed in turning the company around.

FOLLOWERS WHO CAME, SAW, WON *AND* MOVED ON

This has to be compared with the BMW management that turned a half-bankrupt motorcycle manufacturer 30 years ago into an extremely successful car-maker today by constantly setting their sights on Mercedes-Benz. An important feature of this spectacular use of positive aspects of the *feindbild* attitude is the relative coolness in strategy execution, avoiding the dangers of hate–fear emotions, and the management's ability to avoid fixation by moving on to their next target after surpassing Mercedes in 1993. BMW's spectacular acquisition of Britain's Rover has simply turned it into a different company in a different ball park with different targets to follow.

The Texan computer-maker Compaq fits into this category as well. Facing rapidly diminishing returns caused by a simultaneous onslaught from the cheap Asian manufacturers like Acer and aggressive mail-order firms, offering more service like Dell, it tried to better both approaches and won by all accounts, almost doubling its annual revenues to an unprecedented $700 000 per employee/per year and becoming an undisputed leader in the highly dynamic computer hardware market. Once again, not stopping there, it selected another target—IBM's mainframes. As a result, the company will have tripled its revenue in the past four years to an estimated $10 billion in 1994, turning itself into a leader in a dynamic market. The future will tell whether Compaq can sustain this position by moving onto an offensive strategy and starting to set the pace (like Microsoft or Swatch—other leaders in their dynamic market segments do) instead of managing the competition.

Sculley's (1987) description of the 'cola wars' in the 1970s gives a classic of a well-orchestrated and beautifully executed use of *feindbild*—Coke. Pepsi's managers have never concerned themselves with questions such as 'what are they doing to us, and what in the world are we going to do in response?' Instead they have consistently asked themselves 'knowing all this about them what can we do differently or better?' The result was a spectacular almost hundred-fold growth of an obscure and puny ($300 million in annual sales in 1963) company to a giant with over $25 billion in annual sales—twice the size of Coke today.

COMBINATION OF A *FEINDBILD* WITH STRATEGIC NETWORKING

Most interesting is the approach by Novell—a Utah-based main competitor of Microsoft. This firm has cleverly combined the mobilizing energies of a *feindbild* (Microsoft) with an organization of a strategic network of other firms competing in the same market. All the firms are united by the common dislike of the standalone, often-brutal Microsoft and the well-executed network organization skills of the Novell management. Novell's recent successes in stabilizing its position as an increasing alternative to Microsoft and its efforts to further strengthen ties with the larger members of its network (via mergers, acquisitions and cross-shareholdings) will help define the software market's future after it moves to a more stable state.

SUMMARY

Following the analysis above, the answer to the question of the usefulness of war attitudes in competition is 'Yes', 'No', and 'Yes and No'. There is no simple formula that would give an answer; given a competitive position, however, the simplified model discussed in this chapter gives a general direction. The figures adapted from the Kienbaum study are extremely compelling, but so are the cases where managers try to blame someone else for their own mistakes and draw no correct conclusions from their failures.

Mobilizing the employees around the idea of a well-identifiable target will bring results in the short run. It is management's responsibility to use this concentrated energy in an optimal fashion, recognizing that today's enemy could be a network partner tomorrow (or will simply lose its relevance in the long run) and shifting the priorities as well as targets along with changing environments.

Firms with a placid, gentlemanly attitude towards their competition may find themselves nudged aside by the more aggressive followers. As the experiences of IBM, Pan Am, and Polaroid have demonstrated, there are really no long-term safe havens in today's competitive landscape where firms can relax and enjoy a peaceful break. Or, returning to Bismarck, *'War is everywhere. And if we want to go on living, we must brace ourselves for more fighting'.*

REFERENCES

Bentivogli, C., Hinterhuber, H. and Trento, S. (1994) The Watch Industry: A strategic analysis. *International Review of Strategic Management*, Vol **5**, Hussey, D.E. (ed.) 133–167, Wiley.

Berth, R. (1993) *Erfolg—Überlegenheitsmanagement: 12 Mind-Profit Strategien Mit ausführlichem Testprogramm*, pp. 83–8, Econ Verlag, Düsseldorf.

Haedrich, G. and Tomczak, T. (1990) *Strategische Markenführung*, Bern/Stuttgart.

Hinterhuber, H.H. (1990) *Wettbewerbsstrategie*, 2 ed Aufl, p. 4, Berlin/New York.

Hinterhuber, H. and Levin, B. (1994) Strategic networks—The Organisation of the Future, **27**, 3, 44–53. *Long Range Planning.*

Kurz, H.R. (1984) Feindbild–Bedrohungsbild–Kriegsbild–Lagebild. *Schweizer Soldat*, N. 12, 4–5.

Lele, M. (1992) *Creating Strategic Leverage*, New York, Free Press

Ohmae, K. (1988) Getting back to strategy. *Harvard Business Review*, November–December.

Rüssli, F.M. (ed.) (1991) *Brauchen wir Feindbilder?* p. 79, Münsingen/Bern.

Sculley, J. (1987) *Odyssey Pepsi to Apple*, London, Fontana/Collins.

Stalk, G. and Hout, T. (1992) *Competition Against Time*, London, Collier-Macmillan.

Ungarelli, M. (1992) *Storia maestra di management*, Rizzoli, Milan.

6

CLASSICAL COMPETITIVE STRATEGY IN NEWLY DEREGULATED INDUSTRIES – DOES IT APPLY?

Dolores O'Reilly

University of Ulster

BACKGROUND

This chapter assesses the applicability of classical competitive strategy in a deregulated industry: the airline industry. The question of competitiveness has been central to strategy in recent years and this has been especially evident in industries that have recently been deregulated.

Few other industries have experienced a more global deregulation than the airline industry. The US Airline Deregulation Act of 1978 acted as a catalyst for global restructuring on an unprecedented scale. The effect of deregulation has been to expose the airline industry and many other industries, particularly utilities, to extreme competitive pressures.

THE PROCESS OF DEREGULATION

Today, deregulation has become so extensive that it is possible to

Rethinking Strategic Management
Edited by D. E. Hussey. © 1995 John Wiley & Sons Ltd

discern recurring structural changes irrespective of the industry in which the deregulation has occurred. From a strategic perspective this observation is important in that it should enable strategic planners in regulated industries to develop appropriate strategies for the deregulated era. On the basis of deregulations that have taken place, with particular reference to the airline industry, the process can be categorised into the following stages:

Stage 1: Regulated strategic torpor: This stage is characterised by little competition, high entry barriers, relatively poor financial and operating performances by most competitors, lack of buyer power, high prices and non-price competition.

Stage 2: Pre-deregulation jockeying: Incumbents and potential new entrants engage in pre-emptive strategies such as: the acquisition of new assets, promotion campaigns, political lobbying, staff recruitment, promotion programmes from incumbents in order to deter new entrants and build brand loyalty, and finally assiduous searching for linkages with other carriers to give anticipated necessary critical mass.

Stage 3: Advent of deregulation: This is characterised by many new entrants, severe competition throughout the industry, strategy variety as players seek distinctive strategies to follow and niches to exploit and severe profit erosion as price becomes the premier axis of rivalry.

Stage 4: Shakeout: This is characterised by an increasing orientation towards low price as the primary competitive strategy with the consequent shakeout of weakest players and relentless acquisition and merger activity.

Stage 5: Relative competitive stability: This is characterised by a more stable pool of players, the rules of the game have evolved and competitive stability among the remaining winning players becomes an undeclared but real common objective. This is reflected in price-matching strategies and other relatively mild competitive rivalry. However, this stability is relative as deregulation has lowered barriers to entry and the threat of new entrants places a constraint on the freedom to deviate strongly from purely competitive strategies.

This process of evolution is shown in schematic form in Figure 6.1. In the figure the vertical axis—Intensity of competition—is a reflection of the variety of strategies that airlines employed. Thus, in the Regulated Torpor stage there was little variety in the strategies

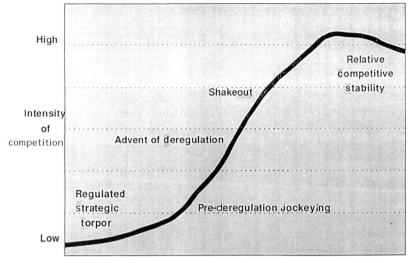

Figure 6.1   The process of deregulation

employed, they were mainly monopolistic or duopolistic international agreements, whereas in the Shakeout stage, strategies included regulation, price wars, and frequent-flyer schemes.

The focus of this chapter is that the competition that prevails in the airline industry in the USA and the European Union has followed the above life cycle model and that currently the USA and the European Union are in the third and fifth stages of their deregulation life cycle respectively. The chapter examines this issue by analysing the airline industry using a Porter (1985) model. More precisely it asks the question: 'Is the Porter model of competitive strategy reflected in the deregulated airline industry?'

> *The European Union has gradually moved to liberalise regulation of air transport in an attempt to achieve a single market in the industry. This deregulation has taken the form of a number of 'packages'. The 'First Package' (14 December 1987) contained measures by the Council on fares, capacity, market access, block exemptions and application of competition rules. The 'Second Package' (27 July 1990) contained more liberal rules in the same basic areas, leading to the 'Third Package' of 23 July 1992. The 'Third Package' came into force on 1 January 1993: it offered open market access except for a temporary exception for pure cabotage, and a free rein on capacity and pricing.*

COMPETITIVE STRATEGIES IN THE AIRLINE INDUSTRY

Contemporary developments and strategic moves in the airline industry as it has moved from being regulated to deregulated are analysed below using a standard Porter framework. Thus the forces are analysed under the following headings:

- The threat of new entrants
- The threat from substitutes
- The power of buyers
- The power of suppliers
- The degree of rivalry

BARRIERS TO ENTRY: PRE-DEREGULATION

Historically the airlines have been one of the world's most regulated industries. 'Probably no other world-wide economic activity of comparable magnitude is more thoroughly regulated, less free of official constraint and guidance than is world air transport' (Lissitzyn, 1968). The degree of regulation has been a universal characteristic of the industry world-wide from its earliest days. Indeed, Sawers (1987) maintains that governments do this in order to '...increase the share in air traffic of their country's (generally state-owned) airlines rather than to promote an efficient industry that meets the demands of the consumer'.

Government regulation of the airline industry has been so pervasive that before deregulation occurred barriers to entry were almost impenetrable. Under regulation, governments froze the structure of the airline industry: prices were harmonised and then fixed, effectively denying customer choice, national airlines were restricted to particular *quid pro quo* routes. Indeed, so rigorous was the regulation that between 1958 and 1978 no new scheduled carriers entered the US domestic system (Breyer, 1992; Pickrell, 1991).

BARRIERS TO ENTRY: POST-DEREGULATION

The Airline Deregulation Act 1978 signalled the start of the era of competition in the airline industry. Perhaps the clearest demonstration of the new competitive era in which airlines would operate was reflected in the great reduction in the height of the entry

Table 6.1 The number of new entrants to the US airline industry and the total number of exiting competitors between the years 1979 and 1992

Year	Number of new entrants
1979	22
1980	17
1981	16
1982	10
1983	18
1984	19
1985	18
1986	7
1987	5
1988	4
1989	5
1990	7
1991	5
1992	15
Total	168
No. of exits	112
No. remaining	56

Source: US Department of Transportation (1993).

barriers. Thus Table 6.1 shows the number of new entrants to the US airline industry between 1978 and 1993.

With deregulation and the erosion of the entry barriers, many new entrants commenced operations and oversupply quickly developed. Because of the high capital investment necessary to operate in this industry, capacity utilisation became a primary concern of all carriers and in a classic PIMS manner and price became the primary competitive weapon as firms fought punitive and often pyrrhic battles to maintain load factors. (PIMS argues that investment intensity is the largest single cause of profit problems: see Buzzell and Gale, 1990.)

In general the airlines have found it difficult to erect sustainable barriers to entry which would provide them with attractive returns. Indeed, the erosion of entry barriers was the overwhelming competitive dynamic which caused firms to increase their investment intensity, which in turn led to loss making and overcapacity. Tables 6.2 and 6.3 highlight the losses incurred by the eleven biggest carriers in the USA and by the 'flag-carriers' in the European Union from 1990 to 1992. The competitively injurious

Table 6.2   Yearly net income (losses) of major US airlines 1990–92 (US $ million)

Airline	1990	1991	1992
America West	(74.7)	(213.8)	(131.8)
American	(76.8)	(239.9)	(935.0)
Continental	(1236.4)	(305.7)	(125.3)
Delta	(154.0)	(239.5)	(564.8)
Eastern	(1115.9)	—	—
Northwest	(10.4)	(3.1)	(383.0)
Pan Am	(638.1)	(283.1)	—
Southwest	47.1	26.9	103.9
TWA	(237.6)	48.2	(239.8)
United	95.7	(331.9)	(957.1)
US Air	(410.7)	(305.3)	(1,230.0)

Source: US General Accounting Office (1993).

effects of this overcapacity were exacerbated by shifting power from the airlines to their buyers: an issue which is considered next.

BUYER POWER

Buyers in the airline industry can be divided into two major categories:

(1) *Corporate buyers,* i.e. travel agents, tour operators, large company travel managers (serving both the public and private sectors)
(2) *Individual buyers,* i.e. individual flyers who book on an individual basis, normally through travel agents or directly through the airlines.

Although there is great deal of heterogeneity in the purchasing requirements of each group, it has tended to be the case that the additional power that the corporate buyers have accumulated has also been enjoyed by the individual buyers. Consequently in this section no distinction is made between these two buyer groups.

Buyer Power Pre-deregulation

Pre-deregulation buyer power was extremely limited. In the United

Table 6.3 Yearly cumulative net income (losses) of 'flag-carriers' in the European Union 1990–92 (US $ million)

Airline	1990	1991	1992
Aer Lingus	8.300	(18.500)	(195.600)
Air France	(132.100)	(121.146)	(617.000)
Alitalia	(81.700)	(27.900)	(11.900)
BA[a]	169.600	687.300	297.700
Iberia	(137.700)	(346.800)	(339.800)
KLM	(346.900)	66.200	(319.00)
Lufthansa	9.400	(257.700)	(250.400)
Luxair			600
Olympic	(164.300)	(133.900)	(224.800)
SABENA	(205.700)	(68.600)	11.700
SAS	(144.800)	(239.000)	(127.400)
TAP	(15.300)	(38.000)	(199.800)

Source: Airline Business, ICAO (1994).
[a]British Airways is 100% privately owned while all the others are either wholly or partially owned by national governments.

States neither travel agents nor individual buyers had any influence on the fares charged for the two-thirds of bookings made directly with the airlines. In the case of bookings made through the automated Computer Reservation System (CRS) service provided by airlines, travel agents received an identical amount of sales commission irrespective of which carrier's flights were booked.

Buyer Power Post-deregulation

Post-deregulation buyer power was greatly enhanced by two major influences (Table 6.4): the strategies of the airlines and the actions of governments and consumer bodies such as the Air Transport Users Council (AUC) in the UK and the Federation of Air Transport User Representatives in the European Community (FATUREC). FATUREC was created in 1983 and it unites user groups from ten member states. It meets twice a year and is consulted by the European Commission (DG VII) in order to consider the air users' perspective when drafting legislation.

Buyer Power in the United States

From 1978 to 1986 airline payments to travel agents rose greatly as a cost per revenue passenger mile (RPM) and as a percentage of total operating costs. In a period in which total costs per RPM increased

Table 6.4   Factors causing an increase in buyer power

Airline forces boosting buyer power	Government/consumer forces boosting buyer power
Investment intensity: overcapacity	Application of EU competition law
Entry of 'rogue' players	Promotion of competition by national governments (e.g. U.K.)
Variety of airline strategies	Growth of consumer bodies (e.g. AUC, FATUREC)
Standard products	
Low switching costs	
Product often unimportant to buyer	
Buyer has full information	

by only 35%, the commission to the bulk purchasers—travel agents—rose by 143% and the percentage of commission payments in total costs by 83% from 4.7% in 1978 to 8.6% in 1986. These changes are set out in Table 6.5.

An additional way of looking at the increasing power of buyers is the actual percentage commissions paid by airlines to agents over this period. Thus in 1978 the average rate of commission paid by airlines in the United States was 8.3% and this had increased to over 10% by 1986. Even this understates their increase in power, as the

Table 6.5   Airline commission payments to agents

Year	Commission costs per RPM (US cents)	Commission as % of total costs
1978	0.416	4.7
1979	0.478	4.8
1980	0.663	5.2
1981	0.820	5.8
1982	0.850	6.2
1983	0.907	7.0
1984	0.994	7.6
1985	0.993	7.6
1986	1.009	8.6

Source: IATA (1987).

share of total sales through agents in 1978 was 57% and by 1986 it had increased to almost 80%.

Buyer power in Europe

Increased buyer power is also seen clearly in Europe. This has occurred because of the extension of choice made possible by the opening up of previously impenetrable markets. Traditional duopoly agreements on fare fixing at uncompetitive rates are being eroded slowly by the arrival of the 'third carrier' on thick, popular routes where historically there was no choice between fares.

Responding to buyer demands for lower prices, new carriers have reduced their prices and hence have won buyers away from the incumbents (see Figure 6.2; MORI and Wagonlit Survey, 1994). In order to retain or win back market share, the incumbents have reacted by matching their fares. This enhanced buyer power is clearly illustrated in Tables 6.6 and 6.7.

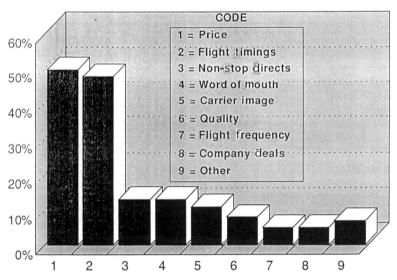

Figure 6.2 Factors influencing the choice of an airline. (*Sources:* Compiled by author using data from MORI and Wagonlit Survey, 1994)

THE THREAT OF SUBSTITUTES PRE-DEREGULATION

In the pre-deregulation era although it could be argued that substitutes in the form of rail, road, and sea did exist, at that time

Table 6.6   Fare structures on selected routes which have a third carrier, British Midland

Route	Carrier	Fare (£) 28.10.1992	Fare (£) 6.6.1993
Heathrow–Paris	BM	256	240
	BA	316	240
	Air France	316	240
Heathrow–Amsterdam	BM	236	204
	BA	274	204
	KLM	274	204
Heathrow–Frankfurt	BM	—	330[a]
	BA	366	364
	Lufthansa	366	364

[a]BM started on this route in March 1993.

Table 6.7   Fare structures on selected routes which have no third carrier

Route	Carrier	Fare (£) 28.10.1992	Fare (£) 6.6.1993
Heathrow–Rome	BA	524	524
	Alitalia	524	524
Heathrow–Milan	BA	416	416
	Alitalia	416	416
Heathrow–Munich	BA	436	436
	Lufthansa	436	436
Heathrow–Copenhagen	BA	452	452
	SAS	452	452

none of those services could have been considered as an adequate substitute for air travel as the differences in the journey time were so great. Consequently there were no genuine substitutes.

THE THREAT OF SUBSTITUTES POST-DEREGULATION

The only realistic substitute mode of travel considered in this study is the European high-speed train. Since the introduction of the

French TGV (Train à Grande Vitesse) in 1981, and with the extension of this type of network throughout Europe there is now a more realistic substitute for air travel, especially on city-centre to city-centre routes of 300–350 kilometres (Institute of Air Transport Report, 1991).

Factors Influencing the Choice between High-speed Train and Aircraft

Research shows that when there is a choice of travel mode, i.e. air, rail, car, and boat, a number of key factors tend to influence passenger decisions, namely:

- Journey time
- Convenience of schedule
- Price

(Data from the Association of European Airlines, 1990.) There are of course other factors—city to airport links, journey costs, punctuality, standards of comfort and reliability, and consideration of safety—which often influence choice of transport. However, in this study only the AEA report factors will be considered.

JOURNEY TIME

Improved journey times on European railways have made rail a major substitute for air travel, as time is considered to be the primary factor influencing the choice of travel mode. In highly populated Europe where the distances between large cities are relatively short, the introduction of sophisticated high-speed train networks is likely to increase the popularity of rail over air as illustrated by the substitution that has taken place between the French TGV and air travel (see Table 6.8).

Table 6.8 Changes in the travel patterns, train and aircraft on the Paris–Lyon route, 1981 to 1984

	1981	1984
Air (%)	21	7
Rail (%)	47	74
Road (%)	32	19

Source: Compiled by author using data from Air Inter (1993).

Table 6.9   Projected km of high speed railtrack in the
EU, 1994–2010

Year	Projected km of high-speed railtrack: EU
1994	13000
2010	24000

Thus since September 1981, when the TGV commenced operations between Paris and Lyon, progressive savings of train journey times have been achieved. The effect of this has been significant reductions in the absolute volume of air traffic (a decrease of 54% by 1984) whereas prior to the introduction of the TGV air traffic had been increasing by 8.7% per annum. This pattern is also replicated, internationally, on the Paris–Geneva link which began operating in 1982: the airline route share of 61% fell within two years to 42.5%. Thus the high-speed train has already emerged as a clear substitute for air travel and its influence will increase as the European networks are extended (see Table 6.9).

The future impact of this threat is one of great concern to airlines and already there are many examples of the competitive reactions of pre-emptive predatory pricing. For example, British Midlands, in February 1994, introduced a £69 return fare for London–Edinburgh, matching the Intercity return saver ticket. This move is likely to be repeated by other airlines competing for city-to-city commuters.

In passing, it should be noted that the strategy of 'deterring' the train companies is likely to be unsuccessful because of the enormous investments which are now being made available in railway infrastructure (total expenditure by the European Union (which includes Austria and Switzerland and all Member States of the EU in Mainland Europe) of ECU 180 billion by the year 2010—European Commission DG VII, Brussels, 1994).

CONVENIENCE OF SCHEDULE

The extension of the European high-speed rail network is expanding rapidly in scope and also in the variety and convenience of the rail schedules. This is illustrated in Table 6.10.

Table 6.10 A comparison between TGV services and competing air services

Year	Paris–Lyon Distance (km)	TGV time (hours)	Daily direct frequencies TGV	Air
Winter 1982/3	512	2.36	13	10
Winter 1983/4	425	2.0	18	9
Winter 1984/5	425	2.0	20	6
Winter 1985/6	425	2.0	24	11

PRICE

Substitutes place a ceiling upon the price that can be charged for a service. The pricing consequences of the high-speed train as a substitute for air travel are well documented. Thus Table 6.11 shows comparative fare structures for the high-speed train and selected air routes.

Table 6.11 A comparison between air and rail fares on the London–Manchester and Paris–Lyon routes for 1993

1993 prices at FFr 8.10 = £1	Air fare (£)	Rail fare (first class)
London–Manchester	85	65
Paris–Lyon	93.30	46.6[a]

[a]Plus a small compulsory registration charge.

THE POWER OF SUPPLIERS

Suppliers in the aviation industry can be divided into two groups:

(1) *General suppliers of products and services* to the industry without reference to any particular airline
(2) *Suppliers of specific products and supplies* to specific airlines.

Each of the above is now discussed.

General Suppliers

These suppliers provide the utilities that all airlines need to operate and include the following:

- Air traffic control
- Airport facilities
- Police and security
- Immigration
- Customs and excise
- Supporting travel infrastructure
- Regulatory licensing bodies

Specific Suppliers

These provide supplies purchased by individual airlines from individual firms or governments, i.e.

- Products: aircraft and associated equipment,
- Aircraft consumables (i.e. food, etc.)
- CRS systems

The Power of Suppliers Pre-deregulation

In the pre-deregulation era it could be argued that the power of general suppliers was almost absolute in that for an airline to operate, approval by the various licensing authorities was essential. This power was manifested at many levels: global, inter-regional, national, regional and finally at the level of the individual airline.

The Power of Suppliers Post-deregulation

Supplier power in the post-deregulated industry, although weaker than before, is still a major profit pressure on airlines and on smaller and newer ones in particular. This power can be considered under the classical Porter headings shown in Table 6.12.

Suppliers of Licences

Civil aviation is a global industry and safety standards are regulated on a world-wide basis. The International Civil Aviation Organisation (ICAO) was established after the Second World War as an

Table 6.12 Dimensions of supplier power

Dimension of supplier power	Licences and safety	Airport facilities	Fuel	Ground handling	CRS
Highly concentrated	X	X	X	X	X
No substitutes	X	X			
Not an important customer	X	X	X	X	X
Supplier product important	X	X	X	X	X
Supplier products differentiated	X	X	X		
Supplier switching costs	X	X		X	X
Threatens forward integration					
Government as a supplier	X			X	

intergovernmental body to perform this co-ordinating role. ICAO establishes detailed specifications for standards and procedures but it is the 140 individual member governments who enforce these regulations. In the UK, the Civil Aviation Authority's (CAA) mission states that its primary purpose is 'to maintain and where possible improve existing standards of safety' (CAA Document. No. 535, 1992). The rigour, hence the power of their licensing, is seen in its more detailed regulations, excerpts of which are set out below. The CAA states that it will:

(a) Provide and manage a safe air traffic control system in the UK.
(b) Set standards for and monitor the airworthiness and operational safety of all UK registered aircraft.
(c) Ensure the maintenance of high levels of safety in:
    (i) The operation of UK aerodromes;
    (ii) The licensing of UK air crew, air traffic controllers and maintenance engineers;
    (iii) The UK design, manufacture or overhaul of aircraft, engines and equipment.

The conditions for granting an Air Operators Certificate under the

138 DOLORES O'REILLY

European Union's legislation are as follows:

- European Union ownership must be evident
- Financially sound operations must be obvious
- Safety requirements must be met.

The regulation also includes rules on country of registration for aircraft operated by EU carriers. In general, liberalisation has allowed greater freedom in the use of equipment registered in other EU member states and in the transfer of aircraft from one EU register to another. However, the supplier of licences still retains power by allowing member states to restrict the use of owned or leased aircraft registered in a non-EU country.

Suppliers of Airport Facilities

The price that air carriers must pay for airport facilities is controlled by the supplier. While the airlines, acting together through the International Air Transport Association (IATA), may try to restrain landing fees or en-route charges in particular countries, individual airlines have almost no power to negotiate superior rates. As airport charges are a function of two variables—airport costs and government policy regarding recovering costs or generating profits—they tend to vary significantly from airport to airport as illustrated in Table 6.13.

The Suppliers of Computer Reservation Systems

Computer Reservation Systems (CRS) provide immediate access to flight information, seat availability and fares. The system has the characteristic that it allows a small number of privileged suppliers— major airline carriers—to achieve considerable market dominance by promoting their own services and by selling the CRS to other carriers.

Although there are a number of CRS systems, the market, especially in the United States, has tended towards domination by a small number of players. For example in the United States it is dominated by two majors: Sabre, owned by American Airlines, which in 1986 had 35% of the market, and Apollo, owned by United, which at that time had 25% (Wardell, 1987; Feldman, 1987). Not only does CRS enhance the relative power of the owning airline but it also gives power over non-CRS owning airlines, in that the latter have little choice but to assign their seat-reservation functions to one of the CRS suppliers.

Finally, their power is also considerable outside the airline

Table 6.13   Representative airport charges 1990

Airport	Landing plus passenger fees[a] (US$)	
	Boeing 747	MD80
Manchester (peak)	8157	2190
Manchester (off peak)	7035	1725
LHR (peak)	6477	3080
Frankfurt	6470	1524
Tokyo–Narita	6305	1062
Montreal	5238	1768
Amsterdam	5147	1321
Paris	4758	1109
Zurich	4568	1230
Rome/Milan	4030	1188
New Delhi/Bombay[b]	3297	384
Buenos Aires[b]	2732	338
Cairo	2343	729
Singapore[b]	1876	254
Rio de Janeiro[b]	1754	295
Bangkok[b]	1513	220
Kuala Lumpur[b]	1320	184
New York	1297	219
LHR (off-peak)	1221	795
Caracas[b]	1140	192
Hong Kong (peak)[b]	1022	356
Nairobi[b]	529	72
San Francisco	490	83

[a]Based on 70% seat factor.
[b]Excludes passenger charge because paid direct by passenger to airport.
Source: IATA *Airport and En-Route Navigation Charges Manual.*

industry itself, particularly in relation to travel agents. This power is exercised through the provision of additional services such as car rental and hotel reservations. Evidence of the necessity for travel agents opting into such systems is evidenced by the growth in their participation rates: in 1977 just 5% of US travel agents used CRS and by 1987 the corresponding figure was 95% (Feldman, 1987).

The Suppliers of Fuel

The cost of fuel supplies have a major effect upon airline costs and the variations in costs between airlines and where they fuel can be considerable, as shown in Table 6.14. Airport aviation fuel prices are determined by the companies supplying the fuel and the national

Table 6.14   Variations of fuel prices.

Posted fuel: per US gallon $ US (exclusive of duties/taxes)

Airport	Cents
London	170
Manchester	170
Entebbe (Uganda)	145
Manila	100
Singapore	95
Brazil[a]	84

[a]Posted fuel price was 84 cents at any Brazilian airport because of the government's policy.
Source: Compiled by author using data from Shell 1990.

government. Although the price of crude and refinery costs tend to be similar globally, the distribution and handling costs vary considerably, leading to great variations in supplier prices based upon volumes and geographical location.

Governments also influence the fuel prices through such measures as duties, tax, and price fixing to conform with government policy. For example, during the 1970s oil crises the US and Australian governments maintained the price of domestic crude refined products at below world levels.

In general, suppliers of fuel are in powerful positions as they can impose escalation clauses in fuel-supply contracts which permit fuel prices to move in response to changes in the price of crude oil in addition to price adjustments due to fluctuations in supply and demand.

The Supply of Slots

Take-off and landing slots control the competitive potential of airlines as they determine every airline's scope of operations. The increase in the number of airlines and in traffic since deregulation has led to a major increase in the demands for slots and runway capacity. Betts and Gardner (1992) have commented: 'Congestion at such busy airports as Heathrow or Frankfurt could squeeze out new entrants because of the lack of available take-off and landing slots. At the same time, airlines with a dominant position will have an important competitive advantage.' In addition Lockwood (1992) has emphasised the importance of slots as a success determinant. 'The slots...are the key to any air service. Those who hold them will not give them up without a fight.'

Table 6.15 A comparison of slot allocation at London's Heathrow Airport for summer 1992 for incumbents and newcomers

	Number	% total	% UK total
Total slots	233185	100.0	
UK airlines	128741	55.2	100.0
British Airways	87661	37.6	68.1
Brymon	1380		
Dan Air	1260		
Sub-total	90301	38.7	70.2
British Midland	30667	13.2	23.8
Manx	1360		
Sub-total	32027	13.7	24.
Virgin Atlantic	1200	.5	.9

Source: Virgin Atlantic Presentation to the AUC UK, summer 1992.

Smaller carriers and new entrants generally regard the restriction of slots by the majors as a primary barrier to their development. Thus Table 6.15 shows that the British Airways group of carriers has approximately three times the number of slots as the British Midland group and approximately 70 times as many at Heathrow as Virgin Atlantic. Physical restrictions would indicate that this will be a permanent bottleneck in the development of new entrants.

Conclusions on the Power of Suppliers

Every indicator of supplier power given in this section indicates that supplier power comes from a diverse set of sources, is powerful, and is likely to become more powerful in the future.

THE DEGREE OF RIVALRY

The airline industry, like most industries, claims that since deregulation it has faced unique and unprecedented levels of rivalry

142

resulting in the severe profit erosion set out in Tables 6.2 and 6.3 above. Table 6.16 considers the *causes* of the rivalry and shows that all the classic causes of rivalry are present to a significant degree.

Consequences of Intense Rivalry

A consequence of this intense rivalry is that many airlines have sought strategies to structurally redefine their operations and increase their power in their markets through the active pursuit of

Table 6.16   Classic causes of rivalry in the airline industry

Generic causes of rivalry	Applicability to the airline industry
Numerous/equally balanced competitors	Similar competitor structure in EU countries. Big 10 in USA
Slow industry growth	EU ave. growth rate 1992/1—0.5% US ave. growth rate 1992/3—1.2%
High fixed costs	Ave. price Boeing 757, 1992/3 $42 million
Lack of differentiation	Comparable services and prices on many routes
Lumpy capacity augmentation	Ave. price jumbo jet, 1995 $140 million
Diverse competitors	Major differences between airlines in structure, scale, missions, goals and objectives
High strategic stakes	National prestige
High exit barriers	Expensive dedicated assets

Table 6.17 Selected examples of structural changes in the airline industry

Airline	Subsidiaries/trade investments
Aer Lingus	80% Aer Turas Teoranta; 25% Futura; 49% Pegasus; 100% Aer Lingus Commuter; 100% Irish Helicopters
Air France	75% Air Inter; 95% Air Charter; 51% Air Berlin; 33.1% Sabena; 11.5% CSA; 3.48% Air Madagascar; 12.77% Air Mauritius; 1.5% Austrian Airlines; 25% Cameroon Airlines; 6.25% Corse Mediterranée; 28.5 Middle East Airlines; 35% Aeropostale; 3.97% Royal Air Maroc; 5.6% Tunis Air
Alitalia	100% ATI; 45% Avianova, through ATI; 45% Eurofly; 27.6% Air Europa, through Eurofly; 30% Malev
British Airways	100% British Asia Airways; 100% Caledonian Airways; 100% BA Regional; 49.9% TAT; 49% Deutsche BA; 49% GB Airways; 33% Air Russia; 25% Qantas; 24.6% US Air; 49.9% The Plimsoll Line (owner of Brymon European)
Iberia	100% Aviaco; 100% Binter; 100% Viva; 45% Viasa; 35% Ladeco; 30% Aerolineas Argentinas.
KLM	100% KLM Cityhopper; 20% Northwest; 14.9% Air UK; 80% Transavia Airlines; 40% ALM; 35% Martinair
Lufthansa	100% Condor Flugdienst; 100% German Cargo Services; 100% Lufthansa City Line; 49% Euro Berlin; 40% Sun Express; 26.5% Lauda Air, through Condor; 24.5% Cargolux; 13% Luxair
Luxair	24.53% Cargolux
Olympic	100% Macedonian Airlines
Sabena	71.4% Sobelair; 79% DAT; 49% DAT Wallonie
SAS	40% Airlines of Britain Holding (owners of British Midland); 43% Lans Chile
TAP	22% Euroair

global and regional strategic alliances while simultaneously extending customer choice (Table 6.17).

CONCLUSION

This chapter has examined the competitive structure of the airline industry from a Porter perspective and the conclusion is that the industry has, in most respects, behaved as the theory predicted. Thus the effect of the heightening of the intensity of the five forces was clearly seen in the financial returns earned by all players in the industry and also in the number of carriers who exited the industry or formed strategic alliances. The robustness of the theory is also reflected in the relative success of those carriers which resolutely followed Porter's classic generic strategies and which pursued clear and distinctive strategies of:

- Focused differentiation (for example, Southwest in the United States)
- Differentiation based upon branding (for example, Virgin Atlantic on the London City–Dublin route,
- Scale (for example, British Airways).

This suggests that in future when deregulation is likely to increase, those carriers who have so far failed to pursue a strategy of focus, differentiation, or scale must now make that decision. In terms of assisting that decision the next stage in this research will be to disaggregate the industry into significant strategic groups and examine each group's competitive intensity. In addition, this research template will also be verified by applying it to other recently deregulated industries.

REFERENCES

AEA Report (1990) *Impact of High-Speed Trains on Air Transport in Europe*. Brussels, Association of European Airlines.

AEA (1993) *AEA Year Book 1993*, Brussels, Association of European Airlines.

AER Inter (1993) In *Impact of High Speed Trains on Air Transport in Europe*, Brussels, Association of European Airlines.

Airline Business, ICAO (1994) International Civil Aviation Organisation. In *Expanding Horizons: A Report by the Comité des Sages for Air Transport to the European Commission*, January, Brussels.

Betts, P. and Gardner, D. (1992) Clouds over open skies. *The Financial Times*, 24 June, London.

Breyer, S. (1992) 'Regulation and deregulation in the United States'. In Majorie, G (ed.), *Deregulation in Europe and the United States*, London, Pinter Publishers.

Buzzell, R.D. and Gale, T. (1990) *The PIMS Principles*, New York, The Free Press.

CAA (1992) *Safe Journey: The Work of Britain's Civil Aviation Authority*, CAA Document No. 535, London, Civil Aviation Authority.

Department of Transportation USA (1993) New competitive fares in the US. *The Avmark Aviation Economist*. March, London.

Fieldman, J. (1987) CRS in the USA. *Travel and Tourism Analyst*, September, New York.

GAO (1993) US General Accounting Office in *The Avmark Aviation Economist*, April, London.

IATA (annual) *Airport and En-Route Navigation Charges Manual*, Geneva, International Air Transport Association.

IATA (1987) *Deregulation Watch*, International Air Transport Association, Fourth Report, Geneva.

Institute of Air Transport Report (1991) *Rail/Air Complementarity in Europe: The Impact of High Speed Train Services*, Institute of Air Transport: For the Commission of the European Communities, Paris.

Lissitzyn, O. (1968) Freedom of the air: scheduled and unscheduled services. In McWhinney, E. and Bradley, M (eds), *The Freedom of the Air*, New York, Oceana.

Lockwood, C. (1992) Open skies, crash landings. *Director*, January, London.

MORI and Wagonlit Survey (1994) What factors influence your choice of airline? *The Evening Standard*, 16 January, London.

Pickrell, D. (1991) The regulation and deregulation of US airlines. In Button, K. (ed.) *Airline Deregulation: International Experiences*, New York, New York University Press.

Porter, M.E. (1985) *Competitive Strategy: Techniques for Analysing Industries and Competitors*, New York, The Free Press.

Sawers, D. (1987) *Competition in the Air: What Europe can learn from the USA*, Research Monograph 41, London, Institute of Economic Affairs.

Shell (1990) *Shell Aviation Service Handbook, Part 2. Prices Guide*, London, Shell International Trading Company.

Wardell, D. (1987) Airline reservation systems in the USA. *Travel and Tourism Analyst*, January, New York.

Virgin Atlantic (1992) The anti-competitive era lives on. Presentation to the Air Transport Users Council (AUC), London.

7

BENCHMARKING AS AN INSTRUMENT FOR STRATEGIC AND OPERATIVE IMPROVEMENT

Bengt Karlöf

Karlöf and Partners

The field of leadership is wide open to methods and approaches whose popularity is attributable to their novelty value rather than their effectiveness. Leadership is an art, not a science. In science you can quantify the variables, discover correlations, and arrive at optimum solutions. In leadership the variables are fuzzy, the correlations unknown or unknowable, and you have to look for satisfactory solutions. In leadership, then, much necessarily depends upon judgment as well as analysis. This leaves scope for a variety of methods in fashion from time to time, with an equally great variety in their actual effects on the success of the organization.

Now that benchmarking is spreading all over the world like wildfire, there is a serious risk that this tremendously powerful method may come to be regarded as just another management fad. That would be most unfortunate, in view of its proven effectiveness. In this chapter I shall deal primarily with the reasons for the outstanding success of benchmarking rather that with how the method is used in practice. The book *Benchmarking* (Karlöf and Östblom, 1993) covers the practical application of the method; you can get the details from it or another book on the subject. Here I shall confine myself to explaining why the method has proved so very effective.

Rethinking Strategic Management
Edited by D. E. Hussey. © 1995 John Wiley & Sons Ltd

EFFICIENCY AS A MEASURE OF SUCCESS

On a global level we have seen how Japan has actively pursued benchmarking ever since that country opened itself to impulses from the West in the middle of the nineteenth century. The Japanese made notes, took photographs, and dissected products made in the West in order to establish a platform for their own further development.

In Russia, on the other hand, the prevailing view was that the Soviet system was best, that they had nothing to learn from others, and that they should therefore do everything themselves. Comparing Japan to Russia today, we find that the Japanese possess hardly any natural resources of their own. It is by exporting added value that they have achieved the world's highest standard of living, or have come close to it.

Russia, by contrast, has everything. You name it, they have it: uranium, oil, diamonds, gold, arable land, timber, the lot. Yet Russia cannot feed its own population—not even with root vegetables. The conclusion to be drawn from this is that it is efficiency, not natural resources, that generates success, and with it economic prosperity and personal freedom. The interesting thing is that the same lesson applies to aid to developing countries. In contrast to what many economists have long believed, and still believe, the relative backwardness of Third World countries is due not to lack of resources but to lack of efficiency. The transaction barriers and uncertainties are so great that economic activity falters and grinds to a halt. In many countries it takes more than a whole year of a person's life to start a company. In those circumstances, no new companies are started.

Still following the same line of reasoning, we can conclude that the planned-economy systems of the East imploded because they failed to deliver what people want, i.e. economic prosperity and personal freedom. The burden of inefficiency simply grew too heavy, whereupon the systems collapsed under their own weight.

Efficiency is defined here as a function of value and productivity. Value, in turn, is the quotient of utility and price, while productivity is the quotient of costs and number of units produced. These relationships are illustrated in Figure 7.1.

It is important to define the concept of efficiency because benchmarking utilized both axes of the efficiency matrix, both value and productivity. Note that utility or quality must always be set in relation to price, i.e. to people's willingness to pay. We have seen in recent years how the concept of quality has been bureaucratized, with the result that organizations have received quality awards

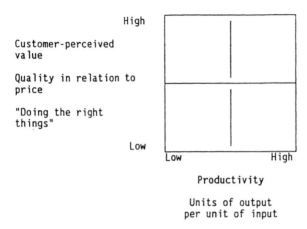

High

Customer-perceived
value

Quality in relation to
price

"Doing the right
things"

Low

Low   High

Productivity

Units of output
per unit of input

Figure 7.1   Efficiency matrix

while operating at a loss. If articles of the finest quality are produced with no customers prepared to pay for their quality, the term becomes meaningless. A high degree of subjective valuation prevails in the area of quality, and this makes it difficult to measure. The parameters of productivity, on the other hand, are much easier to quantify in hard figures.

An interesting conclusion to be drawn from recent world events is that systems which are not efficient enough do not survive. This applies to nations as well as to organizations and companies.

BENCHMARKING AND EFFICIENCY

Having thus defined efficiency and noted its importance to success, let us proceed to consider benchmarking in relation to efficiency. The Xerox Corporation was taken by surprise in 1979 when the Japanese suddenly started selling medium-sized office copiers at a price of US$9600 apiece. At first they did not believe the reports, for the price was lower than Xerox's manufacturing cost. Production director Frank Pipp was sent to Japan to investigate the background to what looked like a Japanese dumping drive in the United States. On his return, he reported that the situation was just as serious as had been feared. Xerox then initiated a comprehensive process of benchmarking which proceeded from the observed gap in productivity. We can thus say that it was Xerox who launched benchmarking, although Motorola, IBM, and several other American corporations began to use this approach at about the same time.

In a fully developed market economy, companies compete on a market and can read their efficiency from the bottom line of their profit and loss accounts. The key factor that makes market economy so greatly superior to planned economy is that customers can choose freely among alternative suppliers. The ones who are not chosen, or who are chosen too seldom, must either become more efficient or go out of business.

I have lectured widely to corporate executives from countries of the former Eastern bloc, especially the Baltic States. Although they readily admit the superiority of market economy, many of them do not understand why the apparently chaotic market economy system has prevailed over the planned economy, which seems so orderly and logical. Leaders from Lithuania and Latvia have asked me how their countries can achieve a decent standard of living when they lack natural resources. I have answered them by citing the comparison between Japan and Russia, and they have gradually begun to understand the importance of efficiency.

It is also important to understand that the question of ownership is theoretically irrelevant to efficiency, although in practice there is nearly always a correlation. It is theoretically possible to conceive a combination of state capitalism and market economy in which the state owns all the companies but where the latter compete with each other and are forced to operate under the rules that apply in a fully developed market economy.

The fundamental point about this line of reasoning in connection with benchmarking is that market-economy mechanisms do not operate *within* companies. What I mean by this is that departments of companies have planned-economy relationships with their immediate business environment in that the users of goods and services produced in-house do not have a free choice of suppliers.

The technical division of an airline supplies airworthy planes to the operational side. The latter does not have a free choice of suppliers. Finnair, for example, cannot send its aircraft to Lufthansa or SAS for servicing. Similarly, the invoicing department of a European telecom service must buy data processing services from its own data processing department: it is not at liberty to buy them from anyone else.

One possible substitute for the efficiency-driving effect of market forces is to construct an internal pricing system. This is much better than nothing at all. It is a way of simulating a market economy which creates something resembling a buyer–seller relationship. Experience indicates, however, that such internal pricing systems are nearly always arbitrary and thus encourage power-oriented behaviour. The freight manager of an airline once admitted that it was much easier for him to buy the Group Controller dinner and talk him into adjusting the internal settlement balance by £3 million than to put in a lot of hard work improving the efficiency of freight terminals around the world. Power orientation is a characteristic of individuals and groups who put their own success before the best interests of the organization. Performance orientation, by contrast, is characteristic of individuals or groups who put the good of the business first and achieve personal success in that way.

Internal pricing systems thus lead to power-oriented behaviour and sub-optimization. The alternative approach, that of finding benchmarks of efficiency in the outside world, stimulates performance-orientated behaviour instead. Figure 7.2 illustrates the effects on both operative content and psychosocial behaviour. Benchmarking, then, unlike internal pricing, promotes true efficiency, total optimization, and performance-orientated behaviour.

What we here call benchlearning is the psychosocial effect of benchmarking behaviour. Benchmarking helps to define gaps in efficiency, to describe successful methods of operating, and to close the gaps. Benchlearning is an expression of development skills, which takes place either in conjunction with benchmarking or as a separately managed process of corporate culture development.

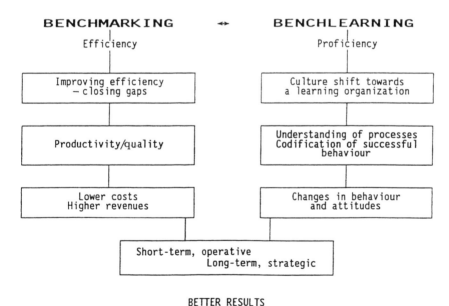

Figure 7.2   Benchmarking and benchlearning

People tend to strip off their blinkers, lay prestige aside, and adopt a new kind of behaviour which involves continual learning and improvement—what the Japanese call *Kaizen*.

BENCHMARKING AS A STRATEGIC AND OPERATIVE INSTRUMENT

Leadership is full of dichotomies—pairs of opposites. The efficiency matrix in Figure 7.1 embodies one of the most important of those dichotomies, the one between value creation and productivity. It is by no means the rule, but rather the exception, to find people who are equally skilled at both creating value for customers and minimizing unit production costs.

Another important dichotomy, though at first it may appear trivial, is that between short and long term. In my time as a consultant I have encountered persons with a high time-span capacity, i.e. the ability to optimize events over a long period of time. They have an ability to consider time that causes them to take action today which will bring success next year, or the year after, or even later. Not infrequently, the operative performance of such people is much poorer. Similarly, I have often met people possessing highly developed operative skills, i.e. the ability to improve this year's results. And just as often, this ability is matched by a lack of ability to foresee the future and think in strategic terms.

Yet successful and sustained business development requires the co-existence of these two abilities and their application at the appropriate times. Having written several books on the subject of strategy, I sometimes find that people presume a bias on my part towards questions of long-term development. I must therefore emphasize the importance of operative skills, which are essential to the avoidance of structural or ownership bloodbaths.

Benchmarking has a short-term operative dimension as well as a long-term strategic one. The short-term aspect consists of identifying efficiency gaps and taking corrective action to achieve better results. The long-term aspect can, to simplify somewhat, be said to lie in the altered behaviour of an organization which guarantees continual learning and change, and thus substantially improves its chances for survival.

DOS AND DON'TS IN BENCHMARKING

A benchmarking process is usually divided into a number of stages.

My associates and I have used five or six stages, others as many as twenty-five. It is simply a question of the chosen level of detailed breakdown, which is a matter of taste. For a description of a systematic approach to benchmarking, I refer the reader to Karlöf and Östblom (1993) but I would like to mention some recipes for success and pitfalls to avoid in benchmarking. These are summarized below:

(1) *A cascade approach is often effective.* By this I mean that you should choose different levels of resolution according to the amount of detail the situation calls for. A Scandinavian telecom service, for example, might want to identify the areas in which it should start to drive to improve its efficiency. In this case the level of resolution can be fairly low. The object is simply to define criteria of efficiency for major areas of operations such as data processing, troubleshooting, procurement of office premises, invoicing etc. This provides an indication of which areas are 'suspect' to be investigated in more detail with a view to improving their efficiency.

(2) *Proceed from correct key indicators to operative processes.* Benchmarking starts with a few vital key indicators. Experience shows that companies tend to use too many key indicators, generating reams of figures that have no effect whatsoever on the organization.

(3) *The difference between sloppy and careful benchmarking is binary.* If the key indicators are imperfect, if due allowance has not been made for differences, and if operative processes have not been properly described, the result of the effort will be zero. Failure to meet the test of credibility will cause the whole of the material to be rejected, and you will have accomplished nothing. A rigorously conducted benchmarking process, on the other hand, can have a tremendous effect on the short- and long-term efficiency of the organization.

(4) *Seek competitive advantage through competitive parity.* You could do worse than follow the example of the Japanese: first copy what others have done well, then process the information to develop a competitive edge. You should, of course, avoid simply being a 'copy-cat', but remember that that is what the Japanese were called before they started applying their own mental powers to what they had learned.

(5) *Benchmarking is good for both individuals and the business as a whole.* The method is ideal for promotion of learning in decentralized systems. In organizations with a multi-branch

structure one often finds an unwillingness to learn from good examples in other parts of the same organization. Benchmarking encourages units of an organization to learn from each other. It has been found, moreover, that benchmarking actually makes life more interesting for the individuals concerned. There is often an initial resistance, which, however, is easily overcome. After this, we have invariably seen how people grow more interested in the operative content of their work and put more and more energy into it.

(6) *Beware of superficial analysis of key indicators.* The intellectual simplicity of the method can be a dangerous pitfall in that it tempts people to make superficial comparisons without understanding the processes. This, as I mentioned earlier, can lead to unreliable indicators as well as causing the process to stop at figures without going on to a concrete drive for change based on understanding of the underlying operative processes. Definitions of operations are extremely important. Inaccuracies in definitions and in distribution costs can easily creep in. If they do, the findings will lack both credibility and effect.

(7) *Admit that somebody else's inventions and discoveries may be better.* There is a type of smugness which affects both individuals and organizations and which deprecates learning from others in favour of finding things out for yourself. The world is full of wheels that have been re-invented simply because people have been unwilling to learn from others. Original ideas are, of course, extremely valuable, but in developing them it is utterly wrong to ignore the very best available information about discoveries made elsewhere.

I am an agnostic as far as leadership methods are concerned. I do not believe in the existence of a sole path to salvation; there are many possible approaches which are effective. I do, however, believe that modern leaders should be well enough informed about available methods and approaches so that they can pick the one best suited to the individual case.

I am convinced that all leaders in the latter half of the 1990s, regardless of the size of their areas of responsibility, must be prepared to answer the question: 'How do you know that your unit is efficient?' The *raison d'être* of all kinds of organized activity will be called into question much more often in the future, and criteria of efficiency must be established. Benchmarking, which has hitherto proved superior to many other methods, will have a definite part to play in that process.

REFERENCES

Karlöf, B. and Östblom, S. (1994) *Benchmarking: a Signpost to Excellence in Quality and Productivity*, Chichester, John Wiley.

8

HUMAN RESOURCES: A STRATEGIC AUDIT

D. E. Hussey

David Hussey & Associates
& Centre for International Management and Industrial Development

A STRATEGIC AUDIT FRAMEWORK

The emphasis of this chapter is on the audit of the strategic elements of human resource management. These are the areas which should alter to reflect changes in the organisation's strategy, and which should also have a proactive relationship with the development of that strategy. They are all areas where the investigator should expect to find differences compared with similar activities. These are not necessarily differences of basic concepts, but of the interpretation of those concepts so that they fit the unique needs of the company.

The strategic elements of human resources are only a portion of the work that goes on within the HR function. Behind the strategic activities stand a host of administrative and support services. The direction of these is, of course, shaped by corporate policy and strategy, but many more would be directly transferable from one organisation to another. For example, the policy towards recruitment may be strategic: the actual processes of recruitment may be very similar between organisations. Record keeping is an administrative task of all HR departments, not very different between organisations: what information goes on the records may be changed by the

Rethinking Strategic Management
Edited by D. E. Hussey. © 1995 John Wiley & Sons Ltd
© D. E. Hussey 1995. Parts of this chapter appear in Chapter 21 of *Strategic Planning: Theory and Practice*, Oxford, Pergamon Press, 1994.

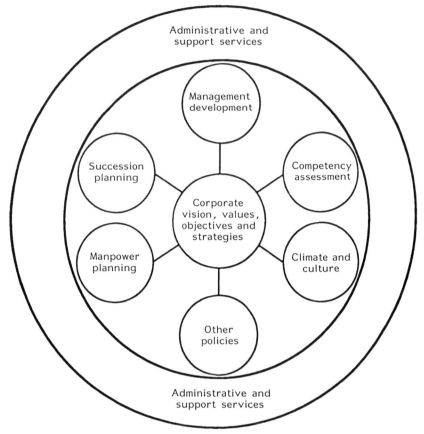

Figure 8.1   Human resource management and corporate strategy. (*Source:* Hussey, 1994)

organisation's specific approach to competencies, manpower planning, and management development.

Figure 8.1 sets out the framework in diagrammatic form. The heart of the model is the vision, values, objectives, and strategies of the organisation. These should drive the strategies and policies of the activities in the middle ring. As mentioned, there is a two-way influence, in that the activities in this ring can affect the corporate strategy. For example, the manpower planning activity may show that the strategic assumptions behind a new strategy are fallible, in that the people needed to implement a new strategy may be unobtainable.

The middle ring activities are management development, manpower planning, succession planning, climate and culture, competency assessment, and a group of policies towards recruitment, remuneration, and industrial relations. The activities in this group may vary in their degree of strategic importance from time to time. The outer ring shows the support activities mentioned above. These will only be dealt with in the context of the middle ring activities in this chapter.

In auditing HR activities a starting point should be the corporate strategic elements at the heart of Figure 8.1. There are a number of steps to go through which are illustrated in Figure 8.2. Most of

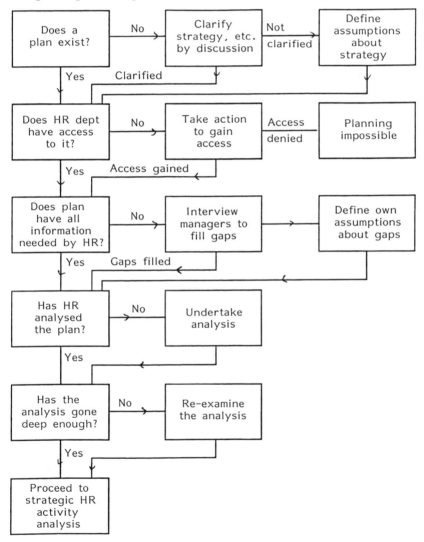

Figure 8.2 Relating HR actions to corporate plans. (*Source:* Hussey, 1994)

this diagram is self-explanatory, but two steps are worth stressing.

• The figure suggests that if the HR department is not given access to the strategic information, the whole audit should be abandoned. It also indicates that if no plan exists, and it is not possible to clarify the strategy officially, assumptions should be made. The different view taken is to do with how the HR department is perceived. If in good esteem, it is worth making assumptions to fill gaps. If not esteemed highly enough to share the plan, then assumptions would be a waste of time because someone else has the true picture, and assumptions from a source that lacks credibility would have no meaning.

• There is a box which questions the depth of the analysis. This is an audit point born from experience and supported by Harbridge Consulting Group research (Tovey, 1991). It is possible to treat a delayering and downsizing decision at two levels. The first is the obvious one, of redundancy actions, early retirement, and communication. The second is more subtle. For example, how do we make the organisation work now that we have delayered? This involves new management processes such as empowerment and performance management, and the training that enables both the empowered and the empowerers to understand how to make the new concept work. The research showed that very few companies were thinking at the second level. It is not surprising that the sort of motivation problems identified in Scase and Goffee (1989) should be found when no action is taken to make the new organisation function.

Table 8.1 shows how to begin to see the corporate plan in HR terms. The example is illustrative only, and the examples are deliberately kept at a simple level to show the method. Behind each tick should be a list of explanations: for example, what is it that management development will have to do to support the delayering strategy?

It is worth mentioning that few strategic plans are written with HR in mind, and that very often HR thinking will not appear in those plans. There is always a need for intelligent interpretation, and it may often be necessary to take the interview route suggested in Figure 8.2 to fill some of the gaps. An alternative to one-to-one interviews is to organise a meeting where senior managers as a group are persuaded to think through the HR implications of the plans. The point is that if this type of thinking is new to the company it may be rather more ragged than the figures suggest. This is how experts earn their keep!

Table 8.1 Using matrix displays (illustrative only)

Strategic sources		HR Areas impacted					
Type	Description	Management development	Succession planning	Manpower planning	Competencies	Climate/culture	Others (specify →) reward
Vision	Customer responsive	✓				✓	
	Global	✓			✓		
Strategies	European expansion	✓	✓	✓	✓	✓	
	New R&D unit			✓	✓		
	Delayering	✓	✓	✓		✓	✓
	Strategic alliance	✓				✓	
Values	People centred	✓	✓	✓		✓	✓
	Performance management	✓			✓	✓	✓
	Integrity				✓	✓	✓
Objectives	25% p.a. revenue growth	✓	✓	✓	✓	✓	✓
	Double market share	✓	✓	✓	✓	✓	✓

Source: Hussey (1994).

RELATING TO THE EXTERNAL ENVIRONMENT

The Human Resources strategy, like other business strategies, is impacted by what is going on in the outside world. It is important that an audit looks at these events and trends, as in most organisations no one else will be doing this from an HR viewpoint.

Figure 8.3 provides a broad checklist under which the factors can be grouped. Under these headings are many sub-headings, and these may be different between organisations, and in the geographical areas that come into the study. As with strategic changes, it is possible to think deeply about these issues or be superficial in looking at the HR impact. For example, the changes in demography in many countries of the world are well documented. It is possible to look at these only in terms of recruitment and retention, and overlook more subtle impacts such as increased diversity in the cultural and ethnic backgrounds of the workforce in certain age groups, making it important that the organisation plan to handle this diversity in the most constructive way. At one extreme there may be a need for training in cultural diversity. At the other there may be a need to modify the workplace and workplace procedures to make people from minority groups feel more welcome. Tovey (1991) in her research found that most organisations in the UK were planning to

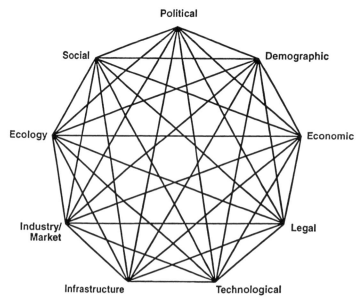

Figure 8.3   The environment. (*Source:* Hussey, 1991)

deal only with the obvious things, and had not considered the less obvious but potentially more important issues.

Another example is that changes in technology may bring a long-term shift in the nature of jobs in a company and in the people who are competent to fill them. Rajan (1990) showed in his research how the financial businesses, such as insurance, were changing to require more knowledge workers where previously the overwhelming requirement had been for clerical people.

Table 8.2 sets out a matrix for considering environmental issues from an HR perspective. The sub-headings given are illustrative, and would need to be expanded to fit the specific situation. Since the external environment is continually shifting, it is essential for the organisation to have access to sources of information which enable it to monitor what is going on. A few questions should be answered before the procedure of Table 8.2 is followed:

- Does the organisation have a unit that monitors external changes?
- Does the HR department have a full understanding of those changes?
- Is there a forum inside the HR department where they can be properly discussed?

Some explanation is needed of Table 8.2. The examples in the checklist column are not meant to be followed slavishly, but to act as prompts for the sort of trend or issue that could be important. The intention is that the investigator would record what is important to the specific organisation in the third column. In the example changes which may be important to the organisation but not to HR have not been listed.

The scoring method for impact, probability and overall importance is:

- Impact

What impact would it have?	Score
Extremely High Impact	6
	5
High Impact	4
	3
Relatively Low Impact	2
	1
Don't know	7

Table 8.2 Assessing the impact of environmental issues on HR activities

Broad headings	Example checklist	The important changes	Impact	Probability	Importance	How does it impact HR?
Demographic	Age structure of population Migration levels Size of population Diversity of population					
Economic	Inflation Reflation/ Recession Wage and salary levels Taxation					
Legal	Employment law H & S legal EC rules Information disclosure					
Technological	IT Production methods Product life cycles					
Infrastructure	Educational system					

Table 8.2 cont

Broad headings	Example checklist	The important changes	Impact	Probability	Importance	How does it impact HR?
Industry/ market	Competitor employment practice Industry norms					
Ecology	Environment movement Pressure groups 'Green' attitudes Smoking attitudes					
Social	Work attitudes Cultural differences Educational values					
Political	Likely pressures Government changes					

Source: Hussey (1994).

- *Probability of it happening*

A Certainty	100%	6
Very Likely	84%	5
Quite Possible	67%	4
As Likely as Not	50%	3
Probably Not	33%	2
Highly Unlikely	16%	1
Don't Know		7

Overall importance is calculated by multiplying the impact by the probability scores. 'Don't know' scores high so that something important is not overlooked through ignorance. The final column in Table 8.2 is a notepad for describing how the trend or event will affect HR.

One should not be trapped by the neat mathematics. The tool is an aid to thinking about the right things, and the numbers are a way of helping to focus on the most important.

ENVIRONMENTAL TURBULENCE

Igor Ansoff has done much to develop the concepts of strategic management, and might be termed, with considerable justification, the founder of the subject. Beginning in the 1980s, Ansoff and his colleagues have been researching and developing the concept that the way in which an organisation should undertake strategic management should be related to the degree of environmental turbulence in which it has to operate. The concept has been described in a number of publications, particularly Ansoff and McDonnell (1990) and Ansoff (1991). A summary of eight years of research supporting the models developed appears in Ansoff, *et al.*, 1993.

The Ansoff approach sought to identify the different environmental conditions under which different organisations were operating, and to match these with appropriate approaches to management strategy. The approach suggests a scale of turbulence:

Level	State of turbulence	Strategic aggressiveness
1	Repetitive	Stable, based on precedents
2	Expanding	Reactive, incremental based on experience
3	Changing	Anticipatory, incremental, based on extrapolation
4	Discontinuous	Entrepreneurial, based on expected future
5	Surpriseful	Creative, based on creativity

The approach to strategic decision making is different under each level, as the above description suggests. It follows that the optimum approach to strategic management should also vary with the turbulence level. Ansoff (1991) suggests that for level 1 the appropriate system is management by procedures, since nothing is changing, and the best guide to the future is the past. However, it is doubtful whether this level of turbulence is currently experienced by many commercial organisations. For level 2, the right approach is what Ansoff terms financial control, where the emphasis is on control through budgets, rather than seeking new strategies. At level 3 the approach is extrapolative, and termed long-range planning: the emphasis is on sticking to the historical strategies of success, since the future is a logical extrapolation of the past.

At level 4 it is no longer safe to assume that tomorrow will be a continuation of the trends of yesterday, and the appropriate process is strategic planning. Ansoff (1991) defines this as being '...focused on selecting new strategies for the future and redirecting the firm's energies and resources to follow the logic of the new strategy development...' Thus strategic planning repositions the firm for success in the future environment.

Ansoff argues that even before level 5 is reached forward-looking strategic planning is not adequate to ensure a speedy response to future events. This is particularly true when future changes are both violent and difficult to foresee. He suggests two 'real-time' system responses: issue management, which can begin to supplement strategic planning from level 4, and surprise management. Issue management attempts to anticipate and respond to threats and opportunities. There is a link here with the scenario planning approaches which are used by some organisations.

By level 5 an increasing number of issues confront the organisation without prior warning. To cope with these the firm needs to add a further management system to deal with surprises. Ansoff suggests an emergency communication network, with a top-level strategic task force to cross organisational boundaries to deal with the issue. The key to success is plan the surprise management organisation, and to train people in operating it. In other words, while issue management is a form of contingency planning for a predicted possibility, surprise management is a planned framework to deal with contingencies that cannot be foreseen.

The appropriate approach may vary in different parts of the same organisation. Thus it is quite possible for an organisation to have one strategic business unit operating under level 3 and another under level 5. The approach to strategic management should be varied by strategic business units to take account of this.

In theory, there are organisations operating under all levels of turbulence, and there has also been an evolutionary movement from the lower to the higher levels. Thus there are more organisations in levels 4 and 5 now than there were in the 1970s. It is reasonable to suggest that this increase in uncertainty will continue in the future.

Although not a specific part of the Ansoff model, from observation I would suggest that organisations make temporary shifts to higher levels of turbulence from time to time, sometimes reverting back to their old position when the period of turbulence is over. It is reasonable to suggest that in severe economic recession even organisations that are normally at level 3 will for a period find themselves operating at level 5.

Each level of turbulence calls for different managerial characteristics, because the business has to be managed in a different way. Ansoff and McDonnell (1990) provide profiles of management skills, management climate, and management competence required for each level of turbulence.

The implications for HR management are mainly as we move from the present to the future. If the position on the scale of turbulence is changing, it may be that the nature of management in that organisation must also change. This can change succession plans, may have a training implication, and will alter other aspects such as performance management and recruitment policy.

A STRATEGIC APPROACH TO MANAGEMENT DEVELOPMENT AND TRAINING

Now it is possible to begin to explore the circles on the middle ring of Figure 8.1. All will be approached in a strategic way. It is worth mentioning that this is not the way in which most organisations currently think about HR issues, although Harbridge Consulting Group research (Ascher, 1983; Tovey, 1991) shows that an increasing number of organisations have adopted this view.

The concept for management development is shown in Figure 8.4. The argument is that the philosophy for management development should put emphasis on corporate needs, in addition to the traditional view which looks at individual needs in the context of what the organisation is willing to spend.

In order to make this effective, those drawing up the management development plans and programmes must have an intimate knowledge of the corporate strategy, and the ability to get behind the

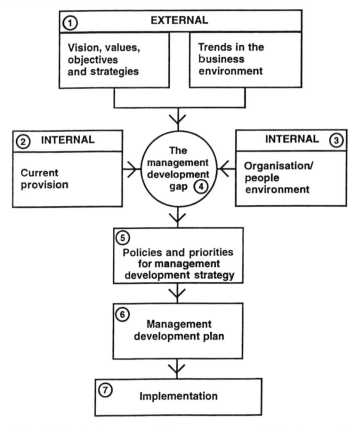

Figure 8.4 Strategic framework for management development. (*Source:* Hussey, 1994)

strategy to the management development action needed to support it. This may require the actions to survey senior managers as mentioned in the first part of this chapter, additional analysis by human resource specialists who have an appreciation of the firm's strategy as well as knowledge of their own craft, and a large supply of common sense. Management development and training people who expect to be able to find a company book with all the answers will be disappointed. It is they who have to be proactive and write the book!

My experience is that once a company begins to adopt this model, it will find that it also has to change how it assesses individual needs. One possibility is the use of company-relevant competencies, which can be used as a basis for assessing needs. These have value in many methods of assessment, including assessment centres. Some brief thoughts on a strategic approach to competencies will be given later. The assessment of individuals remains an important element of the mix, but a strategic view may lead to different ways of making that assessment.

Matrices should be developed to help relate individual needs to corporate needs. Table 8.1 provides a starting point, and the following hypothetical example shows how the corporate need for training in specific skills and knowledge might be derived from the data in this figure. Only the items listed under strategy are considered for the purposes of the example, although in reality all the strategic sources would be covered. I make no claim that the example covers all that the organisation might require from its managers, nor that the answers would be the same for other companies following a similar strategy.

Example:

Strategy	*Corporate management development need*
European expansion	Market planning
	Country cultural differences
	Working of the EC
	Managing change
	Visionary leadership
	Project appraisal
Delayering	Empowerment
	Career management
	Situational leadership
	Interpersonal communication
	Performance management
Strategic alliance	Successful alliance management
	Understanding cultural differences

Such matrices would need to be developed for various levels of management, and possibly for different areas of the organisation, and in some cases for specific jobs. It should also be clear that these matrices are a starting point. Each item needs to be looked at in more detail to specify exactly what the need is, and what sub-topics would also have to be covered.

Another box in Figure 8.4 is the audit of current management development provision. All our research suggests that cost-benefit analysis is not a regular feature of management development management, and that there is a tendency to hold on to training programmes and the resources which teach them even when there is a high level of dissatisfaction.

A framework for auditing all current management development

activities, of which the majority will be training programmes, is offered in Table 8.3. Many organisations find it surprisingly difficult to answer these simple questions, which suggests that the management of the function has been less than professional. (A longer checklist covering the policy issues, will appear in Table 8.4).

From the gap that emerges out of the audit it becomes possible to define new policies and priorities for management development. This leads to another box in Figure 8.4, the development of a management development plan. The final box is a reminder that plans have to be implemented, and to support this some guidance will be given on selecting external resources to help implement the training elements of this plan.

The integration of these various types of information in the approach shown in Table 8.3 allows management development to be

Table 8.3 Audit of current training provision

(1) Aims	For each initiative (2) Results/current plan	
• Objectives	• Number of events	
	Planned	1992
• Corporate goal, KSF or	Actual	1991
strategy supported	Actual	1990
• Other rationale for	• Number of	
initiative	participants	1992
		1991
• Target population		1990
• How is target population	• Participants as %	
identified?	of target groups	1992
		1991
• How are people selected		1990
to attend?		
	• When did the initiative start?	
	• How is it resourced?	
	• Breakdown of costs	
	• What were the course ratings?	
	• How are benefits measured?	
	• How has the initiative contributed to the objectives?	

Source: Hussey (1994).

viewed in a business-oriented manner. Most organisations that work in this way change the priorities they had been following, and alter many of their approaches to development and training. It also allows more initiatives which can be tied directly to bottom-line results, thereby making it easier to demonstrate the value of training to the organisation.

Figure 8.5 suggests three groups of training needs that might be defined from such a study. Without trying to be dogmatic, because the decision will vary by company, I have indicated in the figure possible proportions of corporate effort that should be devoted to each group. Initially, I should like to discuss each circle in the figure as if it were a watertight entity, but later will try to show how initiatives that fall in the overlap areas of the circle may enhance the value of the initiatives, by killing two or more birds with one stone.

By direct priorities I mean initiatives that contribute directly to corporate aims and objectives, such as training events designed to

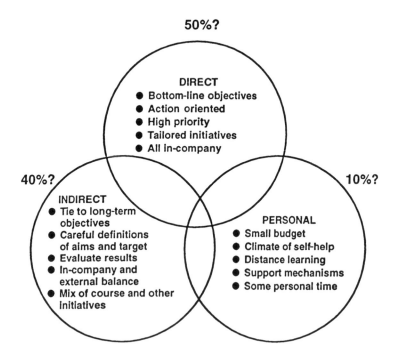

INCREASE AREAS OF OVERLAP TO ACHIEVE MULTIPLE POLICY OBJECTIVES

Figure 8.5   Some policy issues. (*Source:* Hussey, 1994)

implement a strategy or structural change, formulate strategy, deal with an issue from the business environment, implement a policy change, change culture to enable a strategy to succeed, or provide solutions to a specific problem or issue. By their nature, these needs are likely to be met by initiatives that are action oriented, have bottom-line objectives, and have a high degree of urgency. In turn, this affects the solutions, which may well be courses that cascade through several levels of an organisation, are entirely run in company, and have a high degree of tailoring. Only if they have these characteristics can these initiatives deal with the type of issue that is identified as a direct need.

Indirect priorities may be equally important for the company, and many of the initiatives will be more long term in both their objectives and the time over which personnel are involved in an initiative. However, not all will be lengthy initiatives. Under this heading I include induction training, career development programmes, and actions to improve personal performance. I believe that the policy here should be to tie to long-term objectives where appropriate, to be very clear about the aims of and the target population for the initiative. Here there may be a balance between in-company and external initiatives, and a mix of training and development actions. Many in-company courses under this category would benefit from being tailored, but the depth of tailoring may often be less than for a course dealing with a corporate issue. The decision hangs on the learning objectives of the various components of course or programme.

The final category is needs which are identified by individuals in discussion with their managers, but which are personal in that they do not have a high corporate priority. If people are motivated to develop themselves, there is likely to be value to the organisation in giving encouragement. What I believe is appropriate here is not company courses but the creation of a climate of self-help and the provision of support.

Under this heading I should consider giving financial support for distance learning, for example, and perhaps establishing a resource centre where self-study can take place. In return for this support I would expect individuals to give some personal time to the course of study.

Clarity emerges from such an analysis, but the benefits to the firm may be increased if deliberate attention is given to the overlap areas. For example, indirect needs can be tied closer to direct needs through the use of competencies as the standard against which the developmental and remedial needs of individuals are evaluated.

Competency assessment will be the next circle to be considered in our middle ring of strategic areas.

A second way of adding value to 'indirect' initiatives is to build some of the direct issues into the longer-term development programmes through teaching materials and project work. Another example is of an initiative to help business units to develop sound strategies, which, with modification, can be used later for an indirect development need, to train less senior managers in business planning.

Creative thinking can help an organisation to obtain much more from management development than the three-circle diagram may initially suggest, but the value of the planned approach cannot be overstressed. This approach does not mean that organisations should never do any training that can only be looked at as an act of faith. It is a question of balance. Just as it is poor management for the total management development strategy to be built from the bottom up, so it would be equally poor if it were to be totally built from the top down.

There should be a switch from a purely cost-based decision on available options to one of cost-benefit analysis. It is common practice for training managers, for example, to take an out-of-pocket expenses view of training initiatives. The cost of participants' time in attending training initiatives is rarely considered, and almost nobody adds in the real economic factor, the opportunity cost of this time. As a result, many current decisions on training matters are aimed at reducing the cost of the initiative, rather than increasing its benefits. This has led to many decisions which are wrong for the companies concerned.

A DIFFERENT SLANT TO ASSESSING INDIVIDUAL NEEDS

It may be of interest to record that Tovey (1991) found that all her sample of large UK companies used a performance-appraisal method to establish needs, and for 40% it was the only method. Only 10% used competency assessment, and assessment centres, where used, were on a selective basis (which is sensible). Other methods such as surveys and assessments by training managers were used by the 60% that did not rely solely on assessment centres.

The annual appraisal interview is a notoriously poor way of assessing development needs, as it depends on two levels of perception, the subordinate and boss, both of which could be erroneous. Greater use of the competency approach can ensure that the right questions are asked, but does not remove the bias.

We have found that upwards assessment is particularly good at identifying needs that may have otherwise remained hidden, but can only use this method for looking at management and interpersonal skills. On a confidential basis questionnaires are completed by the subject, and by at least three subordinates and/or peers. These are aggregated and the individual reports are not revealed to the subject. What is of value is the 'photograph' of management behaviour, which is often different from the self-perception. This method can be used in a general way, although we also have approaches which are related to researched topics, such as the management of innovation, leadership, and organisation climate. The relationship with individual needs identified using the climate instrument has a direct association with the corporate needs.

Surveys can be a valuable periodic tool, and can be focused on the competencies that are important to the firm. We have found it useful to obtain ratings on perceived abilities and the perceived importance the person places on them. This is particularly useful in a change situation, when management sees the needs for new skills, and this view of relevance is not shared by those below them.

The use of assessment centres is well known. What might be less well known is the way in which they can be designed to mirror the strategic requirements of the organisation, both in ensuring the selection of the right people for a particular situation and in identifying the strategically oriented training needs. Most experts in assessment centres come from the industrial psychology route and they give more emphasis to the individual than to the firm. Put a business orientation to assessment centre design and a very powerful tool is created. *HR Reporter* (1988) showed how Pratt and Whitney used an assessment centre approach to help restore their competitive position. Their response to being pushed out of the number-one position in aero engines by GE was to break down a 21 000-person operation into 52 smaller business units. Managers had to be selected and trained to operate as small business managers, a move considered necessary to respond to the changed business situation.

CONCLUSION

The strategic view postulated here would improve the total approach to management development, allowing this function to add more value to the corporation, without necessarily spending more. At the same time, it would provide a permanent mechanism for aiding the implementation of strategies, and remove many of the problems that currently occur, when the company finds far too late that it has an implementation problem. Bomona (1984) suggests that when a company finds that its strategy has not produced the right outcome it is as likely to assume that the strategy is wrong as it is to recognise that the problem may have been a failure to implement. This often leads to a change in a perfectly appropriate strategy. And this is hardly the way to effective management.

Table 8.4 provides a checklist of questions for an audit of management development using the principles of the model in Figure 8.4.

A STRATEGIC APPROACH TO COMPETENCY ASSESSMENT

The idea of defining management standards and competencies is not new, but in the UK received a new emphasis after the publication of the report into management development by Constable and McCormick (1987). This led to the formation of an organisation called the Management Charter Initiative (MCI), one of whose activities was to research and publish generic management competencies for various levels of management. So far, competencies have been published for supervisory, first-line, and middle management (MCI, 1991a, b, 1992). These competencies are intended to 'provide a basis against which managers may be assessed, their performance improved and their skills more effectively utilised'.

Properly used, competencies have value in management development, staffing and succession planning, recruitment, and performance management. MCI use the following headings to define competencies:

- *Units of Competence*: the broad descriptions of what is expected from a competent person at each level.
- *Elements of Competence*: a breakdown of the units.
- *Performance Criteria*: which specify the outcomes of competent performance that have to be achieved.
- *Range Statements*: which describe the range of instances and circumstances in which the element is applied.
- *Evidence Specifications*: what evidence is required to show that competence is achieved.

The MCI competencies are well loved by government, which likes the idea of standards that can be universally applied, and by many

Table 8.4 Checklist of questions for an audit of management development

---

1. What is management development contributing to the achievement of corporate objectives?

2. Do you know whether it is helping you to gain competitive advantage?

3. How do you know?

4. What explicit connections are there between training initiatives and corporate strategy?

5. When was the management development plan last fully reviewed against the strategic needs of the company?

6. Is there a mechanism for top management involvement in such a review, for example by a regular steering group, or by periodic detailed consideration by the chief executive?

7. How are management development plans determined?

8. Do management development initiatives cascade from top to bottom of the organisation, or is all effort concentrated on one or two levels?

9. When training initiatives are designed to help implement strategies, do you start at the top of the organisation and work down?

10. How are budgets for management development activity determined?

11. Are budgets related to the corporate need, based on a clear management development and training plan, which is broken down into defined and costed projects?

12. What is your total expenditure on management development?

13. Are all elements of expense of management development under the same budgetary responsibility: or is it possible for one part of the organisation to save expense by causing increased costs to another part? (For example, by the training manager choosing a cheaper hotel in the country because this looks better against his budget, but in doing so causing much higher travel costs which fall under other budgets.)

14. Are the opportunity costs of the people attending training programmes identified and considered when planning such courses?

15. Does the control system force actions to minimise the expense of training without any consideration of whether this minimises the return on the opportunity cost?

16. How large is your training budget compared to competitors? In your home country? In other countries?

17. How does your management development effort compare with best practices in the world at large (e.g. benchmarking yourself against the leaders)?

Table 8.4   *cont.*

18. When you require a global training initiative to develop a common approach across all subsidiaries, do you run the programme in the language of the company, or do you deliver a programme which keeps the integrity of the original, but makes adjustments for country cultural difference, and offers the programme in the various mother-tongues of participants?

19. Do you have a clear policy difference for the different categories of need identified in Figure 8.5?

20. How are people selected to attend a programme: in relation to the corporate need or on a 'volunteer' basis?

21. How is management development organised in your organisation?

22. Does the structure enable corporate priorities to be identified and addressed?

23. How are differences of perception, about what is of corporate importance, between different areas identified and resolved?

24. How are management development activities coordinated between corporate, divisional head offices, country offices, and other organisational units of the organisation?

25. What actions are taken to ensure that management training results in changed behaviour in the job situation?

26. How do you evaluate the effectiveness of a management development initiative? .

27. Do you do anything more than give a reactions questionnaire at the end of a course?

28. There are 500–600 providers of training services in the UK alone. Do you understand the differences between the various types of competitor, so that you can relate their particular competencies to your need? Or have you stereotyped providers so that you automatically use business schools for senior management initiatives without evaluating whether there are other high-quality providers who may be more appropriate for the task?

29. Do you insist that when an outside provider is quoting you for a tailored course the proposal shows the effort that will be spent researching the course in the company, and developing the right amount of company-relevant teaching materials? Are your tailored courses really tailored, in the sense of being unique to your organisation and its needs?

30. How long have you used all your present training suppliers?

31. Is there a mechanism so that you can judge their performance?

Source: Hussey (1994).

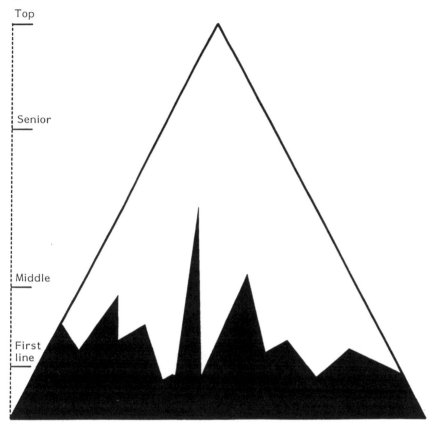

Figure 8.6   Generalised diagram: impact of strategy on competencies at various management levels. (*Source:* Hussey, 1994)

academic organisations, which use them as the basis for developing new educational programmes, in the belief that relevance to industry is thus assured.

While the concept of competencies has undoubted value, the generic approach has serious faults. Figure 8.6 shows in an approximate way how levels of management are affected by the strategic decisions of the firm. While the job of a supervisor may be almost entirely the same, regardless of vision, values, and strategies, it is hard to argue that senior management jobs are equally identical. In the figure the black area shows where generic competencies are likely to be of value: the white area where they have doubtful validity. Exact positions of the boundaries will vary by company, so the argument is not that the generic approach is never appropriate but that how and where it is appropriate will vary considerably between organisations.

A second disadvantage of the MCI approach is that it does not set out to cover all competencies. It aims to deal with the generic rather than the functional skill elements of management jobs. Even if all the generic descriptions were right for a particular organisation, the competencies would still not cover all the things that needed to be done to enable the organisation to achieve strategic success.

One example will suffice to question the value of the generic approach. Two multinational grocery product companies face up to their markets in very different ways. One operates a global strategy, where country differences are subordinate to the overall strategy. The other works on a multi-country basis, with every country operation being an ROI centre, and having a high degree of strategic freedom. The management and business skill competencies for most senior level jobs would be quite different between the companies. A successful country managing director in the global company has to operate in a different way from a competitor in the multi-country company. A successful career in one company does not guarantee success in the other.

Figure 8.7 shows a more strategic approach to competency assessment. Like the strategic management development approach, to which it is related, it begins with a strategic review (step 1). This is fundamentally the process already described. In step 2 the competencies the company requires at each level, in order to implement the strategy successfully, are defined. These are blended in step 3 with the assessment of required competencies at the level of the key jobs. There is a recycling loop at this point, to ensure that the individual competency assessments are properly related to the corporate needs. The most likely issue is that a change of strategy could bring a requirement for new strategic areas of competence which are not seen by those who should be affected, because they are unaware either of the strategy or of its implications for them. The approach, with case histories illustrating different aspects of its implementation has been fully documented in Tovey (1992).

To make sense of competencies derived by the above method requires a way of grouping competencies once they have been identified. Figure 8.8 shows a method which we have used, which is related to research into leadership. The core of the model is flexibility, because it is believed that this is a prerequisite for success in modern competitive conditions. The inner ring consists of the individual skills and attributes each manager should have to perform effectively in the particular company situation. The outer ring shows the elements each manager should possess to be an

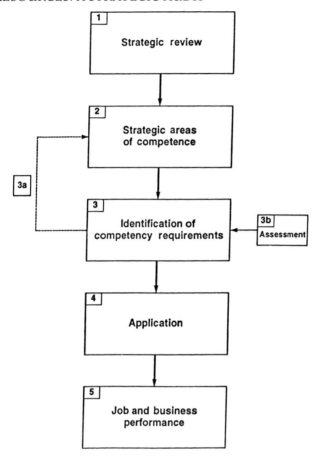

Figure 8.7 A strategic approach to competency assessment. (© Harbridge Consulting Group Ltd: used with permission)

effective leader in the particular company. Other ways of grouping could be used.

Table 8.5 gives an example of the competencies that might be derived for a specific company under one of the sub-headings of the model in Figure 8.8. Although some elements might appear in a similar exercise undertaken for a different organisation, what we find is that there are differences in priorities, detail, and nuances of meaning because of the different business activities and strategies. In the example the company operates in only one country: additional elements would have to be introduced if it were to have a multinational strategy. Similarly, it is a single-industry company. Additional competencies would be needed at the top if the company

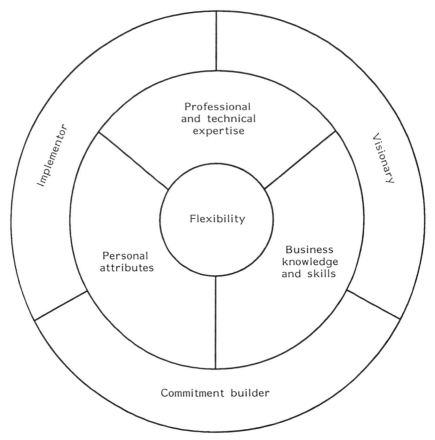

Figure 8.8 Strategic competency profile. (© Harbridge Consulting Group Ltd: used with permission)

operated more broadly, perhaps competencies in portfolio management. The reference to customer focus is not because the consultants considered this to be a good thing, but because it was a key plank in the company's strategy. Similarly, there is no reference to competence in value-based strategy concepts, which there would be in another company dedicated to this concept. A checklist of questions to aid an audit on competencies appears in Table 8.6.

Table 8.5   Example of competencies related to one element of Figure 8.8.

VISIONARY

Conceives longer-term direction for the business in the context of opportunities, competitive factors, and profit requirements: causes a desired future state to be defined that is realistic, motivating, and meaningful to others: shares this with conviction so that people know where they are going and what they have to do to get there.

Strategic thinking

Able to combine analytical method and mental flexibility to produce creative and realistic responses to changing business situations

- Insightful analysis
- Solutions-oriented questions
- Non-linear mind set

Industry and market knowledge

Understands the key external factors and trends which help to shape the direction of the company and underpin the formulation of its vision and mission

- Being customer focused
- Knowing the competitors
- Understanding the external environment

Knowing the company

Understands the key internal factors and issues which enable the best operating decisions to be made for the company, its customers, and the business units and the individuals who work in them.

- Strengths and weaknesses/distinctive competencies

Core values

Behaves in a way which reflects the values and beliefs of the company and is consistent with its vision and mission

- Being credible
- Showing conviction
- Displaying integrity
- Constancy of purpose

© Harbridge Consulting Group Ltd. Used with permission.

Table 8.6   Checklist of questions: competency assessment

1. Are competencies used in your organisation?
2. If not, should they be used?
3. How are they integrated into the management and HR process:
    Performance management?
    Recruitment?
    Job descriptions?
    Training needs assessment?
    Development of training initiatives?
    Personal development?
    Manpower planning?
4. Do the competencies cascade from the top down?
5. How do the competencies relate to the unique situation and strategies within the company?
6. Does the whole company buy into the defined competencies?
7. What mechanism exists to ensure that competencies are updated as the company strategy changes?
8. Do competencies cover the whole management task, as suggested in Figure 8.8, or are only a portion, as in the MCI competencies?
9. Is the company serious about using competencies or simply following a management fad?

CLIMATE AND CULTURE

There are three dimensions to the audit of corporate culture:

*   What is the current culture?
*   What is the desired culture to achieve corporate success?
*   What should be done to change or reinforce culture?

In everyday terms organisational climate can be paraphrased as 'how it feels to work around here'. It is closely related to culture, and some authorities see little differences between the two. It is important because an organisation's climate has a direct impact on what that organisation can achieve. This is increasingly recognised, and some of the major repositioning moves of large companies have been accompanied by a deliberate attempt to change the culture. Examples include the 1980s drives by Jan Carlsen of Scandinavian Airlines and Jack Welch of General Electric. Publicly announced actions in the UK include British Telecom and British Petroleum. It is not easy to change the culture of an organisation, unless there is a crisis situation which is widely accepted, as there are always many factors within the organisation that reinforce the historic situation. What is widely observable are top management groups who assess the culture that they believe is necessary if their companies are to be successful over the next decade and issue edicts which say things such as:

> Our culture will be open and honest, giving appropriate recognition and respecting the rights of the individual. The company puts the customer first, and makes decisions as low down the organisation as it can. It is dedicated to creating an environment which encourages entrepreneurial attitudes and individual creativity.

The reality is often different. Inside the company there is an attitude that the business would be fine if only the customers would stop complaining, no one knows what decisions are being taken at the top, there is no delegation, the people are risk averse, and everyone will always try to pass decisions upwards.

Figure 8.9 shows the dimensions of climate used by Harbridge

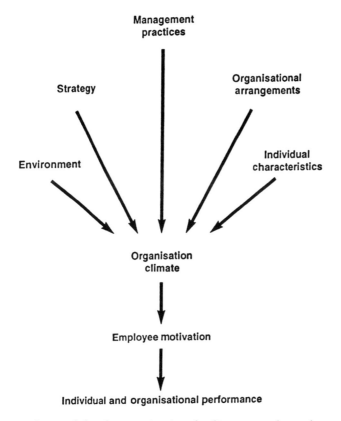

Figure 8.9 A model of organisational climate and performance—the determinants. (© Harbridge House Inc.: used with permission)

House. A critical determinant is the management practices of superior managers. The research shows that certain practices dramatically affect climate, that these can be measured objectively by taking a reading from the people who report to the manager, and that any desired changes to the climate can best be achieved by persuading managers to modify their work practices in the critical areas. The clusters of practices that have been found to be critical are:

- Structure—clarity of roles and responsibilities
- Standards—pressure to improve performance coupled with pride in doing a good job
- Responsibility—the feeling of being in charge of one's own job
- Recognition—the feeling of being rewarded for a job well done
- Support—the feeling of trust and mutual support
- Commitment—a sense of pride in belonging to the organisation.

The advantage of using an objective method to audit climate is that it is easier to see what is compatible or incompatible with corporate strategy; discussion internally on what should change is focused and has more credibility; it is possible to remeasure at some future time to monitor the effect of changes; and it is possible to compare the cultures in different parts of the company.

Because virtually all ways of looking at climate or culture are proprietary or protected by copyright, it is not possible to provide a checklist for the detailed approach to measure climate. Readers may care to refer to Handy (1981), where a different approach to assessing the culture of an organisation is provided. This includes a questionnaire attributed to Harrison. Table 8.7 provides some broad questions to be addressed when climate is considered.

A STRATEGIC APPROACH TO SUCCESSION PLANNING

Succession planning may be considered as one aspect of manpower planning, and is only looked at separately because of its strong links with management development. It is also possible for an organisation to gain considerable benefit from succession planning without necessarily undertaking any other manpower planning activity. As with all other HR activities, succession planning can be either a dynamic and powerful tool which supports the corporate strategic effort, or a bureaucratic exercise which results in neat-looking succession charts which do not contribute in any way.

Since our approach is strategic, succession planning should begin

Table 8.7   Checklist of questions for an audit of climate

---

1. How would you define the climate in the organisation?

2. How would you define any differences in climate between your various organisational units?

3. Compare the existing climate with the corporate vision, values, objectives, and strategies: does the climate support these? is it hostile to them? what, if anything, needs to be changed?

4. How objective is your assessment of climate?

5. When was the last assessment of climate made?

6. Have there been any significant developments in the company which may have affected climate since the last survey?

7. What recent, deliberate actions have been taken to change climate?

8. What effect have these had?

9. Are there any new policies or actions recently applied or under consideration which could affect climate?

10. Has their possible impact been considered?

11. What actions should be taken so that climate becomes supportive to the achievement of corporate aims?

---

with a consideration of the impact of the strategies and changes in the external environment on the structure of the organisation. This by now will be a familiar approach, and much of this consideration will have already been given if the audit has followed the order of this chapter. It is self-evident that any change, or projected future change, in key jobs will affect the skills and qualities looked for in any potential successor to the present incumbent. In addition, the nature and pact of change resulting from the strategy may bring a need for more, or different, managerial positions.

Succession planning also requires a means for identifying people with the potential to move upwards in the organisation. There are dangers if the only means of making this identification is the assessment of superior managers. The dangers include:

• Different perceptions across divisions: a person judged in one area not to have succession potential may in fact be better than another from a different area, judged by his or her manager to be a strong candidate.
• There may be a tendency to judge that people have potential, but that they will not be ready for, say, 2 years. However, when the

exercise is repeated the following year, the same people are still seen as being 2 years away from being ready.

• The perception of the superior manager of another person's suitability to succeed may be based on what the job is now, rather than how it will be by the time that person succeeds.

• Judgements may also be biased because the candidate is compared against the manager's belief in his own capabilities. An interesting sidelight is thrown on this by Ichikawa (1993). He observes that all Japanese business leaders are short people, despite the overall growth in the height of the Japanese population. However, leaders are always selected by their predecessors, and the culture means that a successor will not be appointed if he is in any way seen as superior to the present incumbent. Someone who is taller, unless he has family ties, has little hope of appointment. Western culture is somewhat different, but not so different that selection is always unaffected by using oneself as a ruler against which potential successors are measured.

A more balanced view of potential may be obtained if assessment centres are used in addition to assessment by superior managers, and if there is a review mechanism so that all potential successors are considered by a higher-level management group on a regular basis. Table 8.8 gives a number of questions for use in an audit of succession planning.

Table 8.8   Checklist of questions for an audit of succession planning

---

1. How will key job requirements change as a result of:
   The corporate strategy?
   Environmental trends?
   Changes in environmental turbulence?
2. What are the key jobs which should be included in the succession planning exercise?
3. Which of the following elements are included in the succession planning system?
   Review of all potential successors regularly by a high-level team
   Personal involvement of the chief executive
   Identification of potential by superior managers, and regular review of these judgements
   Additional objective ways of identifying potential such as assessment centres
   Career planning for those identified as having potential

Table 8.8 *cont.*

---

4. Have potential successors been identified for the key jobs?

5. Is the pool of potential large enough to meet expected requirements?

6. Is it too large, so that the company is not meeting the career aspirations of the potential successors?

7. What management development is provided to develop potential successors (tie in with management development plan)?

8. What steps are taken to avoid creating crown prince mentalities among those seen as successors?

9. Have likely changes among present incumbents been forecast?

Retirement
Promotions
Loss through disposal of business
Resignations
Death/disability

10. Are the number of high-quality potential successors appropriate in relation to the expected volume and timing of vacancies?

11. Has the exercise identified a high-flyer pool, who should receive accelerated development?

12. Should high-flyer identification begin early in a person's career, to increase the number of potential successors later?

13. What actions should be taken if there is an inadequate pool of successors?

14. If there is not enough potential now, does this tell us anything about the overall quality of management in this organisation?

15. Does the performance management system support the identification and development of successors?

16. Do senior managers possess the coaching skills necessary to operate a modern performance management system?

17. Is a lack of succession potential a result of the working style of senior managers?

A STRATEGIC APPROACH TO MANPOWER PLANNING

Figure 8.10 offers one way to approach the task of auditing a manpower plan. It suggests certain steps which have to be followed in order to end up with a meaningful and comprehensive plan. As will now be familiar to the point of becoming boring, the critical

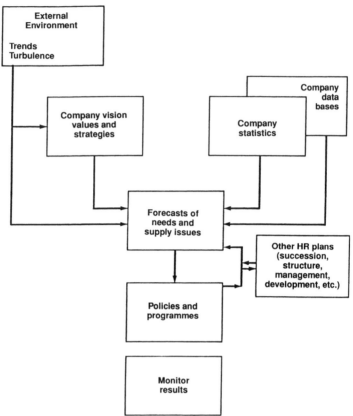

Figure 8.10 A strategic framework for manpower planning. (*Source:* Hussey, 1994)

starting points are the environmental trends and the vision, values, and strategies of the company. The strategy issue has been thoroughly debated, and there is no need to add anything at this point. The environmental box is worth a brief mention as there are some things to consider which have not so far been dealt with at any length.

If the full audit of the environment has been undertaken carefully, most of the trends which affect manpower planning will have been picked up. Obvious trends are demographics, not only changes to population size and the age structure of that population but also changes in the ethnic mix at different age levels. For some businesses, the analysis may have to be undertaken at a local level for certain types of labour. Although overall there may be a surplus of a certain type of low-grade labour in a country, this may be an academic fact to a company which operates in an area where there is a shortage.

The external study should also cover education and skills. Thus it may be important to understand the changes in the expected output of graduates in certain disciplines, or the speed at which the supply of a profession (for example, actuaries) can be adjusted to meet expansion in national demand.

It is almost impossible to make effective use of the information covered in the environment and strategy boxes in Figure 8.10 unless there is a strong base of company statistics. If, for example, you do not know how many people there are at a particular level or function, there is not much that can be done with an assessment that implies that the company will need this particular skill to support its expansion plan. Without knowledge of the rate of labour turnover, and the reasons for people's leaving, it is impossible to begin to estimate the number of people that the company should plan to recruit. Table 8.9 lists some of the statistics that the organisation should be collecting.

Although in most cases the most recent information is the most important, time series can be very useful to allow the study of trends, and to examine the impact of new policies. In addition, there will be a need from time to time for additional information. Behind the regular series of statistics there should be a comprehensive database, which allows the identification of individuals with particular attributes and the collection of specific statistics. In addition to basic employment records, the database might contain details of training given, particular skills (such as language capability), psychological profiles (e.g. tolerance of ambiguity, career aspirations, and particular experience (such as service in a particular country), salary grade and level, and salary history. Competencies could be used as one of the parameters for the database.

Because all organisations are different, the auditor should construct his or her own list of statistics needed. It is not untypical to find even large organisations which have trouble tracking down basic statistics, such as the total number of employees each month, and sometimes two conflicting figures are passed to top management: one from the accountants, based on payroll, and the other from the personnel area. While it is possible for there to be legitimate differences in these figures (such as someone being on the payroll in the month following departure because overtime or bonus payments have to be paid), a good place to start an audit of manpower planning is the availability, timeliness, and accuracy of the HR statistics.

Table 8.9 Some of the internal statistics needed for manpower planning

1. Total number of employees by:
    Grades
    Business areas
    Locations
    Meaningful jobs/skills
    Sex
    Basis of employment (e.g. permanent, part-time, etc.)

2. Age and length of service structure by grades, business areas, locations, meaningful jobs/skills, and sex.

3. Labour turnover rates, by grades, etc.: by age and by service length.

4. Productivity data by grades, business areas, location, meaningful jobs/skills, and sex.

5. Potential of employees in critical jobs (see succession planning), and statistics on promotion.

6. Accidents and other occupational health data, by activity, location, age, etc.

7. Time lost through sickness, by grades, business areas, etc.

8. Industrial relations disputes, by grades, etc.

9. Trade union membership statistics, by union.

10. Recruitment activity and success rates, by grade, etc.: number of unfilled vacancies by grade, etc.

11. Overtime statistics, by grade etc.

12. Contract and agency employees, who are substituting for full-time employees.

13. Number and type of transfers across business units and across functions: across countries.

14. Number of employees by grade, etc. who are on secondment or temporary transfer outside of the planning unit.

Source: Hussey (1994).

The interpretative part of the manpower planning process is in the box in Figure 8.10 where forecasts of needs, and the supply issues in meeting them, have to be drawn together. If good information is available, the main problem here is uncertainty. Even forecasts for one year ahead can be inaccurate in a turbulent environment. Those for longer periods may justify considerable sensitivity analysis, so that the impact of changes can be properly understood.

The policies and programmes which result from the forecasts may cover any or all areas of HR management. For some issues the solution may lie in training: for others it may be recruitment or remuneration. And sometimes the right solution is not an HR issue but a change in the management process of the organisation as a whole.

OTHER POLICIES

There is only one circle left to consider from Figure 8.1, and this cannot be looked at in detail, because what is strategic will vary from time to time. For example, remuneration may, for much of the time, be a purely administrative function. However, it may have strategic importance if the remuneration policy is hindering achievement of a corporate objective, such as a bonus scheme which emphasises individual effort, whereas the required climate of the company is to emphasise team working. Here the bonus system may be driving people to behave in the wrong way.

One way to determine which need attention for strategic reasons is to rate what each activity does to aid the achievement of the corporate objectives. A matrix such as the following may be helpful:

Activity	Scale				
	Hinders		Neutral		Helps
	1	2	3	4	5
Recruitment					
Remuneration					
Benefits					
Welfare					
Industrial relations					
Employee relations					
Communication					
Pensions					
Records					

This analysis will probably need to be undertaken at various levels in the organisation. Any activities that prove to be strategically critical should then be examined using the principles used for each of the other components of the model.

RESULTS OF A COMPREHENSIVE AUDIT

The benefit that comes out of an audit is, of course, directly related to how well HR is already contributing to the strategic aims of the firm.

Our experience and research suggests that the organisations that take a strategic view of all aspects of HR management are still in the minority, at least in the UK. If this is correct, most organisations that make a serious attempt to follow the ideas set out in this chapter should obtain considerable benefits. The model in Figure 8.1 is a good starting point, but the point at which you choose to begin the audit is less important. All the aspects of HR management discussed above are, to some degree, interrelated, and the full picture will not emerge until all are done. Despite this, there is value in applying the methods to specific areas, such as management development, even if it is not possible to audit other areas at the same time.

If every organisation followed the advice of this chapter, there would be a much greater commitment of top management to the critical HR issues, and it would be easier for HR managers to demonstrate the value of their work. Much less would be an act of faith. This seems to be a move towards more business-oriented and professional HR management than exists in many organisations.

REFERENCES

Ansoff, H.I. (1991) Strategic management in a historical perspective. In Hussey, D.E. (ed.), *International Review of Strategic Management*, 2, Chichester, Wiley.
Ansoff, H.I. and McDonnell, E., (1990) *Implanting Strategic Management*, 2nd edn, Hemel Hempstead, Prentice Hall.
Ansoff, H.I., Sullivan, P.A. *et al.* (1993) Empirical proof of a paradigmatic theory of strategic success behaviours of environment serving organisations. In Hussey, D.E. (ed.), *International Review of Strategic Management*, 4, Chichester, Wiley.
Ascher, K. (1983) *Management Training in Large UK Business Organisations*, London, Harbridge House.
Ascher, K. (1984) *Masters of Business: The MBA and British Industry*, London, Harbridge House.
Bomona, T.V. (1984) Making your marketing strategy work. *Harvard Business Review*, March/April.
Constable, J. and McCormick, R. (1987) *The Making of British Managers*, London, British Institute of Management.
Handy, C.B. (1981) *Understanding Organisations*, 2nd edn., London, Penguin.
HR Reporter (1988) Training small business managers for a big business atmosphere. *HR Reporter*, 3, March, Los Angeles, USA.
Hussey, D.E. (1991) *Introducing Corporate Planning*, 4th edn, Oxford, Pergamon Press.
Hussey, D.E. (1994) *Strategic Management: Theory and Practice*, Oxford, Elsevier.

Ichikawa, A. (1993) Leadership as a form of culture. In Hussey, D.E. (ed.) *International Review of Strategic Management*, 4, Chichester, Wiley.
Management Charter Initiative (1991a) Occupational Standards for Managers, Management I and Assessment Guidance, London.
Management Charter Initiative (1991b) Occupational Standards for Managers, Management I and Assessment Guidance, London.
Management Charter Initiative (1992) Management Standards, Supervisory Management Standards, London.
Rajan, A. (1990) *Capital People*, London, Industrial Society.
Scase, R. and Goffee, R. (1989) *Reluctant Managers: Their Work and Lifestyles*, London, Unwin Hyman.
Tovey, L. (1991) *Management Training and Development in Large UK Business Organisations*, London, Harbridge Consulting Group Ltd.
Tovey, L. (1992), *Competency Assessment, A Strategic Approach*, London, Harbridge Consulting Group Ltd.

FURTHER READING

Alexander, L.D. (1985) Successfully implementing strategic decisions. *Long Range Planning*, **18**, No. 3, June.
Bolt, J.F. (1985) Tailor executive development to strategy. *Harvard Business Review*, November/December.
Handy, C., Gordon, C., Gow, I. and Randlesome, C. (1988) *Making Managers*, London, Pitman.
Hussey, D.E. (1988) *Management Training and Corporate Strategy*, London, Pergamon Press.
Nilsson, W.P. (1987) *Achieving Strategic Goals Through Executive Development*, Reading, MA, Addison-Wesley.

9

BENCHMARKING HR PRACTICES: APPROACHES, RATIONALES, AND PRESCRIPTIONS FOR ACTION

Jean M. Hiltrop and Charles Despres

IMD, Switzerland

INTRODUCTION

The 1990s have become a period of global competition, streamlined organizations and efficient work processes aimed at delivering high-quality outputs. The decade is also characterized by sociopolitical fragmentation, troubled new market economies, toppling corporate giants and unprecedented levels of technologically-displaced and jobless individuals. Executives in the midst of this swirling confusion are anxious to maintain or improve their company's competitiveness, and most recognize that the effective management of human assets is a key to success.

Experienced managers also know that measuring an event draws attention to that event, and that tying rewards to the measurement process will both magnify the event and sharpen attention. Traditionally, the object of a performance management system and the measurements employed have been financial in nature. This is no longer the case. Managers now realize that an exclusive focus on such measures as return on equity and cash flow ignores other key success factors in an enterprise, ones which may prove critical to long-term success. Geanuracos (1994, 18) writes,

Rethinking Strategic Management
Edited by D. E. Hussey. © 1995 John Wiley & Sons Ltd

At the heart of this new thinking is an understanding that reliance on financial measures alone often undermines the strategies the company must pursue to survive long term. Today's smart firms are searching for ways to incorporate into their regular performance evaluation non-financial measures such as quality, market share, customer satisfaction, human resources, innovation and learning.

Thus, the danger in traditional methods is that performance management may become finance-driven and myopic, resulting in some organizational factors—less important ones, we would argue—being optimized at the expense of others. Furthermore, when rewards are tied to financial targets the organization often alienates employees who have little understanding of how their everyday transactions connect to overall corporate performance objectives which, consequently, produces little perceived ability to affect the 'bottom line'. One recent study (Geanuracos, 1994) determined that only 30% of executives surveyed expressed satisfaction with their companies' performance management systems: the majority believed that performance measures were, among other faults, still too financially oriented.

Recognition of these problems, and in particular the third, has led to a flurry of writing on the need to move toward a new paradigm of performance management. The call is to supplement the traditional and small set of financial performance measures with non-financial indicators of the processes that lie behind them (Eccles and Nohria, 1992). Authors such as Kaplan and Norton (1992) have even argued for placing non-financial measures (i.e., customer satisfaction, innovativeness, and the development of human resources) on an equal footing with financial criteria when determining strategy, promotions, and the allocation of organizational resources.

The European Foundation for Quality Management (EFQM), formed by fourteen leading West European companies in 1988, agrees on this matter. In 1991 EFQM established the European Quality Award which is '...awarded [yearly] to the most successful exponent of Total Quality Management in Western Europe' (EFQM, 1993, 2), and the criteria for this award are pertinent. EFQM developed the model in Figure 9.1 to depict the performance categories that are deemed critical to excellent organizational performance. Financial measures are rather scarce among the EFQM performance criteria, and so they are. Table 9.1 excerpts certain of these criteria in the first four performance categories.

According to Eccles and Nohria (1992), the justifications for this new paradigm are founded in three fundamental truths about

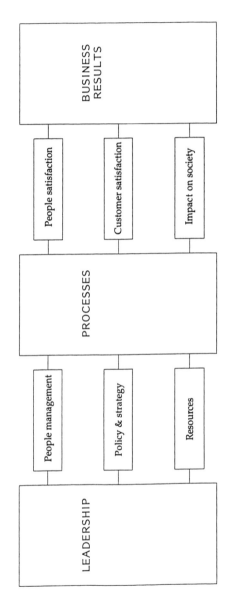

Figure 9.1 The European TQM model. (*Source*: European Foundation for Quality Management)

Table 9.1   EFQM performance criteria

Leadership: how managers take positive steps to:
1. Communicate with staff
2. Give and receive training
3. Assess the awareness of Total Quality
4. Establish and participate in joint improvement teams with customers and suppliers

People Management: how the organization releases the full potential of its people by:
1. Integrating corporate and HR strategy
2. Assessing the match between people's skills and organizational needs
3. Establishing and implementing training programs
4. Achieving effective top-down and bottom-up communication

Policy and strategy: how the organization's policies:
1. Reflect the fundamentals of Total Quality
2. Test, improve, and align business plans with the desired direction
3. Are communicated and instilled in the organization
4. Account for internal and external feedback

Resources: how resources are deployed in support of strategy, including:
1. Financial
2. Informational
3. Technological
4. Material

Source: EFQM, 1993

performance management:

(1) The use of non-financial measures encourages managers to adopts a broad and long-term view of organizational performance.
(2) Measures of non-financial variables target events that are meaningful and actionable in managerial experience, e.g. delivery times, market position, the development of organizational competence, and employee turnover.
(3) Non-financial measures can serve as leading indicators of financial results and thus be made legitimate even to those for whom the bottom line is everything.

However, the task of extending the traditional approach to performance management beyond common financial measures poses significant problems. One of the most difficult facing both academics and practising managers is the development of non-financial measures that deliver realistic data on a company's current position, and which serve well as leading indicators of future financial performance.

HUMAN RESOURCE MANAGEMENT PRACTICES

The human resource management (HRM) function is, at root, a range of activities and approaches that allow a firm to attract, retain, and mobilize a critical mass of human talent. Most efforts to assess HR performance have been limited to (1) general measures of limited value, such as headcount or payroll costs, or (2) sophisticated measures that managers are sometimes unable or unwilling to use. Moreover, experience shows that managers seldom review in a systematic way the intent, impact, or results, of an HR action or policy. As a result, adjustments in human resource policies and practices tend to be based on intuition rather than methodical assessment of concrete and specifiable effects.

Like their counterparts in production, marketing, and financial management, many HR managers are being (understandably) forced to justify in a systematic way the costs of their activities, and to compare their activities and overall performance measures with those of other organizations (Mackay and Torrington, 1986). This need to evaluate the value-added effects of HR practices on organizational products and processes began in earnest during the late 1980s and is becoming critical in this, the age of performance management.

United Technologies, for example, convened a task force with just this issue in mind during the early 1990s (Dailey, 1992). The group surveyed 'internal customers' of the HR function in each of United Technologies' six major businesses (Pratt & Whitney, Sikorsky Aircraft, Carrier, UT Automotive, Otis, and Norden Systems) with the straightforward objective of comparing perceptions of performance between HR and line managers. The eighteen-item instrument used in this exercise is presented in Table 9.2. The performance categories in this instrument are instructive and, generally, the task force found that HR professionals perceived the quality of their services to be higher than did line managers. More worrisome, HR managers were viewed as competent but disconnected from the company's strategic direction:

> HR professionals stood up for the HR perspective, which is good, but did it quite traditionally. They were fairly competent, but didn't measure themselves very rigorously. They did their homework and

Table 9.2   United Technologies: Human Resources Practices Survey

Always: 1	Usually: 2	Sometimes: 3	Rarely: 4

To what extent does the Human Resource organization

— 1. Understand business direction and what management is trying to accomplish?
— 2. Stand up for the human resource perspective on business issues?
— 3. Staff the HR organization with competent professionals?
— 4. Participate actively in the business planning process?
— 5. Take appropriate risks?
— 6. Respond in a timely manner?
— 7. Develop human resource objectives in the context of business priorities?
— 8. Do its homework?
— 9. Provide competent advice and support?
—10. Explore alternative solutions to problems?
—11. Find ways to balance its functional interests with other needs of the business?
—12. React quickly to changes in the needs of the business?
—13. Anticipate business problems?
—14. Help more than hinder the organization in attaining its business objectives?
—15. Have people seek its advice?
—16. Set high standards for evaluating its own effectiveness?
—17. Bring a competitive global perspective to the HR function?
—18. Design solutions to business problems that meet the needs of the business?

Source: Dailey, 1992

came to meetings prepared, but were not seen as very innovative or risk taking. In short, the message from this survey was, "You're not really a strategic partner" (Dailey, 1992, 15–18).

The results of this effort included a two-day conference where 100 HR and 20 line managers discussed the findings, set priorities, charted a new direction, and cascaded the process down to corporate and business units.

As United Technologies illustrates, the competitive environment is intensifying and the development of key HR performance indicators together with their associated monitoring systems is becoming increasingly important. In fact, given the increasing emphasis on cost reduction, quality and excellence in many organizations, it is surprising that human resource management has escaped scrutiny for so long.

APPROACHES TO MEASURING HR PERFORMANCE

How can a forward-thinking organization develop an effective performance monitoring system in the area of human resource management? According to Morgan (1992), there are three approaches.

One is to adopt a stepwise procedure, similar to the scientific method, in which meaningful and reliable variables are identified. The process begins by developing as many measures as possible, particularly in the HR areas of greatest concern. Second, measures whose potential benefit is outweighed by the expense or difficulty of data collection are eliminated. Third, systems are developed which regularly collect the necessary information, preferably devolved to line management, and a commitment is made to the time and effort needed for analysing the data and interpreting its meaning in the realm of HR strategy. After two or three years (often the time required to realize the impact of an HR activity) it becomes possible to reduce the number of measures to four or five key indicators by eliminating those which only confirm the results of others. For example, if employee turnover, job satisfaction, absenteeism, and so forth were all perfectly correlated with one another, only one of the measures would be necessary. By examining this single measure a manager would know the company's performance for all the others. The relationship between performance measures is often complicated and non-linear, however, making multiple measures a virtual necessity.

Although this approach is laudable in its attempt to capture all measurable aspects of HR performance, there is the risk that the task of collecting data, analysing them, and interpreting the results will be costly, time consuming, and result in no clear guidelines for action. There is also the danger of what Eccles and Nohria (1992: 160) called *creeping numeration*, which refers to 'the temptation to turn every measure deemed relevant into a crucial part of an official measurement system'. Indeed, once the decision is made to expand the class of measures from a single (financial) category to three or four, and four or five measures are developed for each category, a company can quickly have twenty or more 'key' performance indicators.

A second approach to performance management involves the identification of key performance indicators that are associated with a specific HR practice, such as recruitment and selection. From this perspective the wisdom lies in keeping things simple and avoiding information overload, and the implication is that only a few measures are needed to help line managers or HR professionals gauge the current state of affairs.

This second approach offers an appealing logic: if objectives have been defined in advance, there should be associated measures and thus no difficulty in collecting and interpreting the data. Most managers simply cannot attend to twenty measures at once—let alone optimize them—despite company rhetoric that may implore them to do so. In fact, imputing significance to each of these measures may only push the problem of devising a meaningful performance measurement system down to the level of each frustrated individual (Eccles and Nohria, 1992). But as Morgan (1992) points out, this method runs the risk of being superficial. It is not enough to know that a specific practice or activity has worked to a greater or lesser extent. To be of real benefit there must be enough information to understand why the specific outcome has occurred, and to incorporate the lessons learned.

A third approach to HR performance monitoring, one which is currently the vogue, is through the process now known as *benchmarking*. Benchmarking denotes a comparison with selected performance indicators from different organizations, typically in the same industry, or with comparable organizations that are considered to be 'best in class'. The most obvious points of comparison are with close competitors, but some organizations have gone beyond their industry group to identify best practice wherever it can be found. Xerox, for example, where benchmarking has been credited as one of the main factors in its 1980s revival, has benchmarked railways, insurance companies, and facilities that generate electric power.

Successful benchmarking requires careful selection and manipulation of comparison measures. A recent study (Geanuracos, 1994) found that while 70% of the executives surveyed reported using benchmarking to evaluate performance, nearly 60% were benchmarking against their own company's historical record as opposed to competitors or industry leaders. Clearly, the greatest gain to be had from a benchmarking exercise is provided through comparison with other firms and different ways of thinking. Indeed, as a programmatic effort benchmarking serves a number of purposes (Glanz and Daily, 1992). First, it enables a company to calibrate how it is delivering HR practices. By examining the way other organizations accomplish tasks and responsibilities, a company can audit itself and identify areas where practices are within or outside a given norm. Second, benchmarking enables a company to learn from others' successes and mistakes. Building a continuous improvement mentality has become an important goal for many organizations in the last decade; benchmarking can open minds and create a climate in which active learning is encouraged.

Third, benchmarking can be used as a tool for creating the motivation to change. By learning what other companies are doing, line managers and HR professionals can build a stronger case for allocating resources to HRM activities in ways similar to those of successful companies. Finally, benchmarking can be used to help set direction and priorities for an HR manager. Rather than fall into the trap of trying to do everything well and please everyone with limited resources (which typically results in no one being satisfied), HR managers can use benchmarking to focus on critical activities (Ulrich et al., 1989). Questions which may indicate a need for benchmarking HR practices in an organization include the following:

(1) What is most critical to business success: Cost reduction? Innovation? Quality improvement?
(2) What areas are causing the most trouble?
(3) Which employees contribute most to the critical success factors?
(4) Which attitudes and behaviours are currently displayed by these employees?
(5) Which attitudes and behaviours are responsible for the trouble areas identified above?
(6) What HR policies and practices are contributing to the current attitudes and behaviours?
(7) Which HR policies and practices need to be changed as a result of the above in order to build on strengths or correct weaknesses in our approach to HR management?
(8) What are the performance measures to determine the effect of our actions?
(9) What are the major cost components of the change program?

Currently, the most common form of HR benchmarking involves salary surveys. It is the rare HR manager who steps beyond this, for two principal reasons: (1) the difficulty of finding standard and acceptable performance indicators similar to those used in financial management, such as return on capital and cash flow ratios, and (2) the reluctance of companies to divulge sensitive information on employee retention, employment costs, and so on. There are other reasons for the lack of HR benchmarking in contemporary organizations, the most prevalent perhaps being the mythology that has developed around personnel work. As Fitz-Enz (1984), observes:

The fundamental belief is that personnel is something of a complex and mysterious art. Allegedly, the true and full value of the work can only be judged by those who perform it. Even then, the appraisal is bounded by subjective criteria. Many of the faithful believe that, like virtue, personnel work is its own reward. Terms used to describe results are satisfied, quick, better, interesting, good, important, creative, and other similar non-specific terms.

There are also people who believe that measuring the effectiveness of human resource management is simply inappropriate. In their eyes, HRM is devoted to stimulating and supporting human happiness and development, and they see no reason to evaluate outcomes in other than humanistic terms.

Benchmarking has its limitations. When used solely to emulate rather than improve performance, advantages may be short-lived, time consuming, and expensive. Moreover, the most valuable information is generally not derived from the actual data, but rather the qualitative information on how and why the data outcomes were achieved. Nevertheless, a well-established benchmarking process can help managers set goals and targets designed to make the company the best in its competitive field, and to initiate focused programs that move the company from its current position. Many firms strive for performance improvements by benchmarking standards of excellence from other firms in such areas as production, research and development, and marketing. HR can be employed to similar competitive advantage, and it is sensible to unearth those HR indicators that contribute relatively more to overall performance than others.

Janssen Pharmaceutica, a wholly owned subsidiary of Johnson & Johnson, undertook just such a benchmarking project in late 1989 (Liebfried and McNair, 1992) as a response to competitive pressures rocking the pharmaceutical industry. Janssen examined in detail the internal components of its administrative overhead and, by comparing benchmarks with a select group of peer companies, addressed what was considered a 'burgeoning problem that is difficult to analyze and control' (Liebfried and McNair, 1992). To begin, the company determined that administrative (white-collar) productivity could be defined through four key elements (Table 9.3).

Management then compared Janssen's performance with that of other companies participating in the project. Janssen's managers soon determined that achieving white-collar productivity improvements would be impossible unless appropriate performance measures were developed and installed. Table 9.4 displays four such measures that Janssen now uses to monitor its performance in this area.

Table 9.3   Elements of white-collar productivity (Janssen Pharmaceutical)

Effectiveness
1. A strong, clear connection between corporate strategy and work activities

Organization
1. Overlap/duplication
2. Fragmentation
3. Inappropriate groupings of functions or alignments of functions
4. Inefficient reporting relationships
5. Excessive management layers
6. Clarity of mission
7. Appropriateness of job design

Motivation
1. Turnover
2. Performance feedback
3. Contribution visibility and recognition
4. Group identity
5. Teamwork
6. Management style
7. Career planning and development
8. Training
9. Communication

Process
1. Value-added activities, operations, and steps
2. Scheduling and backlog control
3. Degree of automation
4. Control and transfer points

Source: Liebfried and McNair, 1992

EFFECTIVENESS CRITERIA FOR HR ACTIVITIES

As noted earlier, developing the specific criteria which define effectiveness for HR activities is one of the most difficult challenges facing line managers and HR professionals alike. In this regard there are two schools of thought. The first school advocates monitoring the costs and benefits of human resource activities—those associated with the attraction, selection, retention, development, and utilization of people in organizations—in economic terms. The underlying assumption is that the ultimate single measure of HR effectiveness is financial...the 'bottom line'. To illustrate this point, consider a

Table 9.4   White-collar performance measures (Janssen Pharmaceutica)

Productivity

1. Units of output/number of employees
2. Units of output/cost to produce
3. Value-added work operations/non-value-added operations
4. Costs to manage/number of subordinates

Throughput time

1. Time required to process work or complete work products

Quality

1. Number of errors/unit of time
2. Error-free work product transactions/work product transactions with errors

Others

1. Deadline accomplishments percentage
2. Customer satisfaction index
3. Degree of employee commitment/involvement (organizational climate)

Source: Liebfried and McNair, 1992

comment by Cascio (1991) in his book entitled *Costing Human Resources*:

> For some time now, I have had the uneasy feeling that a lot of what we do in the human resource management field is largely misunderstood and underestimated by the organisations we serve. In part, we in the field are responsible for this state of affairs because much of what we do is evaluated only in statistical and behavioural terms. Like it or not, the language of business is dollars, not correlation coefficients.

Although methods for estimating the costs and benefits of HR activities have been available for many years (e.g. Brogden, 1949; Cronbach and Gleser, 1965), they are only beginning to appear through the recent writing of academics such as Flamholtz (1985), Cascio (1991), and Fitz-Enz (1990), and in the form of formulas and accounting procedures for measuring the economic worth of the organization's human assets. Table 9.5 gives an illustrative example of conducting simple exit interviews with terminating employees.

This economic approach to measuring HR performance has the advantage of being simple and understandable, but it fails to

Table 9.5 Measuring the costs of exit interviews

Total cost of exit interviews during a given
period = cost of interviewer and interviewee time

1. **Cost of interviewer time** = (time required prior to interview + time required for interview) × (interviewer's pay rate per period) × (number of turnovers per period)

2. **Cost of terminating employee's time** = (time required for the interview) × (weighted average pay rate for terminating employees) × (number of turnovers per period)

provide guidance when implementing effective HR management programs. Many HR managers (and their organizations) understandably feel a need for more detailed and comprehensive means of assessing their performance, and how their performance compares with other companies over time.

The second school, espoused by academics such as Ulrich *et al.* (1989) and Kravetz (1988), is to measure the set of HR practices delivered within an organization and the contribution of each practice to the overall competitive advantage of the organization. A great deal of recent work has appeared which attempts to capture in a single conceptual model the variety of HR practices deployed by organizations to augment innovation, improve quality, and be the lowest-cost producer of goods and services. In 1984, Schuler introduced such a model which identified six categories of HR practices: *planning, staffing, training and development, appraisal, compensation,* and *union–management relations.* He suggests that competitive advantage accrues to companies that identify and develop specific activities in each of these six areas (Schuler, 1984), and that specific activities (such as internal staffing and flexible compensation) become important and advantageous internal competencies. In addition, selection of HR practices should support overall corporate strategy and lead to employee behaviours that are felicitous of it.

After a decade of conceptual and empirical research by Tsui (1984), Kravetz (1988), and others, it is now possible to define key performance indicators in most of the six categories identified by Schuler (Table 9.6). These indicators can help managers evaluate how their HR practices relate to both the operational and strategic level of the enterprise, and lay the foundation for comparing (longitudinally, or sectorially) the effectiveness of HR practices and

Table 9.6   Key HR performance indicators

Recruitment and selection

1. Number of long-term vacancies (over 6 months)/total number of jobs
2. Average length of time to fill vacancies
3. Proportion of vacancies filled internally through promotion, demotion, or lateral movements of personnel
4. Average time spent in a job or function per employee

Training and development

1. Number of trainee days/number of employees
2. Total training budget/total employment expenditure

Compensation and rewards

1. Total compensation cost/total revenues
2. Basic salary/total remuneration
3. Number of salary grades/employees

Employee relations

1. Number of resignations/total headcount per year
2. Average length of service per employee
3. Rate of absenteeism
4. Average length of absence per employee
5. Number of supervisors and managers per employee

Source: Schuler, 1984; Tsui, 1984

policies between companies, divisions, or business units.

Another conceptualization evaluates the effectiveness of HR practices according to six performance criteria (Bernardin and Kane, 1993):

- *Quality of delivery* (in terms of conforming to some practice ideal, or fulfilling the intended purpose)
- *Quantity* (expressed in terms such as dollar value, number of units, or number of completed HR activity cycles)
- *Timeliness* (the degree to which an HR practice is completed, or a result produced, at the earliest time desirable)
- *Cost effectiveness* (in the sense of optimizing the gain or minimizing the loss from each unit or instance of use of human and financial resources)
- *Need for supervision* (the degree to which a person or unit can carry out an HR practice without requesting assistance, or requiring intervention to prevent an adverse outcome)

- *Positive impact* (the degree to which an HR practice promotes feelings of self-esteem, goodwill, commitment, satisfaction, and cooperation among co-workers and subordinates).

Based on this model, the most effective managers or HR professionals are those providing the highest possible *quantity* and *quality* of HR practices at the lowest *cost* and in the most *timely* fashion, with a minimum of *supervision* and with a maximum of *positive impact* on co-workers, organizational units, and the client/customer population.

Ideally, the relative weights to be applied to these six criteria are directly linked to organizational objectives such as increased sales, improved productivity, and, of course, return on investment. Strong linkages in this regard are extremely rare, however. As Ulrich *et al.* (1989) point out, most organizations have difficulty even measuring overall performance in a reliable manner, and few systematically relate individual performance to unit or corporate performance. Moreover, organizations rarely get down to specifics on all six criteria and seldom relate them effectively to the objectives of the firm. Nonetheless, it is widely understood that the linkage is a necessary one if line managers are to be convinced that HR activities are integral to organizational objectives, and that they create and sustain a competitive edge.

In addition to HR practices, Ulrich *et al.* (1989) suggest that benchmarks may also be developed for the HR competencies of individual managers in the organization. Questions that may indicate a need to benchmark HR functions include the following:

(1) Who are the major customers of the HR function: Line managers? Other staff or support functions? Employee organizations? External clients?
(2) What services are provided to these customers? Is there a reason for their existence?
(3) What are the major cost components of these services?
(4) What factors are responsible for customer satisfaction?
(5) What problems have been identified in the operation?
(6) What performance measurements are being used to determine the effectiveness and efficiency of the HR function?
(7) What are the performance gaps and what action is needed to close these gaps?

Under the umbrella of strategic human resource management, three sets of HR competencies may be identified: *knowledge of the business, quality of service,* and the *management of change.* Knowledge of the business refers to the extent to which an HR professional (or a line manager with HR responsibilities) understands the financial, strategic, and technological capabilities of the organization. Quality of service refers to the extent to which the HR or line manager provides high-quality HR policies and services (such as training and development) to the other members of the organization. Management of change refers to the extent to which an HR professional or line manager is able to increase the organization's capability for change through creating meaning, problem solving, relationship influence, innovation, transformation, and role influence.

According to Ulrich *et al.* (1989), measures may be established for specific behaviours in each of these three domains of HR competencies. However, these measures and behaviours have not been as well developed and researched as the performance indicators for HR practices discussed previously. Table 9.7 outlines a felicitous approach discussed by Burn and Thompson (1993), in which the organization defines an indigenous set of indicators, installs measurement standards and monitors performance over time.

In a similar vein, Storey and Sissons (1993) recently proposed a set of activities for benchmarking the organization's HR department. Their intention is to outline a possible approach to auditing the role and performance of the function. According to these authors, a number of steps are involved:

- *Step 1: Decide the composition of the audit team.* There has to be a representative from the HR function and from among senior line managers if the exercise is to have any credibility. But it is not essential (or even desirable) that the team is led by the head of the senior HR managers.
- *Step 2: Identify the function's main customers.* The key decision is to clarify who makes the final decision to buy the services provided by the function. In a decentralized multi-divisional organization, this is likely to be the general managers of the strategic business units.
- *Step 3: Review the HR function's mission statement.* This statement describes the reason for the HR function's existence, its principal activities, and its most important values. For instance: 'To be the HR/Personnel consultant of choice for the firm's line managers by achieving superior levels of customer satisfaction at lowest costs and highest speed in the area of employee attraction, retention, and motivation.'

Table 9.7 A three-tier approach for assessing performance in the HR function

Phase I: Gather fundamental data

1. Specify current activities in the HR department
2. Identify the structure of the HR department
3. Determine the costs of providing HR services in seven key functional areas:
   - Staffing
   - Development
   - Employee relations
   - Organizational evaluation
   - Reward systems
   - Administration
   - Health and safety
4. Determine HR contribution to the 'bottom line'

Phase II: Assess HR service delivery

1. Determine internal clients' *needs* for services in each of the key functional areas
2. Determine internal clients' *reactions to services delivered* in each of the seven functional areas

Phase III: Establish standards

1. Set acceptable standards in each of the seven functional areas
2. Audit HR performance in each functional area over time, and make necessary adjustments

---

- *Step 4: Review the function's role in formulating and implementing the organization's strategy.* The list of questions in Table 9.2 are relevant here. This step will also be critical to establishing the link between HR policy and practices, on the one hand, and the organization's overall business strategy, on the other.
- *Step 5: Review the HR function's role in developing relevant HR policies and practices.* For example, what is the firm's policy with regard to recruitment? Is there a preference for internal or external recruitment? Is this policy sustainable and desirable in the new competitive environment? Does it support the need for high-quality human talent? Is this policy consistent with other HR policies and practices, such as rewards, training and development, performance management, succession, and

promotion? Do these policies and practices focus on improving individual and organizational performance?

- *Step 6: Review the delivery of HR policies and practices.* Questions need to be asked here in relation to all the HR activities currently being undertaken by HR or personnel staff which could perhaps be done as well or better by line managers, by computers, or by external agencies and consultants. For example, one recent survey identified an increasing number of European organizations that have decided to outsource some of their traditional HR services to completely independent businesses. An alternative option is to establish an 'internal consultancy or business unit' in which the HR function sells its services both inside and outside the organization (Adams, 1991). The advantage of this approach is that line managers can go elsewhere if they are not happy with the service they receive from the HR function within the organization.

- *Step 7: Make external comparisons to establish 'best' practice.* As Humble (1988) points out, it does not require an 'espionage' network to get the data. Articles in such magazines and journals as *Personnel Management, Personnel Today,* and *Human Resource Management* carry a great deal of useful information about what other companies in Europe, Asia, and the United States are doing in order to deal with the contemporary HR issues. In addition, a considerable number of research conferences and workshops are currently being organized by business schools and consultancy agencies that allow progressive HR managers to inform themselves and compare their own practices with those of other organizations. At IMD, we are also building and constantly updating a unique database of HR practices that gives an overview of developments within the world's largest organizations today.

- *Step 8: Review the outcomes of the analysis.* Look for performance gaps and discuss the policy implications with the main customers. Gain their commitment for implementing the necessary improvements. This implies that those ultimately responsible for implementing the changes (1) acknowledge the need for improving HR policies and practices, (2) understand the differences between current HR practices and what is desired, and (3) accept and retain full ownership of the practical steps toward implementation.

- *Step 9: Implement the agreed improvements and measure the progress against pre-set targets.* The metrics selected should be the agreed-upon true indicators of the HR function's performance and compare the results with industry averages, competitors, 'best practice' firms, and/or with set targets or previous performance ratings. As shown in Table 9.7, it is usually feasible to produce relevant ratios of HR performance data. The most likely ratios should cover unit costs and appropriate customer-satisfaction measures. If measurements are not clear or difficult to obtain, two alternatives are possible (Camp, 1989). One, the process of determining appropriate HR performance measures becomes a key step in the benchmarking process itself or, two there are approximate measures available from other functional areas that give an indication of how the HR function is performing. For example, lead times may be used as a proxy for the effectiveness of a new delivery-oriented incentive scheme.

LINKING KEY HR PERFORMANCE INDICATORS WITH ORGANIZATIONAL EFFECTIVENESS

Obviously, many managers and investors are interested in knowing if a certain activity or practice can serve as a leading indicator or determinant of financial performance. When such an indicator goes up or down, an organization can take actions to minimize or maximize the impact by changing the relevant practice. Consequently, over the past few years, a number of studies have tried to link specific HR practices and organizational effectiveness in terms of financial performance, productivity, product quality, innovation, and so on. One such study was conducted by Kravetz (1988). In a book entitled *The Human Resources Revolution* Kravetz looked for the correlation between financial results and what he termed *human resources progressiveness* (HRP) in 150 US companies. HRP was defined as the extent to which an organization is:

> . . . operating in concert with the current and future workplace, rather than experimenting with radical programs or spending exorbitant amounts of money on human resources programs. A company high in HRP understands the critical importance of people to the bottom line and operates with this in mind (Kravetz, 1988, 36).

A firm's score on the HRP index was measured through a 50 item questionnaire pertaining to HR practices and policies in the following nine areas:

(1) Degree of openness of communication

(2) Degree of emphasis on people in the company culture
(3) Degree to which management is participative
(4) Emphasis on creativity and excellence in the workplace
(5) Extensiveness of career development and training
(6) Effectiveness in maximizing employee job satisfaction
(7) Degree of recognition and reward for good performance
(8) Usage of flexitime and part-time employment
(9) Degree of decentralization and flattened management hierarchy.

The results showed that human resource progressiveness in these nine areas was significantly correlated with financial success over a five-year period. In particular, Kravetz concluded that highly progressive companies enjoyed significantly higher sales growth, profit margins, equity growth, and earnings per share growth than the less progressive ones. For instance, the annualized sales growth (five-year trend) of high HRP companies was 17.5%, compared to 10.7% for low HRP companies; and the annualized profit growth of high HRP firms was 10.8%, compared to only 2.6% for those low in HRP.

In a second study on the same subject Frederick Schuster (1986) examined the relationship between human resource management performance as measured by the *Human Resources Index* (HRI) and organizational effectiveness. His intent was to lay the foundation for the development of a reliable and practical instrument, which could be used as a benchmarking tool by companies representing a wide range of industries and sizes. The HRI survey contained 64 measures of human resource practices, six of which were the focus of this research:

(1) The assessment centre approach to personnel selection
(2) Flexible or cafeteria approach in reward systems
(3) Productivity bonus plans
(4) Goal-oriented performance appraisal
(5) Alternative work schedules
(6) Organizational development.

These six practices were chosen because they were thought to be related to the general management philosophy which Peters and Waterman (1982) termed *attention to employee needs*, and could therefore serve as an operational definition of this philosophy. Schuster's hypothesis and findings were consistent with those of Kravetz in that he expected and found a small but meaningful relationship between the six HR practices and financial performance (as measured by return on equity and total return to investors). In particular, the total utility of the six HR practices for the average *Fortune 1000* company was estimated at $7.5 million per year.

These two studies represent a small sample of the work currently being done in this field. Their formulations and findings have helped to explore the link between HR practices and overall organizational effectiveness. Or course, it can be argued that better financial performance leads to effective human resource practices (rather than the reverse). While this causal effect is possible, at this point the data indicate that the two types of performance go hand in hand. As Kravetz (1988, 43) argues,

> It is difficult to envision why a company would change its management style, have more employees work out of their homes, or change the company culture to one strongly oriented toward people. Many companies, if they are enjoying great financial success, are not likely to change, figuring that you shouldn't fix things that don't need fixing. They retain their same successful practices until these need to be abandoned to address a static or declining market position. Success is not likely to breed this type of change.

PRESCRIPTIONS FOR ACTION

This final section provides guidelines for installing an effective HR measurement system and is an attempt to offer practical guidance rather than facile prescriptions, since *cookbook* approaches to the matter are inappropriate and ineffective. Based on the lessons we and others have learned, HR managers should consider carefully the following factors when establishing a system for determining the effectiveness of their activities or departments.

First, it is important to recognize that the underlying purpose of a performance management system is change and organizational change of any type requires the active support, preferably involvement, of topmost management. At a minimum, HR managers should have a clear understanding of (1) what the company's principal strategic objectives are, (2) which proposed or actual HR practices and policies contribute to their achievement, and in what ways, and (3) the measures that are or will be linked to these HR policies or practices.

Change programs require clarity of purpose and a good measure of initial momentum in order to achieve success. It is therefore advantageous to focus initial efforts on those HR practices which can be affected by individuals who will be subject to the measurement system. The least desirable course of action is to install monitoring activities that cannot be influenced by the persons involved. By this token, corporate training and development costs should not be allocated to division managers if these individuals have no control over training and development activities in their units.

The performance management systems' measurements should be *robust*. By this we mean that no single measure perfectly captures all aspects of HR performance, even allowing for time lags (Eccles and Nohria, 1992), and an array of different qualitative and quantitative performance measures increases the dimensions along which change can be guided. This principal of *triangulation*—the use of multiple measures to bring a target issue or event under control— also permits managers to gain a broader sense of the HR practices that contribute to company goals, since the likelihood is greater that one measure among the set will relate effectively to their issues and concerns.

HR managers can avoid the *measurement trap* by monitoring key performance indicators, and *only* key performance indicators. The measurement trap springs shut when HR managers are busily occupied monitoring sundry measures which have little impact in the organization. As one counter to this we find it helpful to encourage an open, questioning, even dissenting work culture which challenges the last best idea set forth. Ideally, line and HR managers will feel free to challenge traditional measures (e.g. employee turnover and direct labour costs) since in today's rapidly changing world, the indicators in use may be irrelevant and focusing attention on the wrong activities (Hora and Schiller, 1991).

It should go without saying that line managers need to be actively involved when developing and monitoring an HR performance measurement system; in practice, however, it becomes convenient and easy for HR managers to stay within their function and work with managers of their own stripe. One of the great pitfalls of HR performance measurement systems is opened when HR managers begin to argue that their actions are undiscussable so long as their performance targets are met. For HR measures to have a real impact in the organization, dialogue about the meaning and relevance of programs, activities, and measures must remain open. Some organizations have enforced this dialogue through the use of a cross-functional team which monitors the system and ensures that relevant measures are being used and understood.

Communication is the *sine qua non* of effective change efforts. In this connection HR managers must be prepared to regularly communicate, with a proactive attitude, the purpose and specifics of the performance management system to all involved employees, and be prepared to clarify the measures repeatedly in use. The assumption that managers and employees understand or accept the new system is dangerous and constitutes a serious design flaw.

Analyze the data regularly, at a rate compatible with their impact on decision making, and draw appropriate conclusions by comparing the key performance indicators over time. These comparisons may be made between business units and/or against predetermined targets. Current benchmarking efforts assess the HR performance of business units against comparable units within the same industry, or against units and organizations that are considered best in class.

Finally, be ready to change the measurement system if a particular indicator fails to achieve business goals, or if the costs of collecting and analyzing the data exceed the potential benefits of their use. As Eccles and Nohria (1992) point out, the discipline needed to discontinue irrelevant performance measures should not be underestimated. The benefit of keeping the same measures for a period of time lies in the historical comparability thus afforded, and perhaps in longitudinal evaluation of the impact anticipated by the HR practice. The risk is that attractive new measures can always be found, and unless some existing ones are eliminated creeping numeration will be the result.

AUTHOR'S NOTE

An earlier version of this text appeared in the *Journal of Strategic Change* **3** (3), May/June 1994.

REFERENCES

Adams, K. (1991) Externalisation vs. specialisation. *Human Resources Management Journal*, **1**(4), Summer, 40–54.

Bernardin, H. and Kane, J. (1993) *Performance Appraisal: A Contingency Approach to System Development and Evaluation*, (2nd edn), Boston, MA, PWS-Kent.

Brogden, H. (1949) When testing pays off. *Personnel Psychology*, **2**, 171–83.

Burn, D. and Thompson, L. (1993) When personnel calls in the auditors. *Personnel Management*, January, 21–3.

Camp, R. (1989) *Benchmarking: The Search for Industry Best Practices That Lead To Superior Performance*, Milwaukee, ASQC Quality Press.

Cascio, W. (1991) *Costing Human Resources*, 3rd edn, Boston, MA, PWS-Kent.

Cronbach, L. and Gleser, G. (1965) *Psychological Tests and Personnel Decisions* 2nd edn, Urbana, IL, University of Illinois Press.

Dailey, L. (1992) United Technologies Corporation. *Human Resource Management*, Spring and Summer, 15–17.

Eccles, R. (1991) The performance measurement manifesto. *Harvard Business Review*, January–February, 131–7.

Eccles, R. and Nohria, N. (1992) *Beyond the Hype: Rediscovering the Essence of Management*, Cambridge, MA, Harvard Business School Press.

European Foundation for Quality Management. (1993) *Total Quality Management: The European Model for Self-Appraisal 1993*, Eindhoven, The Netherlands, The European Foundation for Quality Management.

Fitz-Enz, J. (1984) *How to Measure Human Resource Management*, New York, McGraw-Hill.

Fitz-Enz, J. (1990) *Human Value Management: The Value-Adding Human Resource Management Strategy for the 1990s*, San Francisco, CA, Jossey-Bass.

Flamholtz, E. (1985) *Human Resource Accounting*, San Francisco, CA, Jossey-Bass.

Geanuracos, J. (1994) The global performance game. *Crossborder*, Winter, 18–21.

Glanz, E. and Daily, L. (1992) Benchmarking. *Human Resource Management*, Spring, **31**, 9–20.

Hora, M. and Schiller, M. (1991) Performance measurement. In Rock, M. and Berger, L. (eds), *The Compensation Handbook*, New York, McGraw-Hill.

Humble, J. (1988) How to improve the personnel service. *Personnel Management*, February, 30–33.

Kaplan, R. and Norton, D. (1992) The balanced scorecard—measures that drive performance. *Harvard Business Review*, **70**, January–February, 71–9.

Kravetz, D. (1988) *The Human Resources Revolution: Implementing Progressive Management Practices for Bottom-Line Success*, San Francisco, CA, Jossey-Bass.

Liebfried, K. and McNair, C. (1992) *Benchmarking: A Tool for Continuous Improvement*, New York, Harper Business.

Mackay, L. and Torrington, D. (1986) *The Changing Nature of Personnel Management*, London, IPM.

Morgan, J. (1992) Human resource information: a strategic tool. In Armstrong, M. (ed.), *Strategies for Human Resource Management*, London, Kegan Paul.

Peters, T.J. and Waterman, R.H. (1982) *In Search of Excellence*, Harper and Row, New York.

Schuler, R. (1984) Gaining competitive advantage through human resource management practices. *Human Resource Management*, Fall, **23** (3), 241–55.

Schuster, F. (1986) *The Schuster Report: The Proven Connection Between People and Profits*, New York, John Wiley.

Storey, J. and Sissons, K. (1993) *Managing Human Resources and Industrial Relations*, Buckingham, Open University Press.

Tsui, A. (1984) Personnel department effectiveness: a tripartite approach. *Industrial Relations*, **23**, 184–97.

Ulrich, D., Brockbank, W. and Yeung, A. (1989) Beyond belief: a benchmark for human resources. *Human Resource Management*, Fall, **28** (3), 311–35.

10

COMPETITOR ANALYSIS— A CASE HISTORY

D. E. Hussey

David Hussey & Associates
& Centre for International Management and Industrial Development

SCOPE OF CHAPTER

Case histories of industry and competitor analysis are difficult to obtain, because of their confidential nature, and because it is not always ethical to make public one's value judgements of competitors. In this chapter I have tried to demonstrate the results of the practical application of competitor analysis techniques, using mainly real information to illustrate the methods. However, I have used simplified examples in some of the analytical displays, and where necessary for ethical reasons have used fictitious exhibits rather than disclosing my opinions of real competitors. Such exhibits have been reduced to a minimum, and are only included where necessary to ensure understanding of the methods actually applied. The chapter describes experience while I was managing director of Harbridge Consulting Group Ltd, and is written from the viewpoint of that firm.

One of the difficulties of competitor analysis is knowing what information to obtain. The problem often varies between the extremes of having too few data for meaningful analysis and having so much that it becomes difficult to make sense of it. Once a decision has been taken on the information needed, the problem shifts to one

Rethinking Strategic Management
Edited by D. E. Hussey. John Wiley & Sons Ltd, 1995
© D. E. Hussey 1991, 1993, 1994. This paper was published in the *Journal of Strategic Change*, 1, 4, 1992, and in modified form in Hussey, D. E. (1993) *Strategic Planning: Theory and Practice*, Oxford, Elsevier.

of how to obtain it, using legitimate and ethical methods. Finally, we reach the crunch issue of what to do with what we have collected.

The industry is one of two overlapping industries in which we operate. It is typical of many industries in that definition is difficult and there are hazy borders with related industries. It is also subject to certain international forces for change, although it is by no means a global industry. It is fragmented in all senses, and is unusual in having a mix of private and public sector competitors. Within the private sector there are organisations which gain tax advantages from being registered as charities, although this means that they have to operate under certain rules. Among the other private sector businesses are a mix of one-person businesses, partnerships, and limited companies. And like so many other industries, many competitors have operations in other industries, making it difficult to interpret their results. Indeed, most aspects of the situation have echoes in other industries.

It is a professional services business, although there is some competition from "products", such as videos. Many of its characteristics would be recognised by other professional services businesses, such as solicitors, accountants, and surveyors. All the methodologies illustrated have relevance in other industries, and I have used them in client situations that collectively span almost the whole spectrum of business activity.

THE OUTLINE APPROACH

Figure 10.1 shows the outline approach which we have been using continuously on this and other industries since the early 1980s, although some elements of our approach are even older. The analysis of information goes through four linked stages, which also help to identify what information is required to enable meaningful analysis to take place.

All the information sources shown in the figure have been used to a greater or lesser extent in applying these methods to various situations. In our own industry, databases are less helpful than other sources of information, which is a reflection of the structure of the industry, the few quoted companies in the industry, the lack of published statistics, and the relatively small size of most of the players.

Before going deeper into the methods used, I should like to explain the reasons for starting what became an increasingly detailed competitor analysis system.

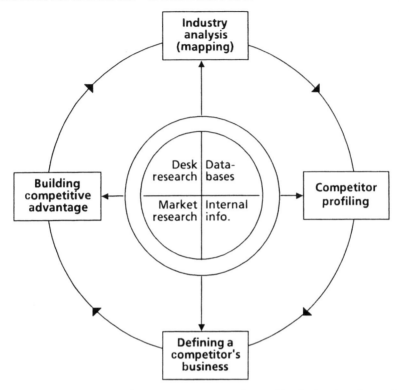

Figure 10.1 An approach to competitor analysis. (© Harbridge Consulting Group Ltd: used with permission)

In early 1980 we had virtually no information about our market in the UK, or our competitors, which made strategic planning a hit-or-miss affair. The UK side of the firm had shown little or no growth for many years. It was also in a classic consultant's situation of basing a business on the skills of its professional staff, and changing emphasis with the departure or engagement of every key employee. What we wanted to do was to position the firm in areas where we could build and sustain competitive advantage, to properly understand the pressures on the industry, and to identify our real competitors from the 600 or so businesses which operate in the UK management training market. We wanted to improve our ability to plan, so that we could do at least as well as the best in growth years, and better than most in the lean years. We wanted to acquire a depth of information that would enable us to speak authoritatively about all aspects of management development.

We had one additional reason, which is probably the only one not similar to any firm in any other industry that contemplates competitor analysis. We needed a "laboratory" in which we could try out some of the concepts we were developing for use with clients. What better laboratory was there than our own business, where we could be freed from the restrictions of client confidentiality, and develop examples which could be shared with others?

My advice to anyone starting competitor analysis is to think through the aims of the exercise first. Competitor analysis may be undertaken for many reasons, and that for purely tactical purposes may take a different form from that for strategic reasons. Our intentions were mainly strategic, although, as I will show later, we did gain some tactical benefit. In addition, some types of analysis are best done as benchmark studies, rather than the method shown here. If, for example, the need is to identify best human resource management practice in the industry, how the best competitors are using information technology, or what is being done about customer responsiveness, a benchmark study to meet this specific objective would be a more appropriate approach. Benchmarking is not covered in this case study. Our approach follows a different course when we undertake such studies, and it is not an approach that we have applied to our own business.

INDUSTRY MAPPING

A journey around the outer circle of Figure 10.1 begins with what I see as the essential first step in competitor analysis: obtaining a detailed understanding of the competitive arena. To do this we used the principles of Porter (1980). For our total strategic analysis we set industry analysis within the context of the outside environment, as in Figure 10.2, although for the purpose of this chapter I will not discuss environmental issues.

Our method explodes the supplier/competitor/buyer boxes of the "five forces" model to mirror the total channel from the first link in the supply chain to the final consumer. The first task is to develop this in block diagram form, using knowledge of managers, logic, and available market information. We tend to incorporate substitutes into this diagram, if they are already significant or appear likely to become so. In addition, we analyse influencers of a buying action. For example, doctors prescribe pharmaceuticals in the UK, but do not sell them: an architect may determine the specifications of a lift in a building, but again is neither a buyer nor a seller of that

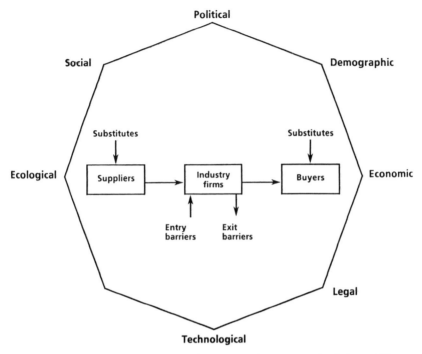

Figure 10.2   The basic elements affecting industry profitability. (Hussey, 1991: used with permission)

equipment. In some industries the influencers may do more to shape the competitive forces than the competitors themselves.

In theory the development of such a block diagram should be easy. In practice we find that many of our clients face difficulty, tending to draw diagrams that reflect their preconceived ideas, or the elements of a channel which they themselves use. When we began our journey towards useful competitor analysis, we found similar problems. We knew what we did, and who some of our competitors were, but surprisingly little about buying decisions, substitute products, or the overall structure of the industry. How we began to collect this information will be discussed later, but the example which appears in Figure 10.3 is the result of several rounds of analysis and is not the original.

As we began to develop our understanding we were able to use the block diagram to record the key information about the industry. Figure 10.3 gives a simplified view of our industry map. The main difference is that the real map contains more competitor assessments, uses a personal system of abbreviations, and includes more analysis

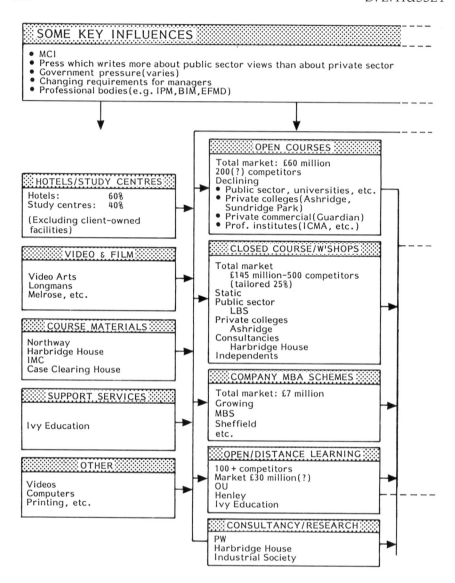

Figure 10.3 Industry map—management training and development. *Notes:* (1) Market estimates are approximate. (2) Market is fragmented (many suppliers, many buyers, multiple buying points in many companies, priority of management development low but higher than in early 1980s). (3) No one supplier dominates (e.g. largest has £12 million turnover). (4) Few suppliers or clients take an international view. (5) High growth 1987–9: now static and some sectors declining. (6) Company names given as examples. (Figure 10.3 continues opposite).

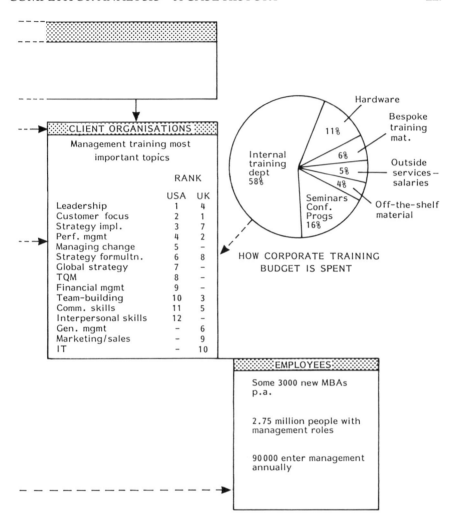

Management training most important topics		
	RANK	
	USA	UK
Leadership	1	4
Customer focus	2	1
Strategy impl.	3	7
Perf. mgmt	4	2
Managing change	5	–
Strategy formultn.	6	8
Global strategy	7	–
TQM	8	–
Financial mgmt	9	–
Team-building	10	3
Comm. skills	11	5
Interpersonal skills	12	–
Gen. mgmt	–	6
Marketing/sales	–	9
IT	–	10

CLIENT ORGANISATIONS

HOW CORPORATE TRAINING BUDGET IS SPENT

Internal training dept 58%
Seminars Conf. Progs 16%
Hardware 11%
Bespoke training mat. 6%
Outside services – salaries 5%
Off-the-shelf material 4%

EMPLOYEES

Some 3000 new MBAs p.a.

2.75 million people with management roles

90 000 enter management annually

of the buying decision. Tables 10.1 and 10.2 show our assessment of the evolution of the market for the type of service we provide. These three diagrams, supported by the additional information which I have omitted for simplification or sensitivity reasons, provide the basis for a detailed strategic evaluation using Porter's (1980) principles. Before I discuss a few of these findings, I should like to mention two decisions that we had to make about the arena we were charting.

There were good reasons for studying the UK as the geographical area, and much of the market is still local to the UK. However, like most industries there is an international dimension. In more recent

Table 10.1 Management training and development market: market sectors
(£ million)

	1990	1991	1992	1993
Open public subscription	57	52	46	
Closed (seen as tailored)	25	30	26	
Closed other	133	137	130	
Distance learning and other	44	70	70	
Management consultancy	55	52	48	
	314	341	320	288

© Harbridge Consulting Group Ltd: used with permission.

Table 10.2 Market for management training and management development
consultancy (%)

Year	Index 1987 = 100	Growth over prior year	Market 1 (£ million)	Market 2 (£ million)
1987	100		169	209
1988	130	30	220	272
1989	153	18	259	320
1990	186	21	314	389
1991	202	9	341	422
1992	189	(6)	320	395
1993	170	(10)	288	356

Notes:
Market 1 is an estimate based on the survey undertaken by the Osbaldeston
working party for the CBI/BIM study *The Making of British Managers*,
supplemented by Harbridge Consulting Group research. This provided a
basis for estimating 1985. The study collected information from suppliers of
company training.

Market 2 is an estimate based on the survey undertaken for the
Department of Employment by Deloittes. This provided a means of
calculating the management training market for 1987, but was based on
employers' expenditure. One reason for the difference is that these figures
would include sponsored academic courses, which were excluded from the
supplier survey, and are excluded from our definitions of the market. The
correct figure probably lies between these extremes.

Growth has been estimated from an index calculated from the annual
revenue of the major competitors over the period 1987–92. The competitors
for whom such figures could be obtained covered some 16% of the total
market. This is not an ideal way to calculate growth, but was subjected to
sanity tests based on the firm's own research, and is believed to be as
accurate as was needed for the analysis. No better figures are available. 1993
was based on conversations with suppliers and buyers in February 1994.

years we have explored this in more detail, in particular researching other countries in Europe, and, of course, we had access to information about the United States through our parent company. These findings have had a profound influence on our strategy, although including the detail of the analysis would expand this chapter to book length.

The second decision was around the problem of industry definition. Figure 10.4 highlights some of the issues. The provision and delivery of management training and development services sounds like a neat industry. However, the suppliers to it, of which a few are illustrated in the figure, are frequently engaged also in related businesses. This has at least two implications: how statistical information is collated; and the gradual merging of some of the activities outside the circle with those inside it.

For example, the Management Consultancies Association publishes statistics on the consultancy industry and included in their figures is a sector that covers management training. Users of these statistics might be tempted to think that this covers the output of the management training industry. Not so: it excludes the activities of the other providers as not only are they not members of the Association but most of them are not eligible to be members.

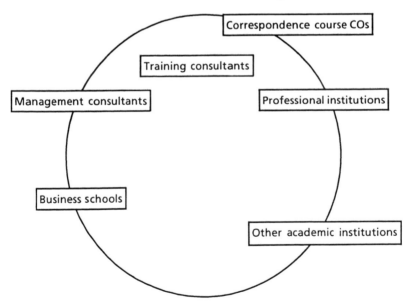

Figure 10.4 How industries overlap. The management training and development industry. (© Harbridge Consulting Group Ltd: used with permission)

Similarly, government frequently looks at the industry as if it were supplied only by the academic institutions (which in the UK are mainly public sector), and often speaks of total UK training when it actually means non-managerial training. The private sector holds a larger market share of the management training market than the public sector, even before we count the in-house training activities of the "buyers".

The related activities of providers change the dimensions of the circle. Three examples clarify this statement.

- As management consultants we frequently combine consultancy and training skills to produce a solution for clients which broadens the traditional use of training, and lies both inside and outside the circle. It is indeed one of the areas of differentiation which we seek.
- Academic qualifications moved into the industry when business schools began to offer tailored MBA degrees to individual companies and consortia of companies. An additional twist is that we run courses for two clients which are accredited by two different business schools towards their MBA degrees.
- Distance learning has been a growth sector of the industry. Not surprisingly, some of the traditional correspondence schools have developed products which compete in the industry, and organisations such as the Open University offer their products to corporate customers as well as to private individuals.

From what I have said it is apparent that the boundary of the industry, even as defined, is constantly changing. It is also apparent that different views could be taken quite logically on what the boundaries of the industry actually are. This suggests a need for careful study of some of the key competitors, including some with whom we do not compete directly, to identify the directions in which they could move and which would change the shape of the market in which we compete. Technological development alone will change the market, and thereby ensure that segment boundaries and competitive positions also change in the future.

INTERPRETING THE INDUSTRY ANALYSIS

It would be boring to most readers if I were to offer a full interpretation of the industry map. What I should like to give is enough of a description of some of the findings to carry the case study along, to help later when we look at how the information was obtained, and to make the value of such industry maps a little clearer. All the points I mention are strategically important to us, and have been used in formulating our own strategies.

- The industry is fragmented. There are numerous competitors, no one organisation has more than a 10% market share (although shares are higher in specific segments), and there are numerous buyers.
- There are no universal patterns by which the buyers organise their management training activity. It is not possible to look at an organisation from the outside and predict whether management training is centralised, decentralised, or a mix of both; or identify the level at which management development decisions are taken, how much training is performed, or what proportion is undertaken by the organisation's own staff.
- Entry barriers to the industry in general are low, but few new entrants are able to grow into significant competitors, although an exception is when the new entrant is a spin-off from an existing competitor. It is probable that there will be a future shift to more outsourcing of training by large organisations, and that this may reduce entry barriers as management buy-outs of training activities establish new competitors.
- Not only do most buyers undertake a proportion of their management training with their own resources, but a number effectively become competitors by offering their services to other organisations.
- In addition to the sectors shown on the map there are numerous segments. Competitors can be grouped roughly into those who offer a "commodity" product and those who are highly differentiated, and who support their activities with proprietary approaches. For example, we do not compete with most of the 600 organisations, and the number of competitors in our chosen segments usually varies between one and twenty. The story would be very different if we were at the commodity end of the spectrum, and I suspect that we would be a much smaller firm.
- There are "switching" costs, although they are not large enough to hold a dissatisfied buyer. The nature of these costs is that only differentiated competitors are likely to benefit from them.
- The product is perishable, in that much of what is offered is time based. Yesterday's unused consultancy time has no resale value.

- There are interesting issues around the way most buyers make their buying decisions. Management development/training departments are controlled through budgets which measure the costs of training rather than the benefits. Not surprisingly, actions follow what the system appears to demand, and most buyers would rather save £500 in the costs of an initiative (on which they are measured), than spend an extra £500 in order to gain an additional £10000 of benefit from the training (on which they are not measured).
- Many relationships between competitor and client exist at the personal level, with the advantages and disadvantages this suggests. The key for an organisation which wishes to grow is to add a parallel relationship between the consultancy and client organisations, while not destroying personal relationships.
- Because the range of subjects and methods within management training is so great, there is always an opportunity to innovate. The cost of concept development is a growth barrier to the independent one-person business.

All this can be summed up in the statement that 600 competitors are not frightening if you can take strategic actions which result in your competing with a manageable number. The opportunities to add value are very great, and the more this is done, the greater the distance the differentiated firm can gain over the bulk of the competitors.

The purists could fairly query whether all these conclusions could have been read from the example of the industry map presented here. Because it is abridged, some could not have been read off this map, although more can be seen from the originals which we use ourselves. However, all conclusions could have been reached through the exercise of completing the map, while the mapping process itself throws up areas where the "facts" do not make sense, shows clearly where there is a lack of knowledge, and often helps missing information to be arrived at by logical deduction.

PROFILING COMPETITORS

From what has been said so far, it is clear that we do not have to study 600 competitors in detail. Many can be grouped, since they behave in roughly the same way. Figure 10.5 shows some of our thinking on competitor groupings in this industry. This diagram could be expanded by adding the dimension of type of ownership,

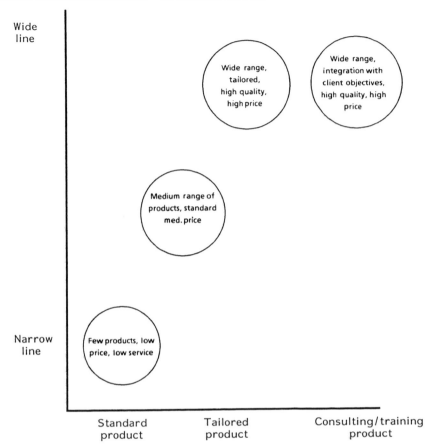

Figure 10.5 Strategic groupings: a hypothetical example from the training industry. The terms low and high are relative to each other and do not imply that one is "better" than another. (© Harbridge Consulting Group Ltd: used with permission)

since public sector organisations, for example, have very different ways of operating to private sector firms. More ideas on competitor groupings are given in McGee and Thomas (1992), McNamee (1990), and Porter (1980).

Currently we keep tabs on about 120 competitors. This includes the 20 or so that are the most significant to us, a number which have the capability of becoming more significant, and enough of the others so that we have a feel for the total situation. We do not keep information on any sole practitioners.

When we started the exercise, we had very little idea of who our competitors were. This may sound surprising to someone used to a

Financial results

	Group – SuperConsult Ltd					Division – Training					Unit				
	19XIV	19XIII	19XII	19XI	19X0	19XIV	19XIII	19XII	19XI	19X0	YR	YR	YR	YR	YR
Sales £m	10.0	9.1	8.7	8.0	7.5	6.5	6.1	5.0	4.0	3.5					
PBT £m	10.8	8	8	7	5										
PAT															
ROA															
ROS															
Prof. empl. no.	85	80	80	75											
Fees per prof. £	118	114	109	107											

Product analysis

	Sales			Direct costs			Contribution			Market share		
PRODUCT	19XIV	19XIII	19XII	YR	YR	YR	YR	YR	YR	19XIV	YR	YR
1 Tailored	5	2	–							1%		
2 Other in co. £M	3.0	2.5	2.0							1%		
3 Public courses £M	3.0	3.4	3.0							0.5%		
4												
5												
6												
7												
8												

Marketing and sales activity

1 Quarterly newsletter

2 Regular exhibits

3 Regular promotional seminars

4 Monthly direct mail campaign

Sources of competitive advantage

SOURCE	NOTES
Infrastructure	
R & D	
Logistics in Operations	Own printing facility
Logistics out	Mainly use own staff for delivery
Marketing	
Sales	Specialist sales force
Services	Strong customer service orientation

Importance of activity to group

SuperConsult is:

10% of UWS revenue
7% of UWS profit

Growing twice as fast as the whole group

Scope of international operations

Total group is strong in North America, UK, Singapore. Weak in the rest of Europe and other S. East Asian countries

typical industry structure where there are clear market leaders, but less so I suspect to someone from a similar fragmented professional services market. The steps we took to find out will be discussed later. It took two to three years from our first researches to developing profiles in the form illustrated in Figure 10.6.

The profile illustrated is a fictitious example, but I have tried to

Key factors	Apparent strategy
1 Own training college 2 Offers training (Management) in all European languages 3 Ties into world network 4 New CEOs in parent and SuperConsult. Watch for changes 5 Clients from bottom half of Times 1000 and similar European companies 6 Prices at high end of their sectors	1 Targeting tailored training market 2 Developing new products (recent advert for development personnel) 3 Will not expand UK college 4 Expected to open French college 19XV 5 Major expansion of Continental client base

Strengths	Weaknesses	Organisation philosophy
1 Reputation in standardised training and open courses 2 Strong financial backing but parent co. wants dividend growth	1 Not well known among larger cos. who buy tailored 2 Employs the wrong people for tailored work 3 High staff turnover	Historically country companies have all reported to US parent Recent announcements suggest a change to a more global approach Do not use external associates – employees only
Implications	**Implications**	
Could solve all problems but corporate cash box only available for quick return projects	Strategy may be defeated by HR issues	

CSF ratings

Factor	Competitor	Own	Index
Quality image	6	9	67
Degree known	8	6	133
Quality of staff	6	9	67
Proprietary concepts	5	5	100
Financial resources	8	4	200

Notes

Assess each factor 0–10 index is
$$\frac{\text{COMPETITOR SCORE}}{\text{OWN SCORE}}$$

Personnel policies

Professional staff have degrees or professional qualifications. Recent adverts seek post graduate degrees

Salaries at academic scales plus profit sharing. Some difficulty recruiting

No equity participation – a quoted US company

Figure 10.6 (see opposite page also) Competitor profile: SuperConsult Ltd (a subsidiary of World Consulting Services). (© Harbridge Consulting Group Ltd: used with permission)

make it realistic by not completing every information cell. Complete information on any competitor is very rare. What the profile shows is where the competitor gains its revenue, and a series of notepads for recording strategic information, focusing on what really matters when we formulate our own strategies Most of the notepad items are self-explanatory, although two deserve further explanation.

(1) Sources of competitive advantage. This is the first step towards
     a value chain analysis, and moves on a little from where we are
     in our own situation towards ideas we are beginning to
     develop. Porter (1985) discusses value chains. In our own
     business we are still some way from having the information
     that makes their use possible.
(2) CSF ratings. This is an abbreviation for critical success factors,
     and is a useful standard for competitive comparisons. CSFs are
     those factors which are essential to success in an industry. They
     are not necessarily the same across all segments. For example,
     the "commodity" competitors require different CSFs to those
     which are essential for us to compete at the differentiated end of
     the market. An example from the detergents industry may be
     clearer. The CSFs of a brand operator like Unilever, part of
     whose success comes from identifying new demand and
     creating a market image, are not the same as those needed for
     success in contract manufacture, where the task is to supply
     own-label products to retailers. The contract manufacturer has
     to be able to produce low-cost products which are similar to the
     brand leaders, and has to react very quickly to new
     opportunities. However, this type of business needs no
     understanding of consumer marketing, since it does not own
     any brands of its own.

     What this profiling has done for us is to provide more discipline to
our collection of information. It has given us the opportunity to
deduce missing parts of the jigsaw puzzle, provided a means of
storing information in an easily retrievable way, and given us a
series of documents that, with the industry map, allow us to survey
a vast array of information painlessly when making our own plans.
It has become easier for us to identify firms in the industry where
collaboration is possible, and to pinpoint appropriate competitors
whom we would recommend to clients (strange as it might seem,
this happens, and if we are making a recommendation we like to be
sure that we are pointing the client to the right people).

     While we have by no means reached perfection in our profiling,
and still tend to update records in blitzes, rather than as a
continuous process, we have been able to develop a much better
understanding of our industry map through this additional work.
We have also been able to draw up some very useful generic
comparisons of strengths and weaknesses between ourselves and
different competitor groups (for example, business schools), while
understanding the individual differences within each competitor

group. In a fragmented market, it is more useful to find a strategy that builds advantages over the majority of competitors, rather than trying to beat each one singly. Products, image, and philosophies that result from this sort of exercise have to stand the test of the market.

DEFINING A COMPETITOR'S BUSINESS

Some of the original thinking about business definition comes from Abell (1980), who suggested plotting businesses on a three-dimensional chart showing customer functions, customer groups, and alternative technologies. Several variations on these themes are possible, and indeed one could delve much deeper into the literature on segmentation to develop the ideas further.

We used simpler matrix displays, which helped us to show the difference between ourselves and other organisations in a diagrammatic way. Figure 10.7 shows some of the actual charts we made, although I have taken off the names. What these did for us was to make us realise the considerable difference in focus of businesses which we had seen as roughly comparable to ourselves. Some, although of high standing and quality, do not really compete with us at all, although we still monitor them because they may change!

In a less fragmented industry, I should have spent more time on this more detailed type of analysis. The number of competitors, and their low market shares, means that the value of going deeper than we have is questionable.

OBTAINING THE INFORMATION

None of this analysis would have been possible if we had been unable to obtain any information. In the beginning the task was somewhat daunting and it would have been easy to decide that nothing could be done as the information was too sparse. In the early years desk research yielded very little, because little was published at that time. This meant that we had to consider primary research, if we were to obtain any information at all. Our first major competitor study was undertaken in 1985, and this set a foundation which helped us make sense of information from other sources. After that time there was an increase in the number of published research studies, which meant that our information was becoming more complete.

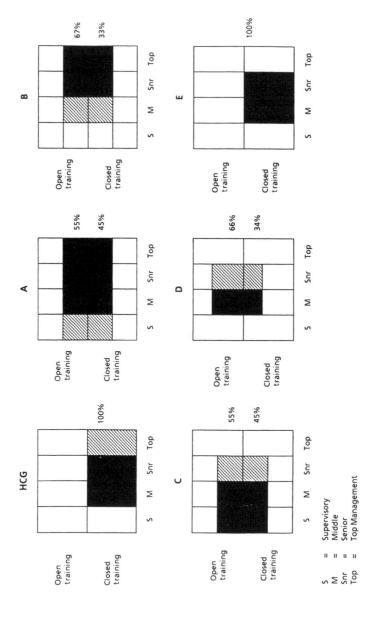

Figure 10.7 Management training activities: a sample of competitors. White = normal activity, black = heavy activity, shaded = some activity. (© Harbridge Consulting Group Ltd: used with permission)

Our first piece of research into the market was completed in 1983. This was not at that time intended to help us follow the sort of competitor analysis described in this chapter, but was the first of a series of reports that we have carried out into management development and training to increase our knowledge of the "state of the art" and to gain marketing information. Most of these reports are published, so that they can be shared with other interested parties, and although they have contributed greatly to our understanding of buyer behaviour, and awareness of changing needs and responses, they are not primarily market research reports.

In 1985 we undertook two interrelated pieces of research. We wanted to find out whether the market for our type of training was expanding. Were we getting our fair share of the growth? What were the factors that the buyers considered when choosing a supplier?

We knew many of our competitors, but did we know them all? There was a great gap between the ones we could list and the columns of names shown in directories. Who were the competitors who might be considered most critical to our future? Who did the buyers think were our competitors, and who did our competitors think were their most serious rivals? We wanted to know if we were competitive in price, quality, speed of response to the client, and in our overall philosophies: and we wanted to answer the same questions for each major competitor. From this, our first intention was to prepare a market-related assessment of our strengths and weaknesses, relative to those of competitors.

A sample survey was conducted by telephone of 43 buyers of our type of training service, exploring aspects of all the research objectives. We interviewed on a personal visit nine major competitors, building up our list of real competitors from information supplied by buyers and competitors. We were able to check much of the information provided by competitors from the interviews with buyers. All this research was done honestly and openly by one of our consultants.

The information from this survey provided the base from which we could build, and develop on the lines already discussed, and led to immediate tactical and strategic decisions. Meanwhile, we continued to add more valuable data from our research for publication, and focused some of this on areas of the industry map which were hitherto blank. We published a report on distance learning, for example, in 1986, and another in late 1989 on consortium and company MBAs. Although not part of the published report, this survey enabled us to quantify the size of this sector of the market. As Table 10.3 shows, many of the earlier studies have been

Table 10.3 Primary research undertaken by us for the analysis

Date	Published	Unpublished
1983	Management training in UK companies	—
1984	MBA and UK industry	
1985		Competitor study
1986	Tailored management education	
1986	Distance learning	
1987	—	Competitor inform project
1988	—	Innovation training
1988	—	Management skills
1989	Consortium/Co. MBAs	
1989		Management training Europe part 1
1989	—	Management training Europe part 2
1989		Hotels/study centres
1990	—	Competitor update
1991	Management training in UK companies	—
1992	Competency assessment	
1993	Company MBA	
1993	Management training in UK businesses	
1993		Competitor update

regularly updated and expanded, so that we are able to note trends and changes in the market.

In 1987 we used an MBA student, to build up the files of competitor information which we had started to compile. This involved collecting brochures from competitors, annual reports (where available), and press cuttings. In addition, we established our first database, using an earlier format of competitor profile. We did the usual searches at Companies House, and probably bored the Charity Commissioners with our complaints about competitors who were registered as charities and who had not lodged their returns for several years.

Most of this activity is typical of competitor analysis generally. Three activities which yielded useful information were:

• Continued direct contact with competitors, including the exchange of the sort of information which would be in the annual report had we all been private limited companies. The competitor analysis system we have built up means that there is somewhere to put the results of all these formal and informal comments, as well as information that comes to us about a competitor from elsewhere in the industry.

- Obtaining feedback from clients when there is a prequalifying exercise or a competitive bid (whether we win or lose). This has been an invaluable source of information. On occasion, buyers have prepared an analysis of all the bidders which they have been willing to share.
- Helping journalists to write about the industry, and suggesting who to approach for the collection of data for league tables. In this way we filled in a number of gaps in our own information, especially as a few firms who had refused to exchange information with us on grounds of confidentiality did not feel the same inhibitions when it was a question of gaining publicity.

Published information and market intelligence have become more important since 1987. A number of studies have been completed, which when supplemented by our own studies have enabled us to quantify the sectors on our industry map. There is still no sound statistical base for the industry, but the combination of all our sources means that we believe that our estimates are as accurate as they need to be for the type of decisions that have to be made.

In 1989 we reworked our competitor database, and now store information in a form similar to the profiles in this chapter. We had hopes of creating a dynamic database that enabled us to update the industry map automatically every time a competitor profile was updated. This is not economic at present. The main conclusion that can be reached from our work is that a competitor analysis system will improve over time if continuous effort is applied, that even small pieces of information can be coordinated and used if there is a mechanism to handle them, and that lack of published information about an industry and competitors may make analysis harder, but need not prevent it.

We have begun to extend the scope of our study to other countries in Europe, and have spent more effort on identifying organisations we can build alliances with than undertaking a complete competitor analysis.

BUILDING COMPETITIVE ADVANTAGE

None of this analysis is worth while unless it leads to actions. The sort of strategic and tactical actions which we took may give an indication to readers of benefits they might obtain from competitor analysis.

- We identified much more clearly where we could gain differentiation, and where there were market segments where we could gain clear advantage.
- As a result, one of the things we did was to build our geographic and language capability, so that through our own resources or alliances with other organisations we are able to run the same course for a multinational company in every West European language. This is especially important when the course is intended to support a European-wide strategy by the client.
- We started many new initiatives to build image and awareness, including our regular publication *Management Update* (10 issues per year, free to management development and human resources personnel). We redesigned all our stationery and literature to achieve a common image.
- A strategy was developed for operations in other countries in Europe.
- A number of different products and concepts were developed.
- The growth of in-company MBA schemes made us seek to become better informed about what was happening, and to find ways in which our work could gain academic accreditation in certain circumstances, without in any way losing our commercial image for that of a pseudo-business school.
- We identified private sector competitors who operated in our sector of the market, and began moves to establish a trade association among those with whom we shared common concerns.

At the tactical level we are now able to identify more accurately which competitors are significant for different types of assignment, and their respective strengths and weaknesses. Even when we do not know who else has been asked to bid, this helps us plan our own proposals and presentation in a way that emphasises our advantages.

We redesigned our basic approach to proposal writing, so that our strengths insofar as they were appropriate to the assignment were presented in such a way as to invite the client to probe to see whether other bidders also possessed them. Our research had shown significant areas where we knew that many of the competitors likely to be asked to bid did not possess similar strengths. Almost immediately after completing our 1985 competitor study we had opportunities to apply these tactical concepts, and won two major assignments on competitive bids in quick succession. We developed strong long-term relationships with both clients.

Our strategy has helped us to grow faster than the market since the mid-1980s, and our concepts of industry and competitor analysis have helped us to develop these strategies. Add this to the benefits which I have observed our clients gain from similar approaches, and the value of competitor analysis becomes clear. However, it is not without cost, and anyone thinking of undertaking it needs to decide whether they are looking for a one-off injection of competitor data into their strategy formulation or wish to set up a continuing system. Either needs a dedication of effort, and the continuing system needs some attention to organisation and resources.

In either case, and whether the aim of competitor analysis is tactical or strategic, the only justification for the costs and effort is the action that results from the new knowledge. I hope that this case history has given some indication of the benefits, as well as a methodology, and that it shows that an initial lack of competitor information can sometimes be overcome.

REFERENCES

Abell, D. (1980) *Defining the Business*, Englewood Cliffs, NJ, Prentice Hall.

McGee, J. and Thomas, H. (1992) Strategic groups and intra-industry competition. In Hussey, D. E. (ed.), *International Review of Strategic Management*, Vol. 3, Chichester, John Wiley.

McNamee, P. (1990) The group competitive intensity map: a means of displaying competitive position. In Hussey, D. E. (ed.), *International Review of Strategic Management*, Vol. 1, Chichester, John Wiley.

Porter, M. (1980) *Competitive Strategy*, New York, The Free Press.

Porter, M. (1985) *Competitive Advantage*, New York, The Free Press.

11

STRESS AND STRATEGIC CHANGE

Marie McHugh

University of Ulster at Jordanstown

INTRODUCTION

The ever-increasing pace of change in world markets and governments has placed renewed emphasis upon the need for organizations to develop dynamic, competitive strategies. However, the competitive environment of most organizations has become increasingly complex and difficult to monitor. Cowen and Osborne (1993) suggest that strategies must be carefully formulated and based upon adequate information incorporating, for example: financial analysis; productivity measurement; marketplace intelligence; trends management; and executive evaluation. Failure to create and respond to information tools which can keep them attuned to change leave organizations in a position whereby they are intuitively managed and thus court catastrophe.

To survive, organizations must address any issue which may impede their performance or threaten their competitiveness, and this may necessitate embarking upon programmes of strategic change. Although such programmes may hold the key to organizational survival and success, it is essential that managers clearly identify what needs to be changed. This may be effected by thorough organizational and environmental analyses, which form the basis for devising a feasible action plan for implementing the change.

Rethinking Strategic Management
Edited by D. E. Hussey. © 1995 John Wiley & Sons Ltd

However, such problem identification and problem-solving activities are often hampered by a host of prevailing environmental forces, not least of which is the world-wide recession, which creates turbulence and places additional demands and pressures upon organizations and their members.

Organizational difficulties associated with this current instability are highlighted by Sillence (1993), who indicates that, under pressure from the international recession and the need for a dynamic response, employee numbers have contracted, and cost and time pressures have quickly increased. Thus, senior management are finding it increasingly difficult to manage the short term and, at the same time, strategically plan for the medium and long term.

While environmental forces have had a significant effect upon privately run corporations, public sector organizations have not been immune to external turbulence and the organization change process. Major governmental changes concerning, for example, health care in the United States, the introduction of a market economy in Russia, and the growing market awareness in China have had a profound effect upon the management of state-owned organizations. Since the late 1970s, numerous changes have swept through the UK Civil Service, incorporated in, amongst others, the Financial Management Initiative (FMI), the Ibbs Report (1988), and the Citizen's Charter. Additionally, it may be argued that environmental forces, such as recession, impact upon public sector organizations through reduced government revenues coupled with enhanced pressure upon available resources (for example, unemployment benefit payments). These changes have diminished traditionally perceived differences between the public and private sectors, and have transformed the functioning of state organizations, placing an ever-increasing emphasis upon efficiency and effectiveness.

For all organizations to weather the current storm and enjoy heightened success in the coming years, it is imperative that managers respond to the diverse range of forces which impact upon their enterprises. However, these forces may create cumulative pressures for organization members through enhanced competitive pressure, technological change, skill obsolescence, and redefined work roles. It would seem likely that the imposition of these pressures will, in turn, pose a major challenge for managers, compelling them to help individual members of staff cope with any difficulties experienced as a result of these demands.

Such pressures come at a time when an organization's people are being increasingly regarded as a major corporate asset which cannot be ignored, and whose creative potential must be exploited. Serieyx

(1987) suggests that quality performance can only be obtained through constant effort and innovation at all levels of the organization, starting with the shopfloor. This view is endorsed by Sparrow and Pettigrew (1988) who highlight a need for a longer-term focus on the management of human resources where people are viewed as assets as opposed to commodities. Furthermore, Goetschin (1987) notes that the management of human resources has become one of the key components of business strategy, where efforts aim to ensure that human resource management is fully integrated with the strategy and the strategic needs of the firm (Schuler, 1992). These sentiments are also emphasized by Serieyx (1987), who suggests that the prosperous enterprise of the year 2000 will mobilize the intelligence and effort of all its personnel. However, given the heterogeneous range of forces at work within the private and public sectors, some (for example, Richards, 1993) appear to be rather sceptical with regard to the possibility of operationalizing such beliefs.

It may be argued that many individuals and organizations perceive the traumatic changes which have taken place to be imposed upon them by external forces, and a cause of deep uncertainty regarding their future. This uncertainty is caused by factors perceived to be largely beyond the control of employees. Thus, individuals within such operating environments are likely to experience a sense of powerlessness, which may erode their ability to cope with the stress caused by threats posed to their organizations and their livelihood. Consequently, it would seem fair to suggest that the pressures placed upon organization members at this time will accumulate and lead to an epidemic of employee stress. Overall, this has created a new and daunting challenge for those associated with strategic human resource management (SHRM). If one accepts that SHRM is concerned with getting everyone from the top of the human organization to the bottom doing things which make the business successful (Schuler, 1992), it would seem fitting that now, more then ever, there is a need to consider work stress, its adverse effects upon human resources, and its management, as issues of strategic importance.

JOB STRESS: A PROBLEM OF STRATEGIC IMPORTANCE FOR ORGANIZATIONS

The pressures associated with recession, enhanced competition, renewed emphasis upon productivity issues, services, and accountability, allied to the uncertainty which is characteristic of organization change, are potential sources of stress. Pressures and uncertainty of this nature may be brought about by increased work targets, threats of job loss, changes in job holders' responsibilities and authority, shifts in the balance of power, and general upheaval. As such, these pressure sources are reflected in many of the core job stressors noted by Cooper (1986), Matteson and Ivancevich (1987), and Fletcher (1991). These include: intrinsic job factors; career development; role in the organization; relationships at work; organization structure and climate; technological change; being redundant; and the home–work interface.

For organizations, the adverse effects of stress may act as an impediment to the formulation and implementation of coherent dynamic strategies, the achievement of competitive advantage, and the change process. These effects may be seen in poor job performance, high levels of absenteeism, discontent among the workforce, high labour turnover with the loss of "good" employees, and a large increase in recruitment and retraining costs (Matteson and Ivancevich, 1987; Brief and Atieh, 1987; McHugh and Brennan, 1992).

Some would argue (for example, Chusmir and Franks, 1988; Arroba and James, 1990), that organizational problems such as sick pay, absenteeism, high levels of labour turnover, and lower job satisfaction may be directly or indirectly related to stress. Thus they may be regarded as costs which ultimately have an effect upon strategy formulation and implementation, and overall organizational performance. The costs associated with stress at work appear to be particularly severe in Britain. To illustrate, the British Heart Foundation has estimated that coronary heart disease (CHD), some of which may be attributed to stress, costs £200 per employee per year (McDubhghaill, 1991). Furthermore, Kearns (1986) suggests that 60% of absence from work is caused by stress-related illness. The magnitude of this problem is reflected in the recent estimate that employee stress costs British industry in excess of £7 billion per year (BBC, 1993). This figure indicates a significant increase from that suggested by the Confederation of British Industry (CBI) in 1990. At that time, stress-related absenteeism and labour turnover was considered to cost British organizations £1.5 billion per year (Summers, 1990). It might be suggested that the recent attention given to the issue of employee stress within occupational health and safety legislation reflects a new level of public awareness and acknowledgement of the importance of individual wellbeing within the work environment.

In an increasingly competitive and fast-changing operating environment, it can be argued that those engaged in SHRM should feel compelled to address the issue of work-related stress through counting the costs and taking appropriate action to minimize its effects. The need to address such a costly organizational problem is presented in the following case studies of two UK-based organizations: a privately owned firm within the giftware sector; and a state-owned organization. The organizations are not named for reasons of confidentiality.

THE CASE STUDIES

In each case, organizational analyses were carried out in March 1993. Secondary data were obtained from each organization regarding:

- Financial status (for example, changes in costs and profit levels)
- Changes in strategy/policy including the stimulus for change, nature and effects of the change
- Employee performance including performance levels, change in performance, and absenteeism.

Additionally, a representative sample of employees took part in semi-structured interviews. Overall, 30% of employees within the private sector and 8% within the public sector organizations were interviewed. The participants represented each functional area and level within the organizational hierarchy. However, within these parameters interviewees were randomly selected. The interviews aimed to generate qualitative data regarding the effects on the organization of:

- The current recession
- Government policy changes
- Efforts to remain competitive/improve customer service
- Restructuring
- Redefinition of work roles.

Interviewees also provided information regarding the personal effects of the issues listed in terms of job performance, motivation, and attitudes to work.

Content analysis was carried out on the interview data. Subsequent findings, together with secondary data, provided two illustrations of the impact of change on the organizations and their employees. These are presented below.

THE PRIVATE SECTOR ORGANIZATION

The Organization

This privately owned company is a relatively small manufacturing firm within the giftware sector which employs 127 people. Originally the company had two divisions: a craft division manufacturing tableware and an alumina engineering division. However, reduced employee performance together with declining demand for the firm's products, partly caused by recession and the increased availability of cheaper substitute products, have impacted upon the organization. These have led to cash-flow problems, a climate of uncertainty and insecurity, restructuring, redundancies, and redefined work roles.

In 1992, reduced product demand, sales and cash-flow difficulties, which were a result of the recession, forced an announcement that the tableware division would undergo downsizing and 39 people would be made redundant. Two members of the management team were to be transferred to another division with their roles redefined. Although these individuals were to receive the same remuneration as before, they were expected to assume additional duties within a division, i.e. alumina engineering, with which they were unfamiliar.

In March 1993 the rundown of the tableware division was underway and the upheaval and uncertainty, coupled with the sense of powerlessness and failure on the part of employees, were perceived to be a source of stress to all organization members, but especially to those facing redundancy. Downsizing of the division has led to the alumina division facing higher overhead costs and a new structure. Many members of staff are having their roles redefined, are assuming additional tasks, with little or no extra monetary reward, and have new superiors and working relationships.

The Stressful Effects of Organization Change

In addition to the threat of redundancy experienced by tableware staff, these individuals are perceived to be vulnerable to additional stressors due to their potential skill obsolescence. Only a very small number of other organizations engaged in similar manufacturing work exist within a 75–mile radius of the company. Thus, in the event of redundancy, these craftspeople are likely to find it exceptionally difficult to find alternative employment without moving to much more distant locations.

The effects of job stress have become evident throughout the organization. The organizational analyses revealed an increase in industrial accidents and absenteeism, compared to previously recorded levels. During interviews individual employees reported a simultaneous decline in productivity and motivation. Meanwhile, the organization has experienced higher costs and lower profits which further threaten its ability to compete and to survive.

A deterioration in physical health was noted by 15% of respondents. This manifested itself through heart attacks, muscular seizure, and gall stones. The timing of these illnesses tended to coincide with rumours of organizational difficulties and announcements of downsizing; this would seem to suggest that work stress was a contributory or causal factor. The sickness experienced by organization members has given rise to long absences of key production staff and increases in sick pay, training, and performance costs associated with increased error rates and material wastage.

The behavioural effects of stress are reflected in declining employee motivation and satisfaction evidenced by comments made during interviews with production staff, especially within the tableware division. People within this division worked hard to boost productivity in an attempt to facilitate survival. However, they consider their efforts to have been defeated by the forces of recession and have given up, perceiving themselves to have failed. They are resentful of their current situation and often attribute the organization's inability to compete, to the perceived incompetence and poor decision making of management. They sometimes refuse to work a period of notice, absenteeism has risen, and theft is rife. Such behaviour is indicative of organizational frustration as described by Chen and Spector (1992).

Within the alumina division employees are constantly under pressure to achieve ever-increasing work targets. In response to current organizational difficulties, external consultants were asked to examine the operation of the division and to make recommendations for performance improvements or, alternatively, selling the division. Meanwhile, management within the division have been asked to justify their past performance, proving that they were efficient and effective. However, inefficiencies have been identified: for example, the consultants revealed that scrap levels were higher than had been assumed, costings were inaccurate, scheduling was inaccurate leading to late deliveries, and much duplication in production existed. Given the vulnerable state of the organization, each of these poses a threat to its survival and to the livelihood of the people within it.

The organizational analyses indicated that many of the key stressors identified by Cooper (1986) were evident, these included:

- Imposed structural change as an outcome of the crisis facing the organization
- Insufficient sales which place the job security of individuals in jeopardy
- New computerized systems which demand the acquisition of new skills, and which potentially usurp manual tasks
- Role ambiguity as a consequence of uncertainty and confusion
- Role overload for managers due to the assumption of additional job tasks
- Role underload for operatives as a result of declines in product and sales demand.

THE PUBLIC SECTOR ORGANIZATION

The experiences of the public sector organization and its employees, although somewhat different from those described above, have been no less dramatic and stressful. As noted previously, many public sector organizations across the world are experiencing ongoing change, the results of which are likely to impact upon individual employees.

The Organization

This organization provides a public service as an agent for a central government department. The collaborative relationship which exists between them is similar to that operationalized by the Next Steps agency initiative.

The organization has a staff of between 2500 and 3500. These are employed at a range of grades and disciplines (for example, managers, technical specialists, manual workers and other support staff). A central headquarters assumes responsibility for policy decisions and local offices deal with enquiries from the general public. Thus, the majority of staff are concentrated at operational level in local offices, dealing directly with the public. A core group of mainly high-level professional staff exists at headquarters.

Effects of Organizational Change

Funding for the organization is provided by the government department and it must work within a specified budgetary framework. In the current economic climate, characterized by cuts in government spending, this budget is becoming worth less in real terms. Frequently staff are forced to bear the effects of this in the form of a reduction in resource provision and, potentially, restrictions on pay. Often it is the case that vacant posts are not filled immediately. Consequently staff are required to assume additional or changed responsibilities. Government policies and changes in the level of need for the organization's services have resulted in a reduction in staff levels by 14–18% since 1988. Furthermore, career development is limited due to redeployments and organizational downsizing, which mean that traditional promotion opportunities have not become available for open staff competition in recent times.

Through its attempts to adopt a more flexible, organic structure, many job roles within the organization have become less well defined. Among qualified professional staff, especially, there is a perception of reduced job status.

The Current Organizational Position

Employees perceived themselves to be experiencing stress and associated this with potential job insecurity throughout the organization. This has been further enhanced by technological advances which have absorbed manual tasks; a development which has occurred at all levels. Thus the generally accepted view that the public sector provides "a job for life" is no longer valid.

In its response to external demands to become more business-like, individual departments have been encouraged to view themselves as business units. All staff are now expected to participate in planning for this process. Such plans are part of the organization's effort to increase its marketability in the face of competitive tendering.

The organizational analyses revealed that, under the UK government's policy to test the competitive tendering process (CCT), it proved uneconomical to keep some key areas of work in-house. Through CCT, the in-house units acted in competition with outside agencies for contracts. They failed in their efforts and consequently the majority of staff in these units were made redundant. CCT is viewed as a major threat and a prominent stressor. It is widely accepted within the organization that the process will affect most elements of its service within the next three to five years, due to the increasing focus on improving public service and response to customer needs and expectations.

Staff in local offices have been exposed to further stressors. These individuals deal with the general public and feel that they have to implement decisions which the organization was forced to make at a corporate level, and which can be difficult to reconcile when dealing directly with the "client" on a daily basis. The often-conflicting demands of client and management are considered stressful by local office staff. Thus, there is often a problem of balancing the competitive demands of the "client" and the "organization".

Individuals perceive recent changes to have acted as stressors. Concerns regarding future prospects within the organization have not been alleviated due to a limited consultation process. Initial indicators suggest that the stress experienced by organization members is evidenced by an increase in labour turnover and absenteeism, and a deterioration in the quality of interpersonal relationships among colleagues. Many employees are disillusioned and have sought work elsewhere. As mentioned previously, vacancies are either being filled through redeployment or individuals are not being replaced. This may be interpreted as a saving in terms of recruitment, retraining, and salary costs. However, an alternative view is that the adverse effects of additional stress experienced by existing staff due to, for example, role overload and thwarted career development outweigh any potential benefits.

Management within the organization consider levels of absenteeism to be relatively high. When placed in the context of the evidence presented by Kearns (1986), referred to earlier, that 60% of absenteeism is caused by stress-related illness, it is suggested that, in 1992, approximately 21 000 days of absenteeism within the organization were attributable to stress. With regard to the quality of working relationships, stress is also evidenced through an increasingly perceived lack of sensitivity in dealing with others and a reported increase in competition between internal departments. Such behaviours have been described by Chen and Spector (1992) as outcomes of organizational frustration and stress which they believe are damaging to the organization.

Employees are generally aware of the cultural changes taking place within the organization and the need for them to play an active role in the change process, rather than being left as powerless victims of externally imposed policies. However, the reality of the change process would seem to suggest that the organization has been thrown into a state of disarray, with individuals believing that too many things are being pressed forward at once, and none of these are being completed satisfactorily.

The Staff Attitude Survey

The conclusions from the organizational analyses outlined above are supported by the findings of a recent in-house staff attitude survey. The latter provided staff with an opportunity to express their views on developments within the organization, and the effects which these are having upon them as individuals.

As with other staff attitude surveys, this required respondents to complete questionnaires covering a number of areas (for example, job satisfaction, organizational change, communications, training, development, and other personnel issues). Through the organization's survey it was revealed that a higher level of perceived stress was evident in offices which directly serve the public, i.e. local offices, as opposed to central headquarters. The survey, which included a 25% sample of all employees, revealed that *all* respondents were, to some degree, affected by job stress. While employee stress was not specifically under investigation, a number of the main survey findings indicate the presence of typical organizational constraints outlined by Peters and O'Connor (1980). Overall:

- 67% were "frequently interrupted" in their work
- 59% considered the volume of work excessive
- 57% complained of having insufficient information to carry out their job properly or not getting it in time
- 40% reported that they did not know how their duties fitted into the organization
- 52% of clerical and administrative staff expressed concerns about their posts becoming obsolete due to technological advances
- 34% indicated that juggling work/home demands presented a problem
- 27% suggested that bringing work pressures home caused domestic and relationship stress
- 40% reported poor communication with their section head
- 67% indicated that an enhanced staff welfare service would help ease problems.

The difficulties cited above were particularly salient among local

office staff. Such constraints are considered by researchers such as
Rizzo *et al.* (1970), Peters and O'Connor (1980), and Fletcher (1991) to
be a source of stress.

MANAGING THE STRESS PROBLEM: AN
ORGANIZATIONAL RESPONSIBILITY

The main causes and effects of stress highlighted within the two
organizations are summarized in Table 11.1. Many of the key
stressors and their effects were common to the private and public
sector organizations. These tended to reflect enhanced competition,
technological change, recession, and organizational change.
Consequently it would seem fair to suggest that the environments
within which *all* organizations operate create similar difficulties for

Table 11.1   Key causes and effects of stress within two organizations

	Private sector organization	Public sector organization
Causes of stress		
Threat of redundancy	*	*
Technological change	*	*
Skill obsolescence	*	*
Poor organizational climate	*	*
Competitive pressures	*	*
Redefined work roles	*	*
Role overload	*	*
Role conflict		*
Limited career development		*
Poor communication		*
Effects of stress		
Ill health	*	*
Absenteeism	*	*
Accidents	*	
Labour turnover	*	*
Reduced productivity	*	*
Reduced motivation	*	
Reduced satisfaction		*
Higher costs	*	
Lower profits	*	
Poor relationships		*

state-owned or private corporations and their employees. Thus, given the universal demand for enhanced levels of organizational efficiency and effectiveness, it is essential that organizations recognize work stress as being an impediment to those organizational processes which facilitate the achievement of these objectives, i.e. strategy implementation. Therefore it is imperative that stress management form an integral part of human resource strategy and consequently becomes embedded in the strategy of the organization.

Within the privately owned manufacturing organization discussed above, stress management provision has been non-existent, with individuals relying heavily upon the social support network. However, it would seem fair to suggest that this approach is totally inadequate, and the current instability and vulnerability of the organization renders it an inappropriate means of dealing with human problems of strategic importance.

The array of operational difficulties currently facing the organization appear to have resulted in neglect of vital human resource difficulties. The organization and its people seem to be caught in a spiral whereby much of the stress experienced by individuals is exacerbated by competitive pressure which, in turn, causes further stress. Thus the cycle of negativity not only repeats itself but its consequences become potentially more disastrous with each twist of the spiral. This organization suffers difficulties devoting time to vital strategic issues which might help safeguard the future of the enterprise. Additionally, it can be argued that the existing social support network must be ineffectual due to the fact that its core components, i.e. the organization members, are themselves likely to be experiencing the adverse effects of stress. Indeed, the network may be in danger of virtual extinction due to current high levels of environmental turbulence which threaten the survival of the organization.

Within the public sector organization, on the other hand, the issue of employee stress has been addressed in a more systematic fashion. It is widely accepted within the organization that it is good management practice to care for the welfare and personal wellbeing of staff. Thus it would seem fair to suggest that there is an "awareness" that individual and organizational wellbeing are interdependent entities. This awareness is reflected in a number of developments within the organization. For example:

• The personnel policy states that the organization recognizes its responsibility to employees to promote health in the workplace.

- Following a health awareness seminar in 1992, a health agenda was devised for the organization with a particular focus on the three A's: raising Awareness; changing Attitudes; and prompting Action.
- A number of internal research papers have recommended a health promotion action plan for 1993. However, as yet, the organization has not engaged in comprehensive stress-management activities, although it is its expressed intention to do so in the near future.

For some organizations, the recognition afforded to the costs of stress in terms of decreased performance, high levels of absenteeism, low morale, and job satisfaction has acted as a stimulus in the development of stress management initiatives. Many American and Japanese organizations have addressed the issue of job stress based upon their increased understanding of the relationship between stress and performance outcomes (Cooper, 1986; Sullivan, 1987). Although the benefits which accrue from such initiatives are substantial, only a limited number of British and European firms have become involved in the provision of stress management programmes. One of the perceived difficulties in implementing stress management programmes is the lack of cooperation from top management and failure to recognize stress as an issue which must be integrated within SHRM. The prevailing notion among many senior managers is that stress is a problem for individual employees, not for the organization. However, evidence such as that presented by McHugh (1993) would suggest that this idea is inherently wrong, stress is a costly organizational problem. As Crawley (1993) suggests, the challenge to organizations is to think and act differently in terms of "managing" and "stress". Thus it is necessary to understand that stress is not just the personal problem of the individual concerned; it is also a problem for the organization.

The presence of stress management initiatives implies that management within *a number of organizations recognize* some or all of the following, i.e. that:

- The negative effects of stress are initially experienced by the individual but they also have costly consequences for their organizations.
- Individual and organizational health are interdependent entities.
- Stress is an unnecessary cost which must be reduced.
- People are a most valuable resource which must be supported and protected.

The conspicuous absence of stress management programmes implies that managers within *many organizations do not recognize* and are guilty of some or all of the following, i.e. they:

- Fail to recognize the costly consequences of stress at work
- Do not perceive individual and organizational health to be interdependent entities
- Do not perceive stress to be an unnecessary cost which must be reduced
- Are unaware of the existence of stress within their organizations
- Are ill informed as to the various courses of action which they should take to solve stress problems
- Do not perceive people to be a most valuable resource which must be supported and protected.

Thus it is argued that for the efficient management of organizations faced with a wide range of additive pressures, managing and reducing the problem of work-related stress must be a deep and all-encompassing issue of strategy which pervades all aspects of organizational functioning. As with other aspects of SHRM, it must link, integrate, and cohere across levels in organizations (Schuler, 1992).

A HOLISTIC APPROACH TO MANAGING STRESS WITHIN ORGANIZATIONS

One holistic approach to stress management within organizations which embraces these concepts is outlined by McHugh and Brennan (1992). Total Stress Management (TSM), which may be viewed as a derivative of Total Quality Management (TQM), is a pervasive organizational philosophy and a practical approach to stress management which focuses upon the elimination of a costly organizational defect. It aims to help organizations achieve optimal stress levels in all areas of organizational functioning, and in all individual organization members so that they may experience enhanced levels of efficiency and effectiveness. As part of the organization's human resource strategy, it may be perceived as a plan which aims to address and solve fundamental strategic issues related to human resource management.

In itself TSM may be viewed as an organization change initiative. Additionally, however, it acts as a necessary accompaniment to other initiatives by facilitating new ways of working, through helping organization members cope effectively with organization change. Thus, given the current climate of competitive pressure, instability, and change, it is argued that TSM is ideally suited to all organizations. The four-stage all-encompassing action model is outlined schematically in Figure 11.1.

Stage One

Stage One of the TSM model concentrates upon *problem identification*

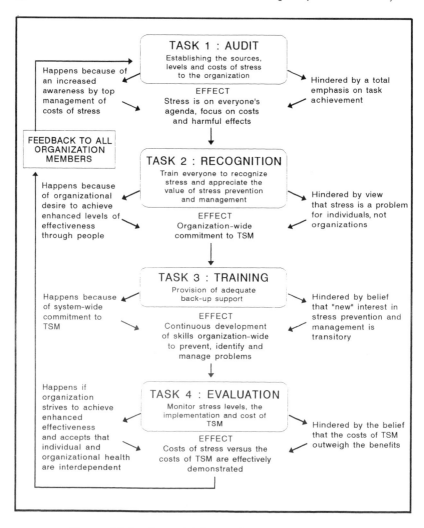

Figure 11.1   A model for total stress management

through a stress audit and organization-wide *acceptance* that stress is a costly defect which interferes with strategy formulation and implementation. This should be effected not only through the collation of data on such factors as absenteeism, labour turnover, and productivity rates but also through investigating underlying causes. While records held by personnel departments should provide the former, it will be necessary to research, develop, and administer an in-house questionnaire to reveal the latter. Alternatively, depending upon specific organizational circumstances, it may prove feasible to use an established psychometric instrument, such as the Occupational Stress Indicator (Cooper *et al.*, 1988) to reveal core stressors and their effects.

Like TQM approaches, an in-depth investigation of this nature will provide the necessary information to lay the foundation for subsequent implementation stages (Pindur and Kim, 1993). It will reveal the current state of the organization by highlighting the dominant stressors and their organizational costs. In doing so it will also serve as a basis for the subsequent targeting of appropriate stress management skills and the training necessary for their development. Analysis of the data should highlight those aspects of the individual's work environment, job role, and personal approach which require "management". Skills which permit this "management" may be developed through a training schedule geared to meet the needs of the individual. The nature of the audit is such that any existing organizational problems in, for example, the communication structure and process will also be revealed. Lastly, the audit will provide an initial reference point for evaluation purposes.

Because TSM affects the organization's most valuable resource—its people—it is thought that the concept should start as a seedling of SHRM which germinates at top management level and eventually grows to the extent that all departments and people become fully acquainted with the meaning of TSM and fully committed to the approach. The communication structure should be such that *everyone* in the organization is "heard". Such communication facilitates understanding, acceptance, and commitment to TSM, a view supported by Pindur and Kim (1993) in their discussion of TQM.

Stage Two

Stage Two of the TSM approach has an educational focus. At this point it is essential to foster acceptance of a new culture which generates the commitment of *all* employees to the necessity of stress prevention and management. This should be accompanied by attitudinal change whereby every staff member in the organization becomes committed to the prevention and elimination of the stress problem.

As TSM advocates organization-wide knowledge and understanding of the stress concept and potential sources, this stage aims to train *all* organization members in *stress recognition* and help them to appreciate the value of a holistic approach to stress management.

Commitment would be fostered by regular organizational and departmental meetings, workshops, and organization-wide training sessions. These sessions provide an opportunity for dialogue with regard to the audit findings: current levels of stress in the organization; dominant stressors; and their effects on the organization and individuals. They should focus upon *problem solving*, explaining the term "stress", its individualistic nature, and its more general causes and effects. In committing themselves to stress prevention and stress management, employees must share the belief that stress is a problem for individuals *and* their organizations. Thus the health of the organization and those who work within them are not independent entities.

When the necessary level of understanding and commitment has been achieved, the organization may move to Stage Three, which emphasizes the need for reinforcement through adequate, on-going back-up training and support.

Stage Three

Stage Three permits organization-wide skills to be developed and continuously augmented to prevent, identify, and manage stress. At this stage employees should be exposed to *generative learning* techniques designed to foster a creative and innovative approach to problem solving, and become able to identify all organizational and personal attributes which contribute to the stress problem for individuals and/or groups. This process will be facilitated by the recognition and understanding of elements revealed by the stress audit.

Such elements may include factors which are intrinsic to jobs (for example, role conflict, ambiguity, overload or underload). Additionally, there may be career-development problems, poor working relationships, an obsolete organization structure, lack of support within the organization, threat of job loss through the forces of recession, competitive pressure, technological change, and/or domestic problems which are carried over into the organization.

Once identified, employees should receive appropriate training and counselling to enable them to acquire and develop skills which permit them to suggest ways in which the stressors may be removed, changed, or managed. This may result in employees at all levels making suggestions to top management which are *"heard"*; these suggestions could signal the need for further change in the organization's operating environment.

Thus Stage Three focuses upon skill acquisition and development, introducing individuals to techniques which permit the active search for stressors and the presentation of creative solutions. As a consequence, they become capable of dealing with problems as they arise rather than letting them stagnate and go unchecked, thereby providing a breeding ground for costly organizational defects.

The adoption of a universal approach to training may seem impossible and very expensive for the organization. However, this is not necessarily true, as training for TSM may be built into existing programmes which must form a part of vital organizational survival and growth strategies for new and experienced organization members. The importance of training activities in the achievement of business objectives has been highlighted by Sillence (1993), who suggests that, among other things, training builds confidence and commitment and helps individuals cope with new demands. Through the training process all employees will become increasingly aware of the need to actively search for sources of stress at organizational, departmental, and individual levels.

Due to the fact that TSM is a system-wide approach involving organization change facilitated by continuous training sessions and workshops, initially it may be relatively costly to the organization, although such costs may be significantly reduced if the organization already has a well-established training mechanism. However, it is expected that the potential savings to be gained from a commitment to TSM are substantial and, like total quality programmes, will far outweigh the costs. Thus the impact and cost of implementing TSM must be measured and evaluated.

Stage Four

Stage Four of the model concentrates upon the evaluation process. This requires the collection of data on current absenteeism, labour turnover, productivity rates, organizational stress levels, and the cost of implementing TSM. When these data have been collected and analysed, results should be compared with the findings of the initial stress audit. A full evaluation of TSM may prove rather difficult to effect, especially if the approach is adopted alongside other change initiatives. In such cases it may be initially impossible specifically to identify and isolate the beneficial effects which are solely attributable to TSM. However, as the approach represents an on-going organizational initiative accompanied by on-going evaluation, the positive outcomes associated with TSM may be more formally identified over time. Thus, the initial difficulties with the evaluation process are not meant to minimize its importance as the fourth stage of TSM.

Once the results of the evaluation are known, the communication structure must facilitate the feeding back of results to all organization members, particularly those at senior management level who are involved in strategy formulation; this is a key feature of the TSM approach. Feedback may be effected by a variety of means—for example, group meetings and/or briefing sessions for group leaders who, in turn, disseminate the findings to employees. This may be further reinforced by posting information strategically on notice boards. The latter should summarize the main findings of the evaluation and outline future goals for organization-wide stress management, thereby emphasizing ongoing organizational commitment to TSM. Thus the process is cyclical, forming the basis for organization renewal.

As human resource management practitioners are most closely attuned to people issues, they are ideally positioned to act as leaders, coordinators, and evaluators in the adoption and implementation of initiatives which move the organization towards TSM. In the first instance, senior members of staff within human resource management departments should ensure that employee stress becomes accepted at board level, as a potential threat to organizational wellbeing and therefore must be regarded as an issue of strategic importance. Consequently it acquires a place on the strategic planning agenda and the challenge of managing stress becomes a core component of SHRM. Second, the members of human resource management departments are often specialized in the design and development of training, workshop, and counselling programmes, therefore it is suggested that these people should play a key role in organizing and coordinating the training activities which are central to TSM. With regard to the evaluation process, it is suggested that one person from each level and function should assume responsibility for the collection of all relevant information. It is expected that this information should be forwarded to the human resource management department, which must play a key role in carrying out the necessary analyses and feeding back results to all organization members. It is expected that human resource management staff should be involved in the collection of all relevant information, carrying out the necessary analyses and feeding back results.

For organizations to derive maximum benefit from TSM, it is essential that the prevailing organizational climate becomes highly supportive whereby everyone is aware of the costs of stress; is encouraged to become totally committed to TSM; and accepts that individual and organizational health are interdependent entities. TSM introduces the idea of a universal commitment to stress prevention and management which become embedded in the strategy of the organization. Within the two organizations discussed in this chapter, it is acknowledged that stress-management issues should be incorporated into a clear policy framework as part of a corporate approach to employee health. The public organization is currently involved in a quality management programme and, as TSM is a derivative of TQM, it would seem that there exists a suitable vehicle for the introduction of the four-stage approach. It is argued, however, that TSM provides a tool and a technique for *all* organizations within the public and private sectors to address the issue of stress effectively.

CONCLUSION

This chapter outlines the implications of recent changes in the operating environments of organizations. It places particular emphasis upon the need to acknowledge stress as one of the outcomes of organization change and stress management as an increasingly important component of human resource strategy. Drawing upon the experiences and views of employees within two organizations affected by major change, the importance of a systematic approach to stress management is outlined. TSM is an example of one such approach which exists as a tool and a technique for helping organizations address the problem of employee stress within the context of SHRM.

For organizations experiencing competitive pressure it can be suggested that current difficulties are perhaps exacerbated by employee stress. Thus it is essential that the latter be addressed through the introduction of stress-management initiatives in order to reduce costs and alleviate threats to organizational survival. Current government support programmes for organizations in the UK and other European countries may provide a source of financial assistance for such initiatives.

It is argued that stress-management initiatives such as TSM reflect an acknowledgement at senior management level of organizational responsibility regarding the management of stress and an enhanced awareness of its associated costs as an issue of strategic importance. Such initiatives also signal managerial awareness that the activities performed by organization members as an outcome of their strategic direction may be stressful. It is hoped that managers will become increasingly aware of the web which incorporates stress and performance outcomes and become committed to problem-solving action. Thus, provision of mechanisms for identifying and dealing with the problem of work stress such as TSM are a necessity for all organizations. Such provision will permit all employees to cope more effectively with the continuous changes and associated pressures which surround them.

It is envisaged that organizations which effectively address the issue of stress management would be characterized by a unique sensitivity to the welfare of people and an acceptance that individual and organizational health are interdependent. As organizations are currently operating in extremely turbulent and hostile environments, it is essential that work stress be considered as a key issue which influences organizational wellbeing and therefore warrants a systematic approach to its detection and management.

To address successfully the challenges posed by currently hostile environments and to be competitive at the international level, organizations are frequently compelled to embark upon programmes of dynamic change. It is essential that those engaged in SHRM first, acknowledge the increased pressures and stress which organization members are likely to experience as a result of the change process, taking cognisance of the interdependence between individual and organizational health. Second, it is imperative that this acknowledgement be followed up by problem-solving action through the use of a mechanism such as TSM. Thus, employee stress becomes accepted as an issue of strategic importance. This acceptance will facilitate the formulation of strategies which permit organizations to deal effectively with existing and future challenges for management.

REFERENCES

Arroba, T. and James, K. (1990) Reducing the cost of stress: an organisational model. *Personnel Review*, **19**, 1, 21–7.

Brief, A. and Atieh, J. (1987) Studying job stress: Are we making mountains out of molehills? *Journal of Occupational Behaviour*, **8,** 115–26.

British Broadcasting Corporation (1993) *The Money Programme—Workplace Stress*, 10 October.

Chen, P. and Spector, P. (1992) Relationships of work stressors with aggression, withdrawal, theft and substance abuse: an exploratory study. *Journal of Occupational and Organizational Psychology*, **65**, 3, 177–84.

Chusmir, L. H. and Franks, V. (1988) Stress and the woman manager. *Training and Development Journal*, **42,** 66–70.

Cooper, C. L. (1986) Job distress: British research and the emerging role of the clinical occupational psychologist. *Bulletin of the British Psychological Society*, **39,** 325–31.

Cooper, C. L., Sloan, S. and Williams, S. (1988) *Occupational Stress Indicator—OSI*, Windsor, NFER-Nelson.

Cowen, S. S. and Osborne, R. L. (1993) Board of directors as strategy. *Journal of General Management*, **19,** 2, 1–13.

Crawley, B. (1993) Lowering stress is good business. *The Independent on Sunday*, 29 August.

Fletcher, B. C. (1991) *Work, Stress, Disease and Life Expectancy*, Chichester, John Wiley.

Goetschin, P. (1987) Reshaping work for an older population. *Personnel Management*, June.

Ibbs Report (1988) *Improving Management in Government: The Next Steps*, London, HMSO.

Kearns, J. (1986) *Stress at Work: The Challenge of Change*, BUPA Series, The Management of Health: 1 Stress in the City, BUPA.

Matteson, J. M. and Ivancevich, M. T. (1987) *Controlling Work Stress*, San Francisco, CA, Jossey-Bass.

McDubhghaill, U. (1991) Stress: the £1bn-a-year disease, *A Supplement to the Irish Times*, 6 March.

McHugh, M. (1993) Stress at work: do managers really count the costs? *Employee Relations*, **15**, 1, 18–32.

McHugh, M. and Brennan, S. (1992) Organizational development and total stress management. *Leadership and Organizational Development Journal*, **13**, 1, 27–32.

Peters, L. H. and O'Connor, E. J. (1980) Situational constraints and work outcomes: the influences of a frequently overlooked construct. *Academy of Management Review*, **5**, 3, 391–7.

Pindur, W. and Kim, P.S. (1993) Total quality management as a vehicle for strategic management innovation in Eastern and Central European countries. *Journal of Strategic Change*, **2**, 5, 275–86.

Richards, S. (1993) Pity the poor bloody infantry. Editorial. *Public Money and Management*, **13**, 2, April-June, 3.

Rizzo, J. R., House, R. J. and Lirtzman, S. I. (1970) Role conflict and ambiguity in complex organizations. *Administrative Science Quarterly*, **15**, 150–63.

Schuler, R. S. (1992) Strategic human resources management: Linking the people with the strategic needs of the business. *Organizational Dynamics,* **21**, 1, 18–32.

Serieyx, H. (1987) The company in the year 2000. *Personnel Management,* June, 30–35.

Sillence, B. J. (1993) Integrating training and development: a practical way to improve business performance. *Journal of Strategic Change,* **2**, 3, 125–34.

Sparrow, P. and Pettigrew, A. (1988) Strategic human resource management in the UK computer supplier industry. *Journal of Occupational Psychology,* **61**, 1, 25–42.

Sullivan, K. (1987) Stress takes its toll on life in the fast lane. *Asian Business,* **23**, 3, 23–4.

Summers, D. (1990) Testing for stress in the workplace. *Financial Times,* 6 December.

RESEARCHING STRATEGIC CHANGE—METHODOLOGIES, METHODS, AND TECHNIQUES

Dianne Lewis

Queensland University of Technology

BACKGROUND

This chapter describes the methodologies, research methods, and techniques used in a longitudinal study of strategic change within an academic institution, ATISIA (A Tertiary Institution Somewhere In Australia) between 1986 and 1990. It also surveys the literature on methods used by other researchers in the study of such change. It is hoped that, while many of the details of the description are specific to ATISIA, they will nevertheless be useful as a guide to other researchers studying similar changes in other organisations.

It is certainly not my aim to offer yet another definition of strategic change, but it seems that any change is strategic to some extent if it attempts to position the organisation better in the external environment. At ATISIA the changes were "strategic", not in the textbook sense of being the product of the minds of managers who are all-knowing, with limitless vision that allows them to see into the future and guide their organisations towards that future while ordinary mortals look on in wonder; but more in the Mintzberg sense of containing the five ingredients of "plan", "ploy", "pattern", "position", and "perspective" (Mintzberg, 1983b). They were

Rethinking Strategic Management
Edited by D. E. Hussey. © 1995 John Wiley & Sons Ltd

probably also "emergent" rather than "deliberate", developing from initial broad goals to more specific ones by the process of "logical incrementalism" (Quinn, 1980, 3).

My research at ATISIA concentrated on the process and effects of change and a detailed examination was made of:

- Management strategies for "managing meanings" (Weick, 1979; Peters and Waterman, 1982; Bennis and Nanus, 1985); that is, transformational leadership strategies
- Effects of these strategies on organisational members
- Effects of the changes on organisational performance as measured against the criteria set by top management.

I chose to undertake such a study for my PhD dissertation because a review to 1984 of the literature on organisational culture, transformational leadership, and strategic change revealed a great gap in the documentation of theories presented there. There seemed to have been very little of substance published on a longitudinal study of strategic change and a study at ATISIA could help fill that gap. Pettigrew's accounts of his studies of British firms were not published before 1985 (Pettigrew, 1985a,b, 1986, 1987, 1988; Sparrow and Pettigrew, 1988; Whipp *et al.*, 1988, 1989).

The research, however, would also serve as a case study of changes being introduced in universities and colleges throughout Australia. With an interest in "excellence" awakened by the writings of Peters and Waterman (1982) and Ouchi and Jaeger (1978), who stressed the importance of a strong culture for successful organisational performance, organisations throughout the Western world have rushed to "seek excellence" by changing—and hopefully *strengthening*—their culture, defined here as:

> basic assumptions that people in an organisation hold and share about that organisation. Those assumptions are implied in their shared feelings, beliefs and values, and embodied in symbols, processes, forms and some aspects of patterned group behaviour (Lewis, 1992a, 3).

Diagrammatically, this view of culture is a three-layered one, expressed in Figure 12.1. Strategic change in this case, therefore, involved *culture* change.

The quest for excellence has not been restricted to the private sector but has also encompassed large sections of the public sector, including government departments and academic institutions. For example, in 1987 the Australian Federal Government distributed a

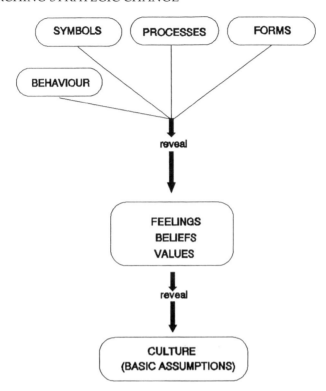

Figure 12.1 The three-layered nature of organisational culture. (*Source:* Lewis, 1992b)

Policy Discussion Paper on Higher Education (the "Green Paper"), stressing the importance of education at the tertiary level that would be "consistent with our economic, social and cultural needs" and would be "efficient" in "performance" (Higher Education: a policy discussion paper, 1987, 1). The Federal Government's aim, as they saw it, was to make all tertiary institutions more relevant and accountable, and, by implication, more "excellent". This Green Paper and subsequent White Paper (Higher Education: a policy statement, 1988) caused many universities and colleges to engage in strategic change and make major alterations in their mission, emphasis, profiles (both staff and educational), and teaching and research content in the hope of strengthening that nebulous phenomenon— their culture.

Parts of the study have been published elsewhere. Lewis (1992b) looked at the strategies used for communicating organisational culture, Lewis and Cunnington (1993) described the transformational leadership strategies used in the process of strategic change, and Lewis (1994) explored the relationship between reactions to change and organisational performance. Therefore, this chapter will not go into details of these aspects, but will concentrate on a description of, and justification for, the methodologies, methods, and techniques used to study, analyse, and interpret the changes at ATISIA during the period 1983–90, a period of rapid change from an institute of technology to a university. Even within these parameters, only superficial details will be given of questions asked at interviews and numbers used for sampling. Full details are available in Lewis (1992a).

I will first explain my reasons for choosing case methodology (in particular, the case of ATISIA) as a way of researching strategic change and, within case methodology, both qualitative and quantitative methodologies. I will then review the literature on research methods and describe and justify the methods chosen. A similar process will be followed for the data analysis. Finally, I will attempt to evaluate the methodologies, methods, and techniques used.

CHOICE OF METHODOLOGIES

"Blessed are the poor in choices, for they will have no trouble making up their minds" ("Halcom's Evaluation Beatitudes", Patton, 1980, 17). "The perfect evaluation design isn't" ("Halcom's Laws of Evaluation Research Methods", Patton, 1980, 90). The study of strategic change is not always a straightforward one, especially if the changes involve *culture* change and the use of *power-based transformational leadership strategies* to effect that change. Methodologies and research methods used for studying such changes have therefore to be complicated and often indirect. According to Limerick (1988, 72), methodology derives partly from the researcher's own world-view, so it is possible that the methodologies used were already fixed in my mind and heart before the study even began. But choice of methodologies also derives from a consideration of the most appropriate way of achieving the desired goal.

Case Methodology

The use of a case study of an organisation from which to develop theories or to build on and fill in gaps in theories that already exist has been described by Glaser and Strauss as "grounded theory", which they define as "the discovery of theory from data systematically obtained from social research" (Glaser and Strauss, 1967, 2). A case study can involve either a single or multiple cases and numerous levels of analysis. For example, some researchers choose a number of cases and analyse them on one particular level; that is, looking at one particular aspect of them and then making comparisons across cases. Peters and Waterman did this in the early 1980s, looking at ninety different companies in the United States to see what factors made them "excellent". Other researchers, like Andrew Pettigrew, have done in-depth studies of a single organisation, analysing that organisation on a number of different levels. In studies of British firms, Pettigrew (1985a,b, 1986, 1987) describes details of a case study of Imperial Chemical Industries (ICI); Sparrow and Pettigrew (1988) describe a study of organisational change at Halfords, a UK retailer of automobile accessories and bicycles; Whipp *et al.* (1988) illustrate change in the UK motor industry; and Whipp *et al.* (1989) present a study of strategic change in the automobile and merchant banking industries in the UK.

Further research on case methodology has been done by Eisenhardt (1989). She believes that case methodology can have a number of strengths, especially in a new area where there is very little theory available, or in an area where existing theory is inadequate. One strength is the likelihood of being able to generate new theories. Because the researcher has to reconcile many different data sources, it often leads to quite creative theory-building. A second strength is that any theories constructed are likely to be testable; the researcher has already tested them many times in the case study. A third strength is that the theories are likely to be empirically valid. Because the researcher has had such intimate interaction with actual evidence, it often produces theory that closely mirrors reality and is reliable. Eisenhardt also believes that the case study is "particularly well-suited to new research areas or research areas for which existing theory seems inadequate" (Eisenhardt, 1989, 548–9). However, as I had chosen case methodology in 1984 for the study of ATISIA, neither Pettigrew's nor Eisenhardt's research influenced that choice. Influences were that ATISIA provided an ideal vehicle for the study of change and I was in a unique position to study it.

First, ATISIA was a relatively self-contained organisation undergoing change. It had originally been a technical college, but in 1965 was set up by the Federal Government as a college of advanced education, one of a number of non-university colleges whose task was to train more scientists, engineers, and business executives than the universities were able to produce. It was primarily a teaching institution and was not funded for research and although new, academically better qualified staff with research interests were appointed during the 1970s, research remained only a small part of the college's activities. In the 1980s, however, with the Federal Government's new emphasis on utilitarian education at the tertiary level, ATISIA's management instigated far-reaching changes—changes that included technical and research excellence and involved ATISIA's becoming a university.

A second, though related, reason that ATISIA was a good case study of change was that preliminary interviews with its top management revealed that ATISIA, in its transcendental, strategic, and operational vision (terms borrowed from Limerick and Cunnington, 1993) was typical of the type of institution the Federal Government was trying to encourage.

Third, its administration had admitted publicly to attempting a top-management initiated change. In November 1984, at a seminar of a professional body at which the Vice-Principal of ATISIA was guest speaker, he said that he and the Principal were attempting to change a "bureaucratic, reactive organisation into an entrepreneurial, proactive one". This statement indicated to me that the kinds of change being planned at ATISIA constituted "transformative" change, defined by Buckley and Perkins (1984, 56) as "major overhauls of . . . basic assumptions and operating policies" and "accompanied by a fundamental shift in consciousness, values or perceptions" (pp. 57–8). De Bivort (1985, 244) says it "requires breaking through existing belief structures"; while Kleiner and Corrigan (1989, 27) call it "profound", "traumatic", and "revolutionary".

Such definitions suggest that *transformation* involves a change in an organisation's culture, as opposed to *transactional* change, which, according to Burns (1978, 4), political leaders use "with an eye to exchanging one thing for another". A transactional leader, therefore, would not attempt to change a *culture*, whereas a *transformative* leader would (Bass, 1985, 1990). Some authors (Argyris and Schon, 1976; Bartunek, 1984; Bass, 1985; Levy, 1986; Bartunek and Louis, 1988; Torbert, 1989) call this "first-order" and "second-order" change. ATISIA's leadership espoused "culture" or "second-order" change.

A fourth reason for choosing ATISIA as a case study of change was that I was in a unique position to study it. With staff connections there since 1968, I had seen it develop almost from its beginnings; and as a part-time lecturer there myself since 1978, I had access to facilities and people. However, I was not affected by the changes in the same way as full-time staff were and so, while I could empathise with them, I was not nearly so heavily involved; and neither was my future so vitally tied up in their outcome. Therefore, I was able to view the culture and the changes from other people's point of view as well as from my own. In addition, I had the enthusiastic support of the Principal and Vice-Principal and it would have been impossible to conduct the research without their wholehearted cooperation. The Vice-Principal asked all senior staff to cooperate with me and gave me access to ATISIA documents and facilities as well as a Letter of Authorisation to show to anyone for whom it might be necessary. The extent of this cooperation will become evident with the description of the specific methods and techniques used.

Within the ambit of the case, both qualitative and quantitative methodologies were chosen. Qualitative research was deemed to be the most suitable tool for studying culture, culture change, and transformational leadership strategies; and a mixture of qualitative and quantitative methodology for studying effects of change on the performance of the organisation. Quantitative methodology was also used to verify qualitative data.

Qualitative methodology

The use of qualitative methodology for studying the culture of ATISIA derives from my belief in the ideationalist view of culture as basic assumptions existing in the minds of people and in the often unconscious nature of these assumptions (Sathe, 1983, 1985; Schein, 1983, 1984). (See also Figure 12.1.) However, the term itself needs definition. Qualitative methodology follows no fixed pattern from one research situation to the next. It is, as Van Maanen says, an "umbrella term" (Van Maanen, 1983, 9), which covers many techniques of describing and explaining situations, people, and behaviour. It uses quotations and narration rather than numbers and does not predetermine categories of experiences, attitudes, values, feelings, and beliefs. Mintzberg describes his own qualitative methodology as "direct research" (Mintzberg, 1983a, 115).

Qualitative methodology brings with it many problems, not the least of which is a problem of ethics. The question of ethics in sociological research has been treated in varying degrees of depth by different authors. Some, like Deetz (1985), see it as fundamental to all research considerations and as much a part of organisational research as theory; while others, like Bogdan, say simply, "Forget your guilt—listen to everything" (Bogdan, 1972, 39). Perhaps the differences in opinions on ethics arise from a difference between *pure* research and *action* research.

Argyris (1970) suggests studying change by intervening in the change process as a consultant to see if the organisation is accomplishing its goals, whether the performance evaluators really do measure effectiveness, and to help the organisation create new goals. Dorson, however, argues strongly against such *action* research because "the folklorist . . . is unequipped to reshape institutions" (Dorson in Jones, 1985, 235).

However, there are ethical considerations other than whether the researcher has an effect on the situation. According to Jones, the methods used to elicit information and the assumptions on which the strategies are based are more important than the actual conduct of the researcher in fieldwork (Jones, 1985, 237). Mirvis and Seashore (1980) believe the future will demand the development of a code of ethics for social research, but at this time, fifteen years later, we have still not come to any agreement on such a code.

Conscious action research was not suitable for studying culture, culture change, or transformational leadership strategies in this situation for two main reasons. First, I had no legitimate power to affect the organisation in any way: and second, it was not the purpose of the research. During the period of data collection, therefore, I tried to have as little effect on the situation as was possible.

Other problems associated with qualitative methodology are the labour-intensive nature of collecting the data, the sheer volume of data to be analysed, and the lack of any tried and proven methods of data analysis and measurement (Miles, 1983, 118). These problems will become obvious later in the chapter.

Advocates of quantitative methods criticise what they see as the subjective and imprecise nature of qualitative methods and it is granted that bias and perception can be an obstacle to qualitative methodologists. Findings do often seem subjective and imprecise. A problem with subjectivity that I faced was that, as the study progressed, I found myself identifying with many of the subjects of the research. While this would be considered by some quantitative methodologists as detrimental to the data interpretation, others, such as Adams and Ingersoll, believe that the researcher cannot possibly hope to understand people's feelings, values and beliefs without becoming personally involved. They admit that there is the danger of bias, but that this is a "natural consequence of examining a human phenomenon" (Adams and Ingersoll, 1985, 225). Qualitative methodologists see their methods as far less subjective than survey questions with restricted categories of answers used by quantitative methodologists. There are also ways of overcoming the problems of subjectivity, which will be discussed later in this chapter.

In answering the criticism of imprecision, Calder (1980, 400–401) says that because qualitative research deals with imprecise things such as perceptions, meanings, and interpretations that people give to the world around them, its imprecision is merely a reflection of the imprecision of those phenomena it is describing. Qualitative approaches were therefore adopted as methods for unearthing both the culture and transformational leadership strategies. While quantitative methods were found to be useful for verifying qualitative data and for gauging the effects of the changes on the organisation, they were not the dominant paradigm. I was aiming for a more holistic view and found most quantitative approaches unsuitable for the following reasons:

- Culture's esoteric nature
- The unconscious nature of basic assumptions
- Possible discrepancies between people's "espoused theories" and "theories-in-use" (Argyris and Schon, 1976)
- The diversity in the effects of the changes
- The possible inaccuracies of people's information due to their perceptions
- Intentional deception by the informants.

First, there is the esoteric nature of culture. With very little agreement on what exactly constitutes culture, but with fairly wide agreement that its nature is complex and embodied in a large number of indicators—some concrete, some symbolic, some procedural—quantifiable methods of studying it appeared to me to be reductionist. I did not believe I could construct an accurate picture of people's feelings, beliefs, and values—and therefore certainly not an accurate interpretation of the underlying basic assumptions—from a direct approach such as written questionnaires or direct survey techniques.

The major problem in constructing preconceived categories is that the categories differ from organisation to organisation. Ed Schein, in an interview, put it very succinctly when he said:

> The reason you cannot use instruments (questionnaires, surveys) is because culture covers everything. You don't know ahead of time what categories are going to be important in that particular

organisation, and you should not bias their thinking toward your own favorite categories......clients may be led into irrelevant areas if consultants imply that the dimensions that are built into their questionnaire instruments are in fact the relevant dimensions of that culture (Schein, 1989, 71, 72).

And Frost *et al.* (1985, 15) believe that questionnaire-survey techniques can neither explore nor explain "deep meaning".

A second reason for the unsuitability of using quantitative methods to study culture is that, according to my definition of culture, basic assumptions are often taken for granted, non-debatable, and unconscious. People possibly could not have given information to me even if they wanted to. I also realised that some topics would be taboo, others considered not worth discussing, and others again seemingly self-evident. During data collection I experienced such responses, which provided a very valuable understanding of basic assumptions. I believe that the rich information yielded by these experiences could not have been gained using quantitative research methods.

Third, there is the possibility of discrepancies between espoused theories and theories-in-use. According to Argyris and Schon (1976), people's behaviour is governed by a number of "theories of action". Two of these theories are our "espoused theories" (the ones we *say* govern our actions); and our "theories-in-use" (those that actually *do* govern our actions). Problems in interpretation of data arise because espoused theories and theories-in-use are not always the same, and quite often the informants are not even aware of any incompatibility themselves. Asking people directly what they think in responses that can be quantified could be not only useless but also counter-productive.

A fourth reason for not using quantitative methodology is the diversity in the effects of the change. Patton (1980, 88–9) says that if it is expected that different participants will be affected in qualitatively different ways, then qualitative evaluation methods are appropriate. Preliminary research at ATISIA showed that different groups *would* be affected in different ways, so it was necessary to describe and evaluate these groups separately. Evidence of such diversity of effects would also need to be described in detail by reference to particular case studies, a process not suited to quantitative research methods.

Fifth, people perceive things according to their own world-view and even though they may believe they would answer questions, either written or oral, honestly and factually, the best they can do is answer as *they* see things. Roethlisberger's "X-Chart", first published in 1941 and reproduced in Davis (1981, 200), depicts people's response to change as a result of their attitudes rather than a result of logic. Even in qualitative research there are dangers in believing what people say, because what people tell us is only their perception of events as they are prepared to tell us at that particular time (Dean and Whyte, 1969, 105–6). The dangers in quantitative methods, which rely heavily on people's responses, were considered to be even greater.

Finally, I realised that informants, for one reason or another, would not always be prepared to tell the truth, even if they were aware of it. The protection of vested interests would be a strong motivating factor in either withholding the truth or telling an untruth. Management strategies for effecting change could be an example of such a case. Some people could intentionally deceive through fear of reprisal, a desire to seem more knowledgeable or accomplished than they really were, or a desire to punish or reward someone or some group. Other people could intentionally hide the truth because they did not want certain pieces of information to be known, especially if their espoused theories differed from their theories-in-use. Therefore, the use of standardised measuring instruments such as questionnaires would be a help to people in hiding their real feelings, motives, or actions, and a hindrance to me.

Quantitative methodology

While qualitative methodology formed the basis of the study of culture, culture change, and transformational leadership strategies at ATISIA, a mixture of qualitative and quantitative methods was used to gauge the effects of the changes on the performance of the organisation and to help verify the qualitative data. Such a mixture can often produce much more reliable results than either qualitative or quantitative methods could alone (Sieber, 1980, 444), because the two method-types are able to "build upon each other" (Reichardt and Cook, 1979, 21). Such use of data is an example of methodological triangulation, described later.

According to Cooke and Rousseau, "quantitative approaches may be more practical for purposes of analysing data-based change in organisations" (Cooke and Rousseau, 1988, 246). Top management of ATISIA had listed a number of indices of performance change by which they planned to measure the success of the changes, and most of these were quantifiable.

CHOICE OF RESEARCH METHODS

Using the qualitative and quantitative methodologies described, a number of specific methods were chosen to collect information on the culture of ATISIA at a particular time, on the changes in the culture, and on the transformational leadership strategies used to effect these changes. The published literature from the early 1980s to the present abounds in suggestions for such studies, some of which are outlined below. However, I was limited in my choices to the literature before 1987.

Studying Culture

A review of the literature to 1986 indicated that, almost without exception, a study of behaviour was included in the methods suggested for diagnosis of a culture, and behaviour is not always a good indicator of values and underlying assumptions. No issue is taken with the study of behaviour as a *possible* embodiment of values, but while behaviour is one embodiment of culture, culture is not the only determinant of behaviour. People's behaviour may not be an expression of their feelings, beliefs, and values at all, but may be a contingency measure that they adopt to cope with situations as they arise. Attribution theory argues that we perceive the behaviour of others as being caused either by the other person themselves, by the environment, or by a combination of both (Wrightsman and Sandford, 1975, 83). We therefore tend to make conclusions based more on circumstances and past events than on observable behaviour itself (Cook 1979, 60). This point alone demonstrates the danger in inferring feelings, beliefs, and values from behaviour.

In spite of the almost universal acceptance of behaviour as implying the culture of an organisation, it is argued here that the methods with the greatest chance of success of unearthing a culture are those that attempt to unearth the underlying assumptions. Techniques for diagnosis have to go deeper than observation of behaviour and analysis and classification of responses to questions. According to Uttal (1983, 69–70), the task is nearly impossible; yet some authors have suggested methods of diagnosis that are worthy of consideration, their main weakness being that most of them rely too heavily on interpretation of behaviour.

Overall, it was considered that the qualitative methods suggested by Louis (1981), Schein (1983, 1984), and Sathe (1983, 1985) would provide a suitable means of gathering the information required for the study of culture at a particular time. These methods were chosen because they are broad enough to encompass the many facets of culture and deep enough to unearth the basic assumptions that are at the heart of culture. Both Sathe and Schein also provide details of the methods used in uncovering the hidden assumptions. Louis (1981) believes we need to look at culture as a whole: its components, how it came about, its manifestations and effects. She suggests a variety of methods, including phenomenological and ethnographic methods as well as interaction analysis and experimental methods. Sathe (1983, 1985) and Schein (1983, 1984) believe that, as a culture consists of a number of underlying, often unconscious assumptions, one has to infer them from observable manifestations. Sathe (1983, 16, 1985, 17) uses shared sayings, things, doings, and feelings as his manifestations while Schein (1983, 16, 1984, 6) provides a list of categories for studying assumptions as well as ten mechanisms that founders and management use to embed and transmit values and assumptions (1983, 22).

Around 1985—after methodology and methods had been chosen for the case study at ATISIA—the published literature on culture took a more utilitarian approach, with researchers asking the question "what *use* may be made of the gained information?" (Hofstede, 1986, 254). Along with this new emphasis on utilitarianism came the first attempts to measure culture quantitatively. Most of the literature here is concerned with measuring culture change, but recognises the need to take a measurement of the culture at the beginning of the change process. Among authors who suggest some use of quantitative measures are Amsa (1986), Desatnik (1986), Hofstede (1986), Reynierse (1986), Reynierse and Harker (1986), Reynolds (1986), Barnett (1979, 1988), Cooke and Rousseau (1988), and Wiener (1988). Hofstede, in his editorial to the special issue of *Journal of Management Studies*, says:

> The message to University and corporate research departments is that . . . there is a strong need for speculating less and measuring more (Hofstede, 1986, 256).

Reynierse and Harker use a combination of quantitative and qualitative measures. The qualitative methods involve interviews and group discussions, while the quantitative method, which they call *Organizational Dynamics*, is a survey questionnaire using 95 items on a 5-point ordinal scale of definite agreement to definite disagreement. The method aims to provide managers with tangible feedback in their attempt to manage culture, and their justification for the method is that "you can't manage organizational culture unless you can measure it" (Reynierse and Harker, 1986, 1).

Another attempt to measure culture quantitatively is outlined by Reynolds (1986), who aims to measure culture differences between organisations to see if the measured differences relate to differences in performance. His method of measurement is also by questionnaire and is described in some detail in his paper. Barnett (1979, 1988) outlines details of what he calls a "Galileo tm" or "Galileo Analysis" for accurately measuring culture. Some of the methods are common to those used in qualitative approaches, but Barnett quantifies the results. I considered that the method was too narrow, using only language, symbols and concepts as measurable elements. Wiener claims to be able to measure culture by measuring the *intensity* and *breadth* of "key" or "pivotal" values in an organisation. The greater the sharing of these values across the organisation, the stronger the "central value system" (Wiener, 1988, 535). Cooke and Rousseau (1988) measure behavioural norms and expectations.

The literature since 1989 on the study and diagnosis of culture has not been particularly abundant. Perhaps this is because there has been so much emphasis on the characteristics of a "quality" culture that managers are no longer concerned about the kind of culture they *have* but only about the kind of culture they *want to have*. Perhaps managers contemplating strategic change are "cutting corners" by omitting one of the early steps. Some researchers, however, have suggested methods for studying and diagnosing a culture. Nossiter and Biberman, for example, use a technique they call "projective drawing and metaphorical analogy fantasizing" (Nossiter and Biberman, 1990, 13), where questionnaires ask participants to draw an image and name an animal representing their organisation and department. They believe that the creativity involved may motivate employees to think more about their organisations. Tucker *et al.* (1990) have designed a comprehensive questionnaire, developed from interviews and discussions with fifty managers of organisations. They believe results from the questionnaire, which are quantified, will help provide some preliminary information on the organisation's culture to managers attempting to deal with particular situations and problems with their cultures. Brink (1991) develops Porter's colour-coded theory of motivation (Porter in Brink, 1991) and applies it to organisations. The techniques suggested by Nossiter and Biberman, by Tucker *et al.*, and by Brink are as yet too recent for much empirical testing to have been carried out on them.

Studying Culture Change and Change Strategies

Research methods I used to study culture change and change

strategies also relied heavily on the qualitative methods suggested by Sathe and Schein. Most of the literature avoids the question of measuring the effectiveness of culture change and therefore, by implication, how to *study* the changes. At the time I was considering methods, a few articles dealing with particular cases mentioned a monitoring process of studying change, but did not give details of exactly how it was done (Vroman, 1983; Main, 1984; Carby and Stemp, 1985). In fact, many of the superficial methods of monitoring that have been used to herald great changes in culture are actually measures of *behaviour* change. Also, while behaviour may be indicative of culture change, it may also be occurring in the presence of a dissonant culture. Sathe, for example, sees behaviour change as only the *first* step (Sathe, 1983, 1985); and Lundberg (1985, 179) says that "a new conception that does not reach the value and assumption levels of cultural meaning is really not true culture change".

Until recently, all measurements of culture change have been qualitative and among the more detailed descriptions of these are the methods of Sathe, Hagedorn and Little, Silverzweig and Allen, and Wiener. Silverzweig and Allen (1976) base their measurement on a combination of both employee perceptions and organisational performance; Sathe's three tests of culture change are concerned with analysis of behaviour (Sathe, 1985, 398–401); Hagedorn and Little's (1984) culture profile is a test designed specifically to measure culture change; while Wiener's (1988) intensity and breadth index—described earlier—measures key values in the central value system.

All the quantitative measures described in the literature to the time of the completion of data collection (that is, mid-1990) used either questionnaires or structured interviews and failed to take account of the pervasiveness of culture, the unconscious nature of basic assumptions, the gap between espoused theories and theories-in-use, the ambivalent nature of behaviour, or the reluctance of people to commit their real feelings to paper (even if they *can* recognise them).

The quantitative measurement of culture and culture change remains problematic, but some serious research is being conducted in the area. Hofstede *et al.* (1990), for example, have recently made efforts to overcome some of the problems. Their study of twenty units from ten different organisations in Denmark and the Netherlands specifically aims at finding out whether culture can be measured quantitatively or described only qualitatively. They use a combination of in-depth interviews and questionnaire surveys. The report of their methodology and methods is impressive and the findings and conclusions are encouraging for future researchers in quantitative measurement of culture and culture change.

Quantitative methodology seemed appropriate in gauging performance change, as some of the indicators used were the performance indicators top management had set for themselves in gauging success, most of which were quantifiable.

Research Methods Chosen

The methods finally chosen were a combination of methods that had been suggested by a large number of researchers and of original ideas I developed myself. Undoubtedly, however, I owe much to Louis, Sathe, and Schein. This technique of using several different methods, called *triangulation*, is defined by Denzin (1978, 291) as "the combination of methodologies in the study of the same phenomena". The term is derived from military and navigational practices of using a number of different reference points to find an exact position of something (Smith, 1975, 273). Triangulation was used in this research for two main reasons.

First, I believed that no one method of studying culture can cover every aspect. This was the major criticism I had made of the literature on studying culture; no single method suggested seemed sufficiently encompassing. Putnam (1983) recommends a pluralistic approach to methodology when conducting interpretative research and Eisenberg and Riley (1988) believe that a variety of methods is essential, particularly when studying organisational symbolism. According to Rose (1982, 309), "no *one* method is infallible, so the use of several methods gives more conclusive results".

The second reason for using triangulation was that it helps avoid misinterpretation of the data due to the use of a particular method (Smith, 1975, 272–4; Reichardt and Cook, 1979, 21). Jick believes the technique can be traced back to Campbell and Fiske's "multiple operationalism" in a 1959 study, which argued that the use of more than one method would ensure that any measurements would be of the trait being measured and not of the method used to measure it (Jick, 1985, 136).

Denzin (1978) distinguishes four types of triangulation:

- Data triangulation; that is, using as many different data sources as possible
- Investigator triangulation; that is, using different observers to collect the same information in order to reduce bias

- Theory triangulation; that is, using multiple theories to test data against
- Methodological triangulation; using "within methods" and "between methods" triangulation. The "between methods" technique involves the use of a mixture of qualitative and quantitative research methods, and the "within methods" technique uses a number of different techniques within both qualitative and quantitative research methods (Denzin, 1978, 295–304).

I chose to use data, theory, and methodological triangulation, and, within methodological triangulation, both "between" and "within" methods. The selection of techniques was thus as wide as possible. This choice of methods has been strengthened in subsequent literature by Whipp et al. (1989, 60–61), who say that any study of strategic change should consciously use methodological and theoretical triangulation.

The "within methods" techniques, described below, aimed to satisfy the requirement of internal reliability, or "the degree to which other researchers, given a set of previously generated constructs, would match them with data in the same way as did the original researcher" (Goetz and Le Compte, 1984, 210). The "between methods" technique, also described below, aimed to satisfy the requirement of external validity, or "the degree to which [representations of a reality] can be compared legitimately across groups" (Goetz and Le Compte, 1984, 210).

Working from a basis of data, theory, and methodological triangulation, an operational framework was devised. In accordance with my definition of culture, it was decided to study culture from its tangible manifestations of "symbols", "processes", and "forms" (see Figure 12.1). From these, the basic, often unconscious assumptions would be distilled. Some of these tangible manifestations that would serve as indicators were inspired by Schein's ideas on embodiments of culture (Schein, 1983, 22), but others emerged or were widened and formalised as the study progressed. They finally reached the form in the operational framework shown in Table 12.1.

As can be seen from this framework, indicators have been divided into symbols, processes, and forms, three of the four tangible manifestations of culture, and under each of these headings a number of specific manifestations have been identified. The fourth manifestation, aspects of behaviour, has not been given a separate category, as not all behaviour can be considered cultural. Those

Table 12.1 Operational framework for diagnosis of culture and strategic change at ATISIA

$\left\{\begin{array}{l}\text{Symbols}\\\text{Processes}\\\text{Forms}\\\text{Behaviour}\end{array}\right.$ reveal	$\left\{\begin{array}{l}\text{Feelings}\\\text{Beliefs}\\\text{Values}\end{array}\right.$ reveal	$\left\{\begin{array}{l}\text{Assumptions}\\\text{Meanings}\\\text{(Culture)}\end{array}\right.$

SYMBOLS

1   Logo
2   Slogans
3   Name of organisation
4   Use of language
4.1 Commonly used phrases
4.2 Commonly expressed sentiments
5   Stories, myths, fables
6   Ceremonies
7   Rituals—meetings, lunch habits, informal communications
8   Exemplars
8.1 Criteria for appointment
8.2 Criteria for sidelining
8.3 Criteria for rewarding
8.4 Power-holders
9   Perceptions of identity and role of ATISIA
10   Perceptions of work expectations
11   Descriptions of one sub-culture by another
12   Indicators of counter-cultures
13   Indicators of sub-cultures
14   Priorities
14.1 Top management's priorities, goals and perceived problems
14.2 Perceptions of top management's priorities
14.3 Personal priorities
15   Perceptions of management's goals

PROCESSES

Formal procedures
16   Management's overall strategies for managing
17   Strategies for effecting changes
17.1 Interventions pre-1987
17.2 Interventions post-1987
18   Recruitment procedures
19   Socialisation procedures
20   Formal communication channels, formal support systems

Informal processes
21   Work and coping practices in different discipline areas
22   Basis for allocation of scarce resources and perks
23   Management's criteria for evaluating success of changes
24   Procedures for handling deviants

Table 12.1 *Cont.*

$\left\{\begin{array}{l}\text{Symbols}\\\text{Processes}\\\text{Forms}\\\text{Behaviour}\end{array}\right.$ reveal	$\left\{\begin{array}{l}\text{Feelings}\\\text{Beliefs}\\\text{Values}\end{array}\right.$ reveal	$\left\{\begin{array}{l}\text{Assumptions}\\\text{Meanings}\\\text{(Culture)}\end{array}\right.$

FORMS

25   Architecture
26   Structure of the organisation
27   Formal documents—staff newspaper, new corporate statement and mission statement, corporate identity manual, submissions to Council, summaries of Council decisions, manual of procedures, proposals, student newspaper
28   Observable rewards
29   Observable punishments
30   Pronouncements
31   Staff profile
32   Written history of ATISIA
33   Formal speeches
34   Performance indicators

aspects of behaviour considered relevant to culture are included in the three categories listed. Many of the categories are, of course, specific to ATISIA and would vary with the specific case being studied. They are presented here as a model only.

Because some indicators were developed out of data collected, and concepts were derived from the indicators, the methodology bears some relationship to Glaser and Strauss's "grounded theory". However, because some guiding propositions had already been formulated after a review of the literature and before the commencement of data collection, a decision taken on which variables to address, and ideas borrowed from the research of Schein and other authors, the research cannot really be called pure grounded theory. I agree with Einstein and Popper in rejecting pure "grounded theory" on the basis of its non-existence. Einstein (in Magee, 1975) wrote in a letter to Popper: "theory cannot be fabricated out of the results of observation, but that it can only be invented" (p. 33) and Popper (1963) wrote: "the belief that we can start with pure observations alone, without anything in the nature of a theory, is absurd" (p. 46). Thus, while it is conceded that some of the theory is grounded in the data collected, the framework presented here is really building on and filling gaps in theories that already exist.

Methods used for studying culture and transformational leadership strategies and for studying culture change and effects on the organisation will now be described.

DESCRIPTION OF METHODS

Triangulation necessitated a complex methodological pattern with the particular methodology varying with the requirements. For example, in order to study past and future changes at ATISIA and their effects on the organisation and on the people who worked there, it was necessary to study the culture as it existed before the change process began, the culture at the commencement of the collection of data, the culture over the following two years, and transformational leadership strategies employed during the period of rapid change. This required cross-sectional and longitudinal studies.

The study of culture and transformational leadership strategies as they existed at a particular time was a cross-sectional one, using the following methods:

- Daily log
- Phenomenology
- Ethnographic interviews
- Focus group interviews
- Formal documents

These methods were also used to study culture *change*, effects of change on the organisation, and changes in transformational leadership strategies, but here the study was a longitudinal one, using the following additional methods:

- Two culture profiles, using a panel sample
- Manifestations of culture
- Retrospective data
- Quantitative methods

I will describe both cross-sectional and longitudinal studies in more detail, though space does not permit a detailed discussion of specifics. While the studies have been divided into two groups—methods for studying culture and transformational leadership and methods for studying culture change and transformational leadership—there is much overlap between the two groups.

Methods Used to Study Culture and Transformational Leadership

Research into the culture and leadership strategies of ATISIA at a particular time required a cross-sectional study, represented

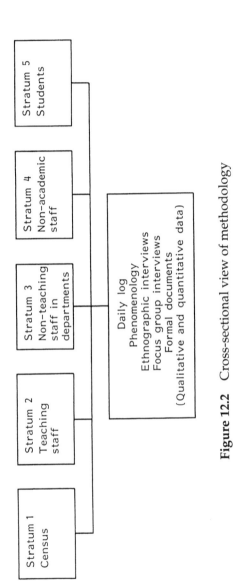

Figure 12.2   Cross-sectional view of methodology

diagrammatically in Figure 12.2. The sampling plan, explaining the strata shown in the diagram, is given later. Within this cross-sectional study, the following methods were used to unearth the culture of ATISIA at a particular time.

Daily log

First, during the period from June 1986 to December 1989 a daily log was kept of observations, informal interviews and other indicators of culture listed in the operational framework. The research technique used here was participant observation, defined by Bogdan (1972) as "research characterized by a prolonged period of intense social interaction between the researcher and the subjects, in the milieu of the latter, during which time data, in the form of field notes, are unobtrusively and systematically collected" (p.3).

While participant observation is often criticised as biased by proponents of quantitative research methods, according to Bogdan (1972, 5), quantitative research methods such as questionnaires are also biased because the questions *selected* are determined by the researcher's preconceived ideas every bit as much as the participant observer's *interpretations* are. Participant observation can be made just as scientific and objective if it serves a formulated research purpose, is planned deliberately, is recorded systematically, and is subjected to checks and controls on validity and reliability (Kidder, 1981, 264). In the research done at ATISIA, checks and controls were provided by other techniques used in the methodology (triangulation). During participant observation, my aim was always to unearth the shared feelings, beliefs, and values of the people who worked at ATISIA and therefore to discover the shared assumptions that enabled them to interpret their situation and to behave appropriately. To achieve this aim, ethnographic research was carried out.

The technique of ethnography was first used as a formal approach by Harold Garfinkel in 1967. Garfinkel (1967) defined his research technique, ethnomethodology, in the following way:

> I use the term "ethnomethodology" to refer to the investigation of the rational properties of indexical expressions and other practical actions as contingent ongoing accomplishments of organized artful practices of everyday life (p.11).

According to Spradley (1980, 3), ethnography is a means of understanding "another way of life from the native point of view".

Ethnomethodologists study everyday activities and information that are considered commonplace in order to see how people make sense of them and use them to direct their behaviour. Translated into the organisational arena, it is the way of unearthing and deciphering the shared feelings, beliefs, and values (and their underlying basic assumptions) of the people who belong to the organisation, not as people say they *ought* to be but as they *are*. I tried to employ ethnographic techniques in my observations.

I took notice of the following things:

- *Language* used by people
- *Stories, myths and fables* that people told. These were written down and later grouped into typologies
- *Formal ceremonies.* Two of these were attended. One was a graduation ceremony and the other was the launch of a new logo and the fund-raising arm of ATISIA
- *Rituals* were observed where possible and two that were institutionalised by top management as change strategies were attended:
  −*A departmental visit* by the Principal and Vice Principal
  −*A senior staff conference.* Permission was given by the Vice-Principal for me to attend this as an observer
- *Who was rewarded, who was sidelined and who was appointed.* Interpretations of reasons were written down, to be checked from other sources at a later date if possible
- *Differences between sub-units.* Particular attention was paid to whether the differences were indicative of sub- or of counter-cultures
- *Management's overall strategies for managing.* Much information on this indicator came from simple observation as well as from formal interviews and group discussions
- *Strategies used to effect changes.* Many of these were not decipherable until after the fact, so the detailed log of day-to-day events became valuable in interpreting events
- *Informal processes* such as expected hours of attendance, procedures for handling deviants, methods people used to "cope with" the system, staff support systems
- *Who got the scarce resources and the perks.* This gave a good indication of power-holders other than those with legitimate power
- *Concrete forms such as buildings and offices.* Some members of the organisation who would have been expected to hold power because of their positions did not always have the best furniture

or the most space. Reasons for this had to be interpreted in the light of other indicators
• *Rewards and punishments.* What did management consider a reward and what a punishment?

Information on the other indicators listed in the operational framework came from one or more of the other methods used as well as from the daily log. While no one single observation could be considered "proof" of anything, a large number of observations, made over a period of time, and of a wide range and large number of people, could be considered to give an accurate picture of the culture of the organisation, the changes in it, and the techniques being used to bring about those changes. I also believe that the log entries, while necessarily subjective in places, met the requirements for scientific observation listed by Kidder.

Phenomenological methods

A second method used to unearth the culture of ATISIA was phenomenology, a method of research where the researcher becomes one of the participants in the situation. As a part-time member of staff at ATISIA, I was able to participate in the culture and the changes and experience them first-hand. Before the study even began, there was a good "feel" for some parts of the culture. This would fulfil Husserl's concept of phenomenology as a way of describing the "essences" beneath everyday experiences (Husserl in Cuff and Payne, 1984, 152).

As ethnography was also being used as a research technique, I was required to put aside many preconceived ideas about ATISIA and to try to learn afresh what other members of the organisation felt. This turned out not to be an insurmountable hurdle. Being only a part-time lecturer, I was not subject to many of the restrictions, nor was I privy to many of the shared feelings that full-time staff were. I believe, therefore, that I could see the culture from other people's points of view. The only *real* hurdle was to keep phenomenological and ethnographic methods separate. This required constant awareness of bias and a strongly disciplined approach to note-taking and interpretations. On balance, I feel that the mix of the two methods ("between method" methodological triangulation) was a definite plus, providing a far richer environment in which to gather information than could be provided by either method individually.

Ethnographic interviews

A third method used to unearth the culture of ATISIA was ethnographic interviews, done both formally and informally. Formal interviews were conducted in the preliminary investigations in 1986, when my task was to collect some background information as a basis for the choice of suitable methodologies, methods and techniques. I interviewed 56 people, including the Principal, Vice-Principal, Registrar, Publicity Officer, all senior academic staff and other people selected as holding power or being in possession of knowledge valuable to the study. This group was classified as Stratum 1 (see Figure 12.2).

While I considered at the time that these interviews were conducted objectively, I realised later that the information sought— and therefore received—from them had been affected by prior experience. For example, I had already conducted one review of the literature published up to 1986 and therefore carried with me a number of assumptions and preconceptions about the nature of culture and culture change. These preconceptions undoubtedly affected which questions were asked in the preliminary interviews, how they were asked, and what interpretations were made.

All preliminary research was conducted using individual, semi-structured interviews with most questions being open-ended. This style of interviewing was chosen as a technique because I had already made some conjectures and decided what variables to address. I felt that interviews would provide the most flexible and efficient tool for getting the detailed information that was required, as questions could be prepared beforehand to elicit the kinds of information needed, but the direction of questioning could be changed if new lines of enquiry presented themselves. Interviews with top management were taped because I felt that these people would not be inhibited by having the interviews taped, as they were well practised in diplomacy. It was also important that the information be recorded accurately. Other preliminary interviews were not taped, but recorded in note form and rewritten later.

These interviews varied in length from half an hour to 2½ hours and, while there was much overlap, they differed slightly from group to group and from person to person. The *types* of questions asked at these interviews were those suggested by Spradley (1980):

- Descriptive questions to elicit what people felt about a thing or event and the meanings they attached to it; for example, "How would you describe ATISIA?" "How would you like to be able to describe it?" "What changes have you made so far?" "How are you communicating the changes to staff?"

- Structural questions to elicit people's understanding of a topic or event; for example, "Why is it necessary to make changes to ATISIA?" "How will you know when you have achieved your goal?"
- Contrast questions to elicit people's understanding of the differences between objects or events; for example, "How does ATISIA differ from a university?" "How will the changes you have mentioned make ATISIA a better place than it is now?"

Sample questions from interviews with other senior academic staff are:

- Which members of the management team at ATISIA would you say are responsible for instigating any changes?
- What are these people's views on what ATISIA is or should be like?
- How much do you think your views differ from theirs?
- How much input do you feel you have in instigating change?

Using the answers to these types of questions helped the formulation of the indicators for the remainder of the data collection. It was invaluable in providing information on top management's vision for ATISIA; on who held power in the organisation and on some of the events so far in the change process; in understanding the events that were to occur over the following two years; and in designing the sampling plan.

Ethnographic interviewing, with a semi-structured form, was used in all three interviews with people in Stratum 1.

Focus group interviews

A fourth method used to unearth the culture of ATISIA was focus group interviews. These are defined by Cox *et al.* (1976) as:

> where a group of people (generally eight to twelve) are led through an open, in-depth discussion by a group moderator. The moderator's objective is to focus the discussion on the relevant subject areas in a nondirective manner (p. 77).

Focus groups were used with members of the organisation other than those included in Stratum 1, as I agreed with Calder (1980, 404) that a guided, interactive discussion with approximate peers on the management scale would bring out their shared feelings, beliefs, and values better than individual interviews would. It also meant that more people's opinions could be sought. Selection and composition of these groups is discussed later.

Procedures used in assembling the groups were as follows:

- Step 1: A letter was sent to each person selected in the sample (see sampling plan), explaining the purpose and general direction of the research and asking people if they would be prepared to come to two group discussions, twelve months apart. More people were sent letters than the sample required, as I felt that not everyone would be prepared to take part.
- Step 2: Over the following two weeks, each person was telephoned and spoken to personally. Once a person had agreed to be part of the research, suitable times for group interviews were discussed. This process of a letter followed by a telephone call resulted in an overwhelming 90% acceptance rate. There was only one faculty from which it was difficult to assemble a group of academic staff, the faculty later classified as a "parallel-culture" (Lewis, 1992a).
- Step 3: Times were then worked out for the different group interviews. Where possible, people were allotted a group according to requirements of the sampling plan but, owing to constraints of academic timetables, it was sometimes necessary to modify the composition of a group. Academic staff were, however, always kept in a group of their own faculty.
- Step 4: Each person who had agreed to be in a group was sent a short note two weeks before the group interview, informing them of the time and place of the discussion. As a result of these notes, more changes in the composition of individual groups had to be made to accommodate individuals.
- Step 5: Two days before each group interview another reminder note went out to each person.

In the conduct of the interviews, a number of conditions had to be met:

- The "questionnaire" for these group interviews had to be very general; however, in all groups, the same basic pattern was followed. Sample questions at these group interviews are shown later.
- The discussions had to be taped. The only other interviews taped were the preliminary ones with top management.

- The discussions had to be partly directive to achieve the desired information.

Difficulties faced in focus group interviews were:

- My own inexperience as a moderator of a group
- The organisation of the groups—choosing a representative sample of people, finding times that suited all group members, and ensuring that the selected people came to two discussion groups twelve months apart
- The very time-consuming process of interviewing personally people who, for genuine reasons, were unable to come to the first group interview but who wanted to be part of the research. This process was not followed in the second group interview, but a composite group (from all faculties) was made up and a group interview conducted with them
- The possibility that group responses were distorted by the "Hawthorne Effect", which says that people behave differently when they know they are being observed. According to Davis (1981, 201), the problem is unavoidable. Some of the distorting effects of the problem were overcome by the large number of people who spoke individually to me after the group discussions.

Study of formal documents

A fifth method used to unearth the culture of ATISIA was a study of formal documents. This investigation was carried out in conjunction and concurrently with all other methods used. While participant observation, ethnographic interviews, and focus groups provided information on most of the indicators identified in the operational framework, some of the embodiments of culture and some of the transformational leadership strategies required investigation of documents.

Many people assisted me in this area of research and it would have been extremely difficult to conduct the study without the wholehearted cooperation of a whole range of people from every area and level in the college. The Principal and Vice-Principal, for example, provided copies of papers they had written and/or presented, and speeches they had made. The Planning and Statistics section provided information on staff and student numbers and composition, on courses, and on performance indicators and this information was the basis for the size and composition of the sample chosen. Personnel provided information on individual staff members, essential for choosing members for the focus groups, and on appointment and socialisation procedures; while Central Records (under instruction from the Vice-Principal) provided any document asked for. These included the Manual of Procedures; and letters, memos, speeches, and pronouncements of the former Principals. The Secretariat, under instructions from the Registrar, provided documents on Council submissions and resolutions, and documents chronicling events in the history of ATISIA. The Public Affairs Office put me on the mailing list of ATISIA's newsclippings service, so that up-to-date published information on ATISIA and on tertiary education in general throughout Australia was available to me throughout the course of the data collection. The Office also allowed me to study the Corporate Identity Manual and documents pertaining to the external promotion of ATISIA. Other documents perused were the staff and student newspapers and newsletters from those sub-units within ATISIA that produced such documents.

Methods Used to Study Culture Change, Performance Change, and Transformational Leadership

All the foregoing methods, using the cross-section of the population shown in Figure 12.2, were used to provide me with an understanding of the culture as it existed at a particular time and of the transformational leadership strategies being used by top management as they attempted to intervene in that culture. In order to study the process of strategic change, the effects it had on the people who worked at ATISIA, and the effects on the organisation as a whole, however, it was necessary to do a longitudinal study, shown diagrammatically in Figure 12.3.

The diagram shows five time frames, chosen as convenient periods into which the research could be divided:

(1) The original culture of ATISIA (1965–83)
(2) The culture from the time of the appointment of the new Principal to the commencement of strong data collection (1983–6).
(3) The culture in the first half of 1987
(4) The culture in the first half of 1988
(5) The culture to the end of 1989 and performance to June 1990.

The choice of each of these time frames will be explained in the description of the methods used in the longitudinal study, given below.

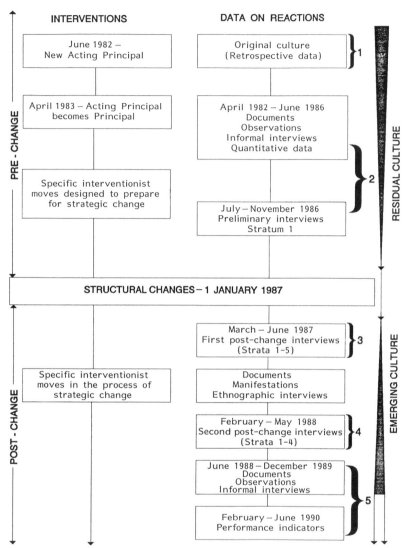

Figure 12.3   Longitudinal view of methodology

Retrospective data

One method used in the longitudinal study of culture at ATISIA was
the use of retrospective data to ascertain the culture in time frames 1
and 2. Data were collected from an examination of ATISIA
documents and by including long-standing members of staff in the
focus groups, to elicit their recollection of critical events in ATISIA's
history, or what Pettigrew (1979, 570–71) calls "a set of social

dramas". Information from long-standing members of staff had to be treated with some caution, as perceptions were naturally coloured by feelings about the present trends and events. It is this preliminary, but essential, step that I believe many instigators and implementors of strategic change eliminate.

Manifestations of culture

Symbols, processes, and forms, the manifestations of culture, were also examined during the same period, using participant observation and via the daily log and a study of formal documents. If culture change or changes in any embodiments of culture had occurred, they should have shown up in the indicators identified in the operational framework.

Culture profiles

A third method used in the longitudinal study was the use of qualitative culture profiles, which were considered useful as *part* but not the *whole* of the technique for diagnosing a culture and measuring culture change. These profiles were constructed from the ethnographic and focus group interviews (see earlier description) and were not an additional technique.

Using the panel method of the same people in each profile, two profiles were taken, twelve months apart (time frames 3 and 4, Figure 12.3). Questions and discussion were aimed at finding out what members felt about changes that were occurring and whether they felt any differently over a period of time. The timing of the profiles was fortuitous, as a major academic restructuring of the college took place on 1 January 1987, which turned out to be a watershed. Before that date, most strategies by top management had been in preparation for change; after that date, intervention was much more open. Figure 12.3 therefore divides the longitudinal study into pre- and post-change, with 1 January 1987 as the division.

Examples of the types of questions asked at the preliminary interviews were given earlier. Below are examples of questions asked of Stratum 1 members in the first profile interview and topics discussed at the first focus groups. As preliminary interviews had already been conducted with members of Stratum 1, the questions in the profiles for these people had to be tailored to the individual person. The examples given below, therefore, are generalisations:

Top management and senior academic staff (Stratum 1) were asked questions such as:

- How has ATISIA changed since our last interview?
- What are ATISIA's main problems now? What are your main problems?
- What feedback have you had from academic staff on the directions that ATISIA is taking?
- What rewards and incentives can you offer staff?
- How can you make sure only suitable people are appointed?
- What can you do with people who won't cooperate?

Questions used in the focus groups (Strata 2–4) were:

- How has ATISIA changed since you first came to work here?
- Which people have been most affected by the changes?
- Have the changes been for the better or worse as far as you are concerned?
- What do you think (top management) want to do with ATISIA? Why?
- What things are important to you in your work here?
- How loyal do you feel to ATISIA? How much trust is there among staff?
- What kinds of people get places at ATISIA? Why?

Examples of the questions asked at the second interviews and topics discussed at the second focus groups are given below. Again, these are only generalisations, as each interview and each group discussion differed according to the information gained from the first profile.

Members of Stratum 1 were asked questions such as:

- What methods do you intend using to communicate your message and then making sure that the substance of the message is followed?
- How are you going to use the Performance Indicators you have chosen?
- What feedback have you had from staff on the directions that ATISIA is taking?
- What problems do you expect to encounter?
- Is there anything that has particularly upset you at ATISIA lately?
- What are the most exciting things that are happening?

Questions used in the focus groups were:

- In what ways has ATISIA changed in the past twelve months?
- What do you think ATISIA's future role is going to be?
- What is of most concern to you now? What is most important?
- What is the atmosphere like in your (department)?
- How enthusiastic do you feel about your work?
- Do staff have freedom of speech? Can you give examples?

I thought that I may have experienced problems with loss of panel members over the period of the study, but this turned out not to be a serious problem. The sample of academic staff was a very stable one. Twelve people of the 120 in Stratum 2 (see Sampling Plan) did leave ATISIA for one reason or another, but five of these contacted me to let me know and to tell me why. This information on why people were leaving was very valuable. There was a greater loss among non-academic staff members, with seven out of a total of 20 of these people leaving ATISIA during the course of data collection.

A more serious problem was experienced with attendance at the second group discussion, so while Stratum 1 (senior and middle management) had almost 100% retention rate, people in Strata 2–4 attended much more poorly. Individual follow-up investigations were carried out with non-attenders in profile 2.

Quantitative methods

A final method used in the longitudinal study was quantitative. Statistics on the indices of performance change mentioned by top management at the preliminary interviews in mid-1986 were analysed in the first half of 1990 (time frame 5, Figure 12.3). The indices and quantitative statistics, while they did not give a comprehensive measure of *culture* change, adequately measured the *performance* change that management had chosen as their goal and which *may* be a sign of a wider culture change. If behaviour change was the end goal of management, then the indices would be the only measurement they would require.

SAMPLING PLAN

Relevant Population

Whenever there are attempts to change the culture of an organisation such as ATISIA, many groups in the community are affected, either directly, indirectly, or sequentially. I considered that in the very early stages of change (the time period being studied), the only groups that would be discernibly affected would be the staff and students of ATISIA and that they were the relevant population for this study.

Sampling Frame

The most recent figures available to me at the beginning of strong data collection were those from the 1985 statistical year, ending 30 April 1986. The sample for the research was therefore based on these figures. In an institution as large as ATISIA, with 1835 employees and 9171 students, both full- and part-time, it was impracticable to survey everyone. Moreover, preliminary research showed that not all members of the organisation would be affected equally by the attempts at change.

Groups deemed to be most affected by the attempted changes were full-time staff, both teaching and non-teaching—particularly teaching—and students. These groups were therefore considered the main target population and data were taken mainly from them. Part-time staff were eliminated because of a lack of a definition of this group. Some departments used part-time staff to teach close to full-time loads, while other departments used them only to take specialist lectures on an occasional basis.

Type of Sample

Preliminary interviews with top management indicated that two main variables would affect how change would be experienced by individual staff members—a person's level on the staff hierarchy and his or her area of discipline; for example, it was assumed that Deans of Faculty would be affected differently from Heads of School, and Heads of School differently from Lecturers and Tutors. One faculty would be affected differently from another.

Such assumptions suggested a compound stratified method of sampling—level × discipline—these being considered at that time to be the principal variables being studied. The advantages would be that there would be homogeneity within strata and heterogeneity between strata, so effects on the different sub-groups in ATISIA could be analysed; and different research methods could be used for each stratum.

The following strata were chosen:

(1)   The power-holders in the organisation (whether their power was legitimate, expert, referent, coercive, or delegated) and

people who had special knowledge relevant to the research
(2) Full-time teaching staff not included in Stratum 1. These people
     were sampled by Faculty
(3) Full-time non-teaching staff in academic schools and faculties
(4) Full-time non-academic staff outside schools
(5) Full-time students

This type of sample resembles Patton's (1980) "purposeful" sampling except that no category of staff was chosen on the basis of convenience. It more closely resembles Silverman *et al.*'s (1990, 64) "focused" sampling of:

- Identifying a set of variables (independent) that are hypothesised to influence the dependent variable(s) being investigated
- Systematically obtaining information about a large number of cases that are eligible for inclusion in the study
- Developing a typology based upon the relevant independent and dependent variables and using it to classify all cases
- Identifying explicit criteria for the selection of cases for inclusion in the study based upon the stated objectives of the research.

Silverman *et al.*'s criteria were not used in selection of the sample at ATISIA, however, as they were published four years after the sample type was designed.

Sample Size

Disproportionate sampling was used in this research because preliminary investigation showed that while some of the strata were very small (for example, top management and Deans of Faculty) their importance was very great. It would have been damaging to the research to interview the same proportion of these groups as Lecturers. By the same token, the preliminary interview with top management showed that non-teaching staff and students were not targeted for the changes as much as teaching staff were. According to Emory (1980, 169), under these conditions disproportionate sampling is desirable.

Stratum 1

This first stratum was a census of 56 people, interviewed individually. While some of these people (for example, the Principal's and Vice-Principal's secretaries, the President of the

Academic Staff Association, the Security Officer) were chosen on a judgemental basis, the remainder constituted those people chosen by top management to attend Senior Staff Conferences. This line of distinction seemed, therefore, the logical one to choose to identify Stratum 1.

Stratum 2

Of 400 full-time teaching staff, 38 were covered in Stratum 1, so 362 was the population from which the sample was drawn. I decided to choose one focus group of 10 persons for every 30 members of this group, giving 12 focus groups spread across the seven faculties and 120 members in the stratum. While this is a far larger number than would be required for a random sample, I considered it necessary to use a much larger sample in order to cover the very wide range of expected categories of staff at ATISIA. The number of groups per faculty was worked out on the basis of probability proportional to the size of the faculty, using systematic sampling with a random start.

Stratum 3

There were 201 non-teaching staff in academic schools and, as numbers varied widely in each school and as the people concerned would not be affected by the proposed changes as much as teaching staff would be in the early stages of change, I decided to choose one focus group of 10 persons for every 100 members of this group, giving two groups in all.

Stratum 4

Full-time non-academic staff outside departments were sampled by one focus group of ten persons. Thirteen people classified as non-academic staff outside departments were covered in Stratum 1. I considered, as a result of the preliminary interviews with top management, that many of the remainder would be largely unaffected by the changes in the next two years and they could be adequately covered in one focus group.

Stratum 5

There were 4265 full-time students at ATISIA according to the latest available figures published in August 1986, and it would have been impossible to sample them on a proportional basis. I decided, therefore, to choose one group of students who were active in the Students' Union. While this was hardly a representative sample, I felt that these students would be more likely to be aware of changes affecting staff at this stage than other, less politically active students were. The total sample size was, therefore:

Stratum 1 (Census)	56
Stratum 2	120
(full-time teaching staff)	
Stratum 3	20
(non-teaching staff in Schools)	
Stratum 4	10
(non-academic staff outside Schools)	
Stratum 5 (students)	10
Total:	**216**

Choice of Participants

In choosing participants for the sample, a purposive, non-probability sampling method was used. The group of 56 people in Stratum 1, as explained earlier, was partly a judgement sample. Focus groups were chosen on a stratified random basis in order to have a selection of people who had worked at ATISIA for a long time and had witnessed changes in the past; and people who had joined ATISIA in 1983 or later. This latter criterion turned out to be critical, as will be explained later. Although I tried to have long-standing and newer staff represented proportionally to their numbers at ATISIA, I was constrained by people's willingness or otherwise to be part of the research. The student group was an attempt to compile a mixture of beginning students, students who had been at ATISIA two or more years, and mature-age and post-graduate students; but as this group yielded very little information, it was abandoned for the second profile.

DATA ANALYSIS

Data analysis is one of the most difficult, and responsibility-laden, parts of qualitative methodology. For example, many of the data are unsubstantiated and it is therefore vital that there are checks and balances to ensure reliability and validity of results.

Data in this research were analysed according to recommendations of a number of authors (Barton and Lazarsfeld, 1969; McCall and Simmons, 1969; Bogdan, 1972; Bogdan and Taylor, 1975; Smith, 1975; Reichardt and Cook, 1979; Patton, 1980; Calder, 1980; Spradley, 1980; Kidder, 1981; Jick, 1983; Miles, 1983; Goertz and Le Compte, 1984). Depending on as much advice as could be gleaned from the literature, I used the following methods to analyse the data.

Reading and Coding of Field Notes

In accordance with advice from qualitative methodologies, all field notes (daily log, transcripts of ethnographic interviews and focus group interview tapes, formal documents) were read carefully a number of times. It became obvious at this stage that stratification by area of discipline and level in the hierarchy was insufficient and that another stratification had to be made—length of service at ATISIA. Fortunately, the distinction had been partly anticipated by having a mix of long-standing and newer staff in the focus group interviews, so the data were at least available.

As the magnitude of the differences between long-standing and newer staff did not become apparent until after all group discussions had been held in 1987, I needed to listen to all tapes again and match comments to specific people. Comments from individual interviews with Stratum 1 were much easier to reclassify. By this reclassification of information, stratification by length of service was compiled.

In order to render the data more manageable, they were then coded according to the indicators of culture and transformational leadership listed in Table 12.1. This process reduced the data to 34 (plus sub-sets) indicators in three major manifestations—symbols, processes, and forms. From these indicators, categories of feelings, beliefs and values were deduced.

Constructing Typologies

The second step in data analysis was to develop some typologies— sets of people at ATISIA who formed "camps". While preliminary research indicated two "camps" (that is, level on the hierarchy and area of discipline) subsequent research revealed a number of others, one of which, "length of service", was crucial to the thesis.

Using the Guiding Propositions

Third, data were checked constantly against guiding propositions formulated after a review of the literature and before the commencement of data collection. Their content is not relevant to an explanation of methodology and research methods, but is discussed in Lewis (1992a, 1994) and Lewis and Cunnington (1993). While most researchers, both qualitative and quantitative, refer to "hypotheses", I prefer to use the term "guiding propositions", as the term "hypothesis" implies that it can be definitively tested.

The guiding propositions, in this research, proved restricting. They had been taken from the literature on culture change and transformational leadership, and the data revealed that they needed modification or addition.

Reaching Convergence

When I felt that the categories and typologies were valid, the final step of inferring the basic assumptions still had to be made. There are few external checks on this step and there is no real logic to it. This ultimate step in unearthing a culture and generalising about change strategies requires an element of creativity, named the "Aha Phenomenon" by Graham Wallas in his "Creative Thinking" approach to problem solving (Wallas in Rosenblatt *et al.*, 1982, 61). Wallas suggested that after all the data are collected, the problem should be allowed to "incubate". "Illumination" may take days or weeks to come, but when it does it should be verified.

Calder (1980, 405), in referring to analysis of focus group interviews, says that there is no real method for discovering patterns in them, but that the researcher's success will depend on their ability to be "intuitive and creative rather than objective and logical". This final step of data analysis is labelled the construction of a "Matrix Formulation" by Barton and Lazarsfeld (1969). Methods used for verification in this research are explained below.

Validating and Verifying Results

"The quantitative researcher's concern for ensuring validity and reliability is comparable to the qualitative researcher's concern for data accuracy, verification and validation" (Silverman *et al.*, 1990, 59). While it is not possible to "prove" causal speculations and conjectures, every effort was made to ensure that neither Type 1 errors (saying something is not significant when it is) nor Type 2 errors (attaching significance to something meaningless) were made. *Triangulation* was employed to ensure multiple data sources, both "between methods" and "within methods", and a generalisation was not considered valid unless there was evidence from more than one source.

Attempts were made to consider *other explanations that would fit the data.* The questions were asked, Is it reasonable to consider that A causes B? Under what conditions?

Negative case analysis became a major consideration in data analysis. The very large number of negative cases finally forced me to modify the original guiding propositions considerably. Negative cases were not easy to identify in the beginning, as the literature had had a restricting effect on me and had blinded me to the actual data. Perceptions were therefore made in the light of prior expectation. An awareness of personal bias enabled a much clearer view and a much more valuable use to be made of negative cases. A careful check was made of the *sampling method* and it was decided that it was wide enough and deep enough to provide a good cross-section of the population.

Quotations from interviewees and members of focus groups were organised and collated under the indices chosen in the operational framework. As the research progressed and more evidence was gathered, more sub-headings under each index were added.

Statistical analysis was carried out on some of the data. Qualitative data do not lend themselves easily to statistical analysis, but, based on my construction of typologies, people and responses were able to be categorised. Category variables ruled out all parametric tests of significance. Therefore to test for significant differences between samples, chi-square tests of independence were carried out where samples were large enough and exact tests of proportions for samples where expected frequencies were less than 5. These were used to test for statistically significant differences between long-standing and new staff at ATISIA and between areas of discipline. They were also used to test for significant differences within those groups between 1987 and 1988. The "within groups" tests were performed with both unmatched and matched samples.

As all non-parametric tests lose data and so tend to hide differences, requiring differences to be much large if they are to be accepted as significant, I realised that Type II errors may occur. I also realised that all tests of significance are negative and do not confirm our hypothesis (or conjecture), but tell us only that the two samples are different for some reason.

Feedback from participants was used as a final method of verification. A semi-final draft of the thesis was given to ten participants in the research for reading and comments. These people were chosen primarily on the basis of trustworthiness and knowledge of the situation around them, though an attempt was made to choose a wide variety of positions on the hierarchy, areas of discipline, and length of service at ATISIA.

These people also represented six of the seven faculties at ATISIA and ranged in length of service from less than 12 months to more than 15 years. Each person read the thesis over a period of 3–4 days (chosen at their convenience) and then an interview was held with each of them. Their feedback, while widely varying, in fact validated the results from other data sources. Some points of the thesis were modified as a result of the interviews, but the overall conclusions were strongly reinforced.

Comments ranged from extremely critical to extremely enthusiastic in agreement. I was in turn congratulated, castigated, warned, patronised, "set straight", advised, and helped. To all those people, I am most grateful; for verification by feedback proved to be the most valuable and the most enlightening of all methods used.

EVALUATION OF METHODOLOGIES, METHODS, AND TECHNIQUES

As the methodology was predominantly qualitative in nature, there was always the danger of subjectivity, the problematic question of ethics, and the difficulties of data collection and analysis. There was also the question of the value of case methodology itself.

In looking at the value of a case, the strengths were discussed earlier, but there are, of course, some weaknesses. According to Eisenhardt (1989), using so much empirical evidence may produce theory that is overly complex and narrow, so that a case study will probably *never* allow one to construct "grand" theory. But, after all, how many people do? According to Kuhn (1970), building on and filling in gaps in theories that already exist is the best that most researchers can ever hope for.

The problem of subjectivity remained throughout the duration of the study. Perhaps, as a part-time staff member at ATISIA, I was closer to the situation than was desirable for total objectivity for, on a number of occasions, I found top management's strategies affecting me more than I had expected they would. Forced self-discipline in analysis may not have been sufficient to eliminate subjectivity.

The problem of ethics was also not entirely overcome. I promised participants in the study anonymity and, where anonymity was not possible, I asked permission to use information if it might identify anyone. The ten people who read the semi-final draft of the thesis as part of the verification process were also asked if they could identify people from the quotations. Yet the finished thesis still annoyed some people.

I also gathered information from people who were unaware they were being interviewed. Informal conversations with staff members were frequently used as part of participant observation and many of these people were not aware that information they gave me was being used. I often listened to conversations among other people and recorded their contents in the daily log.

The difficulties of data collection and analysis were enormous. Data collection was time consuming and mentally and physically exhausting. The specific methods chosen—daily log, phenomenology, ethnographic interviews, focus group interviews, formal documents, retrospective data, manifestations of culture, and quantitative methods—were very wide ranging. However, it is hoped that this mix of a number of different methods (triangulation) ensured that the findings were the result of the trait being studied and not of the method being used. It also overcame the problem of finding one method that would cover every aspect of studying culture and strategic change.

Data analysis was daunting, as the huge mass of information collected had to be not only read and coded but then interpreted and verified. However, I believe that, in spite of the obvious limitations of the research, the methodology, the combination of research methods and techniques chosen, and the process of data analysis yielded as accurate a picture of strategic change at ATISIA as it is possible to get, a picture far richer and more revealing than any that could have been obtained by quantitative methods or by any one qualitative method in isolation.

REFERENCES

Adams, G. B. and Ingersoll, V. H. (1985) The difficulty of framing a perspective on organizational culture. In Frost, P. J., Moore, L. F., Louis, M., Lundberg, C. C. and Martin, J. (eds), *Organizational Culture: The Meaning of Life in the Workplace*, Beverly Hills, CA, Sage, pp. 223–34.

Amsa, P. (1986) Organizational culture and work group behaviour: an empirical study. *Journal of Management Studies*, **23**, 3 May, 347–62.

Argyris, C. (1970) *Intervention Theory and Method: a Behavioral Science View*, Reading, MA, Addison-Wesley.

Argyris, C. and Schon, D. (1976) *Theory in Practice. Increasing Professional Effectiveness*, San Francisco, CA, Jossey-Bass.

Barnett, G. A. (1979) The measurement of organizational culture. In Goldhaber, G. M. and Wiio, O. (eds), *Proceedings of Organizational Communication Conference*, State University of New York, Buffalo.

Barnett, G. A. (1988) Communication and organizational culture. In Goldhaber, G. M. and Barnett, G. A. (eds), *The Handbook of Organizational Communication*, Norwood, NJ, Ablex, pp. 101–30.

Barton, A. H. and Lazarsfeld, P. F. (1969) Some functions of qualitative analysis in empirical social research. In McCall, G. J. and Simmons, J. L. (eds), *Issues in Participant Observation*, Reading, MA, Addison-Wesley, pp. 163–96.

Bartunek, J. M. (1984) Changing interpretive schemes and organizational restructuring: the example of a religious order. *Administrative Science Quarterly*, **29**, 355–72.

Bartunek, J. and Louis, M. (1988) The interplay of organization development and organizational transformation. In Woodman, R. W. and Pasmore, W. A. (eds), *Research in Organizational Change and Development*, 2, Greenwich, CT, JAI Press, pp. 97–134.

Bass, B. M. (1985) *Leadership and Performance Beyond Expectations*, New York, The Free Press.

Bass, B. M. (1990) From transactional to transformational leadership: learning to share the vision. *Organizational Dynamics*, **18**, (3), Winter, 19–31.

Bennis, W. and Nanus, B. (1985) *Leaders: The Strategies for Taking Charge*, New York, Harper and Row.

Bogdan, R. (1972) *Particular Observation in Organizational Settings*, New York, Syracuse University Press.

Bogdan, R. and Taylor, S. J. (1975) *Introduction to Qualitative Research Methods*, New York, John Wiley.

Brink, T. L. (1991) Corporate cultures: a color coding metaphor. *Business Horizons*, **34** (5), September/October, 39–44.

Buckley, K. and Perkins, D. (1984) Managing the complexity of organizational transformation. In Adams, J. D. (ed.), *Transforming Work*, Virginia, Miles River Press, pp. 55–67.

Burns, J. M. G. (1978) *Leadership*, New York, Harper and Row.

Calder, B. J. (1980) Focus group interviews and qualitative research in organizations. In Lawler, E. E. III, Nadler, D. A. and Cammann, C. *Organizational Assessment*, New York, John Wiley, pp. 399–417.

Carby, K. and Stemp, P. (1985) How Hambro changed its name and much more besides. *Personnel Management*, **17**, October, 58–60.

Cook, M. (1979) *Perceiving Others: The Psychology of Interpersonal Perception*, London, Methuen.

Cooke, R. A. and Rousseau, D. M. (1988) Behavioral norms and expectations: a quantitative approach to the assessment of organizational culture. *Group and Organization Studies*, **13**, September, 245–73.

Cox, K. K., Higginbotham, J. B. and Burton, J. (1976) Applications of focus group interviews in marketing. *Journal of Marketing*, January, 77–80.

Cuff, E. C. and Payne, G. C. (1984) Ethnomethodology as a perspective. In Cuff, E. C. and Payne, G. C. (eds), *Perspectives in Sociology*, 2nd edn, Boston, MA, George Allen and Unwin, pp. 151–88.

Davis, K. (1981) *Human Behavior at Work: Organizational Behavior*, 6th edn, New York, McGraw-Hill.

Dean, J. P. and Whyte, W. F. (1969) How do you know if the informant is telling the truth? In McCall, G. J. and Simmons, J. L. (eds), *Issues in Participant Observation: A Text and Reader*, Reading, MA, Addison-Wesley.

De Bivort, L. H. (1984) Fast-tracking the transformation of organizations. In Adams, J. D. (ed.), *Transforming Work*, Virginia, Miles River Press, pp. 243–52.

Deetz, S. (1985) Ethical considerations in cultural research in organizations. In Frost, P. J., Moore, L. F., Louis, M., Lundberg, C. C. and Martin, J. (eds), *Organizational Culture: The Meaning of Life in the Workplace*, Beverley Hills, CA, Sage, pp. 13–25.

Denzin, N. K. (1978) *The Research Act*, 2nd edn, New York, McGraw-Hill.

Desatnick, R. L. (1986) Management climate surveys: a way to uncover an organization's culture. *Personnel*, **63**, (5), May, 49–54.

Eisenberg, E. M. and Riley, P. (1988) Organizational symbols and sense-making. In Goldhaber, G. M. and Barnett, G. A. *The Handbook of Organizational Communication*, Norwood, NJ, Ablex, pp. 131–50.

Eisenhardt, K. M. (1989) Building theories from case study research. *Academy of Management Review*, **14**, (4), 532–50.

Emory, C. W. (1980) *Business Research Methods*, revised edn, Homewood, IL, Irwin.

Frost, P. J., Moore, L. F., Louis, M. R., Lundberg, C. C. and Martin, J. (eds) (1985) *Organizational Culture: The Meaning of Life in the Workplace*, Beverly Hills, CA, Sage.

Garfinkel, H. (1967) *Studies in Ethnomethodology*, Englewood Cliffs, NJ, Prentice Hall.

Glaser, B. G. and Strauss, A. (1967) *The Discovery of Grounded Theory*, Chicago, IL, Aldine.

Goetz, J. and Le Compte, M. (1984) *Ethnography and Qualitative Design in Educational Research*, New York, Academic Press.

Hagedorn, H. J. and Little, A. D. (1984) Profiling corporate culture. *Today's Office*, October, 29–33.

Higher Education: a policy discussion paper (The Green Paper) (1987) circulated by the Hon. J. S. Dawkins MP, Minister for Employment, Education and Training, AGPS, December.

Higher Education: a policy statement (The White Paper) (1988) circulated by the Hon. J. S. Dawkins MP, Minister for Employment, Education and Training, AGPS, July.

Hofstede, G. (1986) Editorial: The usefulness of the 'organizational culture' concept. *Journal of Management Studies*, **23**, 3 May, 253–7.

Hofstede, G., Neuijen, B., Ohavy, D. D. and Sanders, G. (1990) Measuring organizational cultures: a qualitative and quantitative study across twenty cases. *Administrative Science Quarterly*, **35** (2), 286–316.

Jick, T. D. (1983) Mixing qualitative and quantitative methods: triangulation in action. In Van Maanen, J. (ed.), *Qualitative Methodology*, Beverly Hills, CA, Sage.

Jones, M. O. (1985) Is ethics the issue? In Frost, P. J., Moore, L. F., Louis, M. R., Lundberg, C. C. and Martin, J. (eds), *Organizational Culture: The Meaning of Life in the Workplace*, Beverly Hills, CA, Sage, pp. 235–52.

Kidder, L. H. (1981) *Research Methods in Social Relations*, 4th edn, New York, Holt, Rinehart and Winston.

Kleiner, B. H. and Corrigan, W. A. (1989) Understanding organizational change. *Leadership and Organization Development Journal (UK)*, **10** (3), 25–31.

Kuhn, T. (1970) *The Structure of Scientific Revolutions*, 2nd edn, Chicago, University of Chicago Press.

Levy, A. (1986) Second-order planned change: definition and conceptualization. *Organizational Dynamics*, Summer, 5–20.

Lewis, D. (1992a) *Culture change—communication, management and effects: an empirical study of change in an Australian tertiary institution*, unpublished PhD thesis, Griffith University, Brisbane.

Lewis, D. (1992b) Communicating organisational culture. *Australian Journal of Communication*, **19**, (2), 47–57.

Lewis, D. (1994) Organizational change—relationship between reactions and organizational performance. *Journal of Organizational Change Management*, 7(5), 41–55.

Lewis, D. and Cunnington, B. (1993) Power-based change in an Australian tertiary college. *Journal of Strategic Change*, **2** (6), November/December, 341–50.

Limerick, D. C. and Cunnington, B. (1993) *Managing the New Organisation*, Chatswood, NSW, Business and Professional Publishing.

Limerick, I. B. (1988) *Community involvement in education—a study of three schools*, PhD thesis, University of Queensland.

Louis, M. R. (1981) A cultural perspective on organizations: the need for and consequences of viewing organizations as culture-bearing milieux. *Human Systems Management*, **2**, 246–58.

Lundberg, C. C. (1985) On the feasibility of cultural intervention in organizations. In Frost, P. J., Moore, L. F., Louis, M. R., Lundberg, C. C. and Martin, J. (eds) *Organizational Culture: The Meaning of Life in the Workplace*, Beverly Hills, CA, Sage, pp. 169–85.

Lundberg, C. C. (1989) On organizational learning: implications and opportunities for expanding organizational development. In Woodman, R. W. and Pasmore, W. A. (eds), *Research in Organizational Change and Development*, 3, Greenwich, CT, JAI Press, pp. 61–82.

Magee, B. (1975) *Popper*, London, Fontana/Collins.

Main, J. (1984) Waking up AT&T: there's life after culture shock. *Fortune*, December, 34–42.

McCall, G. and Simmons, J. L. (eds) (1969) *Issues in Participant Observation*, Reading, MA, Addison-Wesley.

Miles, M. B. (1983) Qualitative data as an attractive nuisance: the problem of analysis. In Van Maanen, J. (ed.), *Qualitative Methodology*, Beverly Hills, CA, Sage, pp. 117–34.

Mintzberg, H. (1983a) An emerging strategy of 'direct' research. In Van Maanen, J. (ed.), *Qualitative Methodology*, Beverly Hills, CA, Sage, pp. 105–16.

Mintzberg, H. (1983b) Opening up the definition of strategy. In Quinn, J. B. Mintzberg, H. and James, R. M. (eds), *The Strategy Process: Concepts, Contexts, and Cases*, Englewood Cliffs, NJ, Prentice Hall, pp. 13–20.

Mirvis, P. H. and Seashore, S. E. (1980) Being ethical in organizational research. In Lawler, E. E. III, Nadler, D. A. and Camman, C. (eds), *Organizational Assessment: Perspectives on the Measurement of Organizational Behavior and the Quality of Work Life*, New York, John Wiley, pp. 583–607.

Nossiter, V. and Biberman, G. (1990) Projective drawings and metaphor: analysis of organisational culture. *Journal of Managerial Psychology (UK)*, **5** (3), 13–16.

Ouchi, W. G. and Jaeger, A. M. (1978) Type Z organization: stability in the midst of mobility. *Academy of Management Review*, April, 305–14.

Patton, M. Q. (1980) *Qualitative Evaluation Methods*, Beverly Hills, CA, Sage.

Peters, T. J. and Waterman, R. H. (Jr) (1982) *In Search of Excellence*, Sydney, Harper and Row.

Pettigrew, A. M. (1979) On studying organizational cultures. *Administrative Science Quarterly*, **24**, December, 570–81.

Pettigrew, A. M. (1985a) *The Awakening Giant: Continuity and Change in Imperial Chemical Industries*, Oxford, Basil Blackwell.

Pettigrew, A. M. (1985b) Contextualist research: a natural way to link theory and practice. In Lawler, E. E. (ed.), *Doing Research that is useful in Theory and Practice*, San Francisco, CA, Jossey-Bass.

Pettigrew, A. M. (1986) Is corporate culture manageable? Keynote address given to the Sixth Annual Strategic Management Society Conference, *Cultures and Competitive Strategies*, Singapore, 13–16 October.

Pettigrew, A. M. (1987) Context and action in the transformation of the firm. *Journal of Management Studies (UK)*, **24** (6), 649–70.

Pettigrew, A. M. (1988) Researching strategic change. In Pettigrew, A. (ed.), *The Management of Strategic Change*, Oxford, Blackwell, pp. 1–3.

Popper, K. (1963) *Conjectures and Refutations*, London, Routledge and Kegan Paul.

Putnam, L. (1983) The Interpretive approach: an alternative to functionalism, in Putman L. and Pacanowsky M. (eds), *Communication and Organisation*, Beverly Hills, CA, Sage, pp. 31–54.

Quinn, J. B. (1980) Managing strategic change. *Sloan Management Review*, **21** (4), Summer, 3–20.

Quinn, J. B., Mintzberg, H. and James, R. M. (1983) *The Strategy Process: Concepts, Contexts and Cases*, Englewood Cliffs, NJ, Prentice Hall International.

Reichardt, C. S. and Cook, T. D. (1979) Beyond qualitative *versus* quantitative methods. In Cook, T. D. and Reichardt, C. S. (eds), *Qualitative and Quantitative Methods in Evaluation Research*, Beverly Hills, CA, Sage, pp. 7–32.

Reynierse, J. H. (1986) Measuring corporate culture. *The Business Magazine*, September-October, 64–7.

Reynierse, J. H. and Harker, J. B. (1986) Measuring and managing organizational culture. *Human Resource Planning*, **9** (1), 1–8.

Reynolds, P. D. (1986) Organizational culture as related to industry, position and performance: a preliminary report. *Journal of Management Studies*, **23**, May, 333–45.

Rose, G. (1982) *Deciphering Sociological Research*, London, Macmillan.

Rosenblatt, S. B., Cheatham, T. R., and Watt, J. T. (1982) *Communication in Business*, 2nd edn, Englewood Cliffs, NJ, Prentice Hall.

Sathe, V. (1983) Implications of corporate culture: a manager's guide to action. *Organizational Dynamics*, **12**, Autumn, 5–23.

Sathe, V. (1985) *Cultural and Related Corporate Realities*, Homewood, IL, Irwin.

Schein, E. H. (1983) The role of the founder in creating organizational culture. *Organizational Dynamics*, Summer, 13–28.

Schein, E. H. (1984) Coming to a new awareness of organizational culture. *Sloan Management Review*, Winter, 3–16.

Schein, E. H. (1989) Conversation with Edgar H. Schein. Interview conducted by F. Luthans. *Organizational Dynamics*, **17** (4), Spring, 60–76.

Sieber, S. D. (1980) Integration of fieldwork and survey methods. In Lawler, E. E. III, Nadler, D. A. and Cammann, C. (eds), *Organizational Assessment*, New York, John Wiley, pp. 444–70.

Silverman, M., Ricci, E. M. and Gunter, M. J. (1990) Strategies for increasing the rigor of qualitative methods in evaluation of health care programs. *Evaluation Review*, **14** (1), 57–74.

Silverzweig, S. and Allen, R. F. (1976) Changing the corporate culture. *Sloan Management Review*, **17** (3), Spring, 33–49.

Smith, H. W. (1975) *Strategies of Social Research*, 2nd edn, Englewood Cliffs, NJ, Prentice Hall.

Sparrow, P. and Pettigrew, A. (1988) How Halfords put its HRM into top gear. *Personnel Management (UK)*, **20** (6), 30–34.

Spradley, J. P. (1980) *Participant Observation*, New York, Holt, Rinehart and Winston.

Torbert, W. R. (1989) Leading organizational transformation. In Woodman, W. R. and Pasmore, W. A. (eds) *Research in Organizational Change and Development*, 3, Greenwich, CT, JAI Press, pp. 83–116.

Tucker, R. W., McCoy, W. J. and Evans, L. C. (1990) Can questionnaires objectively assess organisational culture? *Journal of Managerial Psychology (UK)*, **5** (4), 4–11.

Uttal, B. (1983) The corporate culture vultures. *Fortune*, 17 October, 66–72.

Van Maanen, J. (1983) Reclaiming qualitative methods for organizational research: a preface. In Van Maanen, J. (ed.), *Qualitative Methodology*, Beverly Hills, CA, Sage, pp. 9–18.

Vroman, H. W. (1983) Primer on changing cultures: the Centrebank case. *US Banker*, **94**, October, 46–53.

Weick, K. E. (1979) *The Social Psychology of Organizing*, 2nd edn, Reading, MA, Addison-Wesley.

Whipp, R., Rosenfeld, R. and Pettigrew, A. (1988) Understanding strategic change processes: some preliminary British findings. In Pettigrew, A. M. (ed.), *The Management of Strategic Change*, Oxford, Basil Blackwell, pp. 14–55.

Whipp, R., Rosenfeld, R. and Pettigrew, A. (1989) Culture and competitiveness: evidence from two mature UK industries. *Journal of Management Studies (UK)*, **26** (6), 561–85.

Wiener, Y. (1988) Forms of value systems: a focus on organizational effectiveness and cultural change and maintenance. *Academy of Management Review*, **13** (4), 534–45.

Wrightsman, L. S. and Sandford, F. H. (1975) *Psychology: A Scientific Study of Human Behavior*, 4th edn, Monterey, CA, Brooks/Cole.

POSTAL ADDRESSES OF CONTRIBUTORS

Graham Beaver *Nottingham Business School, The Nottingham Trent University, Burton Street, Nottingham NG1 4BU*

Charles Despres *International Institute for Management Development, Chemin de Bellerive 23, PO Box 915, CH-1001, Lausanne, Switzerland*

Dr Jean Marie Hiltrop *International Institute for Management Development, Chemin de Bellerive 23, PO Box 915, CH-1001, Lausanne, Switzerland*

Professor H. H. Hinterhuber *University of Innsbruck, Dept of Management, A-6020 Innsbruck, Austria 52*

D. E. Hussey *David Hussey & Associates, 44 Forestfield, Horsham, West Sussex RH13 6DZ*

Peter L. Jennings *Sheffield Business School, Sheffield Hallam University, The Old Hall, Totley Hall Lane, Sheffield S17 4AB*

Bengt Karlöf *Karlöf and Partners, Gamla Brogatan 36–38, 11 20 Stockholm, Sweden*

Boris I. Levin *Am Fuchssteig 4, 82067 Ebenhausen, Germany*

Dr Dianne Lewis *School of Management. Human Resources and Industrial Relations, Queensland University of Technology, Gardens Point Campus, 2 George St, Brisbane, Queensland, Australia*

Marie McHugh *Faculty of Business and Management, University of Ulster, Newtownabbey, Co. Antrim, BT37 0QB, Northern Ireland*

Professor R. J. Mockler *114 East 90th Street (Suite 1b), New York, NY 101128, USA*

Dolores O'Reilly *Faculty of Business and Management, University of Ulster, Magee College, Londonderry BT48 7JL, Northern Ireland*

Professor John E. Prescott *Joseph Katz Graduate School of Business, University of Pittsburgh, 252 Mervis Hall, Pittsburgh, PA 15260, USA*

Charles W. Taylor *Department of the Army, United States Army War College, Carlisle Barracks, Pennsylvania 17013-5050, USA*

INDEX

STRATEGIC CHANGE

Editor DAVID HUSSEY
*Centre for International Management and Industrial
Development (CIMID), UK*

**"...an excellent read...provokes thought and reflection on
contemporary management issues. It has real value for managers
seeking to bring about sensitive, proactive change in their
organisations."**
Graham Beaver, MBA Programme Leader, Nottingham Business School, UK

Recent research by various organisations shows the management of change to
be a major area of concern. *Strategic Change* addresses that concern by
publishing a collection of authoritative and practical articles and case studies.
It covers the whole process of successfully achieving effective and complex
change, including the triggers that bring the **need,** the processes which identify
and plan change within the organization, and the **management of change**
itself. The journal has an international scope, reflecting the current trend
towards intense global competition and increasing global management.

Key topics covered include...
**Managing change, Leadership, Empowerment, Customer service, Cross-cultural
negotiations, Organisational concepts; Management buyouts, Turnaround
management, Process models, Project management, Process models, Project
management, HRM, BPR, Collaboration.**

Strategic Change is the definitive resource for...
• Management consultants • Management directors, CEOs • Business planners

Subscription details Volume 5 (1996) 6 Issues
Corporate Rate: Worldwide US$225.00
Personal Rate: UK £60.00 Outside UK US$90.00
(Personal subscriptions to be paid by personal credit card or cheque)

**To subscribe or receive further information please contact:
Jo Underwood, Marketing Department, John Wiley & Sons Ltd,
Baffins Lane, Chichester, West Sussex, PO19 1UD, UK**

STRATEGIC

MANAGEMENT SERIES

Published in association with *Strategic Management Society* this series provides a key resource of new ideas and issues being discussed by the *SMS* and aims to make them accessible to practicing managers.

STRATEGIC RENAISSANCE AND BUSINESS TRANSFORMATION
Edited by **Howard Thomas** and **Donald O'Neal,** both of University of Illinois at Urbana Champaign, USA
0471 957518   October 1995   390pp   £24.95

STRATEGIC INTEGRATION
Edited by **Howard Thomas** and **Donald O'Neal**, both of University of Illinois at Urbana Champaign, USA and **Professor Edward Zajac**, Northwestern University, Illinois, USA
0471 958069   January 1996   300pp   £24.95

STRATEGIC THINKING, LEADERSHIP AND THE MANAGEMENT OF CHANGE
Edited by **John Hendry**, University of Cambridge, UK, **Gerry Johnson** and **Julia Newton,** both of Cranfield School of Management, UK
0471 939900   November 1993   323 pp   £29.95

BUILDING THE STRATEGICALLY RESPONSIVE ORGANIZATION
Edited by **Howard Thomas** and **Donald O'Neal**, University of Illinois at Urbana -Champaign, USA, **Roderick White**, University of Western Ontario, Canada and **David Hurst**, FedMet Inc, Canada
0471 943991   September 1994   502pp   £24.95

COMPETENCE BASED COMPETITION
Edited by **Gary Hamel**, London Business School, UK and **Aime Heene**, Vlerick School of Management, Belgium
0471 943975   July 1994   358pp   £24.95

(prices correct at time of going to press but subject to change, please contact the New York office for prices in the USA)

All titles available from your bookseller or direct from the publisher

JOHN WILEY & SONS LTD, BAFFINS LANE, CHICHESTER, SUSSEX, PO19 1UD, UK
Tel: (+)1243 779777 Fax: (+)1243 775878
JOHN WILEY & SONS INC, 605 THIRD AVENUE, NEW YORK NY 10158-0012, USA
Tel: (212) 850 6000 Fax: (212) 850 6088